A PLUME BOOK

# THE MIND OF THE MODERN MOVIEMAKER

JOSH HOROWITZ is a writer and television producer. His television work includes producing for *Charlie Rose* on PBS and talk shows on CNBC and the Fox News Channel. His writings have appeared in numerous magazines and Web sites, including *Entertainment Weekly, Interview,* Moviepoopshoot.com, and *Us Weekly.* His musings on popular culture can be read on JoshHorowitz.net. He lives in New York City.

# The
# MIND
## of the
# MODERN
# MOVIEMAKER

*20 Conversations with the
New Generation of Filmmakers*

## Josh Horowitz

A PLUME BOOK

PLUME
Published by Penguin Group
Penguin Group (USA) Inc., 375 Hudson Street, New York, New York 10014, U.S.A. •
Penguin Group (Canada), 90 Eglinton Avenue East, Suite 700, Toronto, Ontario,
Canada M4P 2Y3 (a division of Pearson Penguin Canada Inc.) • Penguin Books Ltd.,
80 Strand, London WC2R 0RL, England • Penguin Ireland, 25 St. Stephen's Green,
Dublin 2, Ireland (a division of Penguin Books Ltd.) • Penguin Group (Australia),
250 Camberwell Road, Camberwell, Victoria 3124, Australia (a division of Pearson
Australia Group Pty. Ltd.) • Penguin Books India Pvt. Ltd., 11 Community Centre,
Panchsheel Park, New Delhi – 110 017, India • Penguin Books (NZ), cnr Airborne and
Rosedale Roads, Albany, Auckland 1310, New Zealand (a division of Pearson New
Zealand Ltd.) • Penguin Books (South Africa) (Pty.) Ltd., 24 Sturdee Avenue, Rosebank,
Johannesburg 2196, South Africa

Penguin Books Ltd., Registered Offices: 80 Strand, London WC2R 0RL, England

First published by Plume, a member of Penguin Group (USA) Inc.

First Printing, February 2006
1 3 5 7 9 10 8 6 4 2

Ⓟ REGISTERED TRADEMARK—MARCA REGISTRADA

LIBRARY OF CONGRESS CATALOGING-IN-PUBLICATION DATA
Horowitz, Josh, 1976–
The mind of the modern moviemaker : 20 conversations with the new generation
of filmmakers / Josh Horowitz.
p. cm.
ISBN 0-452-28681-6
1. Motion picture producers and directors—United States—Interviews. 2. Motion
pictures—Production and direction—United States. 1. Title.
PN1998.2H675    2006
791.4302'33'09973—dc22
2005023782

Printed in the United States of America
Set in Fairfield Light
Designed by Joseph Rutt

*For my parents*
*My mother—whose passion for the arts will*
*always be an inspiration*
*My father—who didn't walk out of* What About Bob?
*Thanks for always indulging me.*

# CONTENTS

# Contents

# ACKNOWLEDGMENTS

There are twenty-two filmmakers whose generosity with their time and candor made this effort possible. I've thanked all of them profusely in person, on the phone, and by e-mail. But here it is, one more time, a thanks immortalized in print.

To each of the filmmakers' assorted agents, publicists, managers, and assistants, my thanks for your patience and cooperation. In particular, I'd like to mention Jason Abril, Raffi Adlan, Rowena Arguelles, Chantelle Aspey, Anders Bard, Samantha Bryant, Ed Choi, Joseph Garner, Todd Gold, Tim David Harms, Marc Hofstatter, Jennifer Howell, Melissa Kates, Suzanne Lehfeldt, Bebe Lerner, Heather Lylis, Phil Raskind, Leslie Rathe, Christine Richardson, Betsy Rudnick, Andy Shapiro, Gale Stanley, and Shannon Treusch.

I was assisted in the transcribing of the interviews by Michael Fontana, Sheena Goldstein, and Priya Sanghvi.

My thanks to everyone at The Creative Culture, most especially Nicole Diamond Austin, for leading me with a sure hand. I am indebted to my editor, Jake Klisivitch, for giving this book a proper home and presentation.

When this book was only a vague idea in my head, several people lent support and advice that propelled me forward. My thanks to Chris Ryall, Keith Gordon, and to the trio of filmmakers who were the very first to agree to be a part of it: John Hamburg, Kevin Smith, and Chris Weitz.

Many friends and colleagues were generous with advice and encouragement for this project throughout. Among them were Lewis

Beale, John Bobey, Alexandra Bresnan, Mark Bryant, Renee Kaplan, Jerome Kramer, the Stuart Krischevsky agency, Cathy Saypol, Liz Topp, Irene Wang, and Cara Weber.

My thanks to Courtney Litz for reading virtually every word of the book in your hands. Her recommendations and support were invaluable.

All the thanks I can possibly muster to my family. To my parents and my brother and sister, I hope it won't surprise you to know that I actually enjoy you all even more than the movies. And I enjoy the movies a whole lot.

I tend to obsess and agonize over most aspects of my life. This project was no different. Sadly for the patient, lovely, and wise Jenny Powers, she had to hear most of the whining. In the many highs and lows of this book, she never failed to be there for me. This book is better for her existence. And so am I.

# INTRODUCTION

I have always found it remarkable that the experience of watching a film in a theater, unlike so many other experiences in life, has never really changed for me. Though I'll never again be ten, the rush of different emotions going to a movie elicits remains astoundingly constant. When the lights dim, I am back where I have been a thousand times before. I could be about to watch one of the most dismal wastes of celluloid in history, but for those first few moments, I'm watching *Citizen Kane*. It has me in its grasp, and whether it lets go of me is, in the end, up to the director. I walk into that theater with the expectation of greatness, that there may be at least one moment of brilliance. It's what director Luke Greenfield calls "the chill." It's those moments where, as he told me, "your hair stands up on your arms, and you feel like you can fucking fly."

I wanted to do this book because I love how films can both excite and disappoint me, how they somehow can make me feel a little bit more alive, even if I've spent the last two hours sitting by myself in a dark room. There are clearly distinct and powerful voices emerging in film today, and it is time for attention to be paid. Was it such a different feeling for an audience member walking out of 2004's *Eternal Sunshine of the Spotless Mind* as it was for the patron leaving 1954's *On the Waterfront*? *Eternal Sunshine* tapped into something as honest and real and true as Marlon Brando did when he picked up Eva Marie Saint's glove a half century before. While *Eternal Sunshine* was clearly an astonishing creation of originality, other films discussed in this book more clearly echo the past. They are, in their own way, no less original. Each generation puts its unique stamp on genres, whether it's Joe Carnahan's call back to *The French Connection* in *Narc* or Todd Phillips's counterculture comedy *Old School*, a film which owes an obvious debt to *Animal House*. The fact that they stand up so well to (and often surpass) their inspirations is a testament to the craft of these modern moviemakers.

Countless books have been written about the seminal filmmakers of the 1970s, a period worthy of examination even if, as Paul Weitz said to me, we often conveniently remove from our memories the subpar work that came out of that era alongside the classics. But the book I always wanted to read about my heroes of the 1970s was the one written then. As fascinating as it is today to hear someone like Spielberg or Scorsese or Coppola or DePalma reflect on the past, what were they thinking at the time and in the moment? They are fully formed filmmakers now, resolute in their methods and ideologies but surely it must have been fascinating to hear from them as they were learning, while they were experiencing the early ebb and flow of a career. That is what this book is all about.

There is astounding work being done today and great filmmakers are emerging every year. I wanted to capture the young talents of today before we know how it all pans out, before their Oscar acceptance speeches or their $100 million flop. The filmmakers in this book are still developing. For many, their best work is yet to come, and that is what is perhaps most exciting about them.

Hindsight is 20/20. We ask how and when and why brilliant directors of the past lost their way. How could the talents behind such films as *The Godfather*, *The Last Picture Show*, and *The Exorcist* be the same artists responsible for *Jack, The Cat's Meow,* and *Jade*? Several of the filmmakers I spoke with worry about similar fates. Most agreed it was simply a matter of keeping in touch with the world around them. David Gordon Green said, "I think there's a point in your life as an artist when you're aggressively reacting to the world around you—and who you know or what you know and who you hear—and there's a point when you're not listening anymore and you're just Woody Allen." This sentiment was echoed by filmmakers as different from Green as McG and Brett Ratner. Can today's film-makers avoid the mistakes of the previous generation and remain in the moment?

Whether a filmmaker can maintain any degree of individuality in today's system was another topic very much on the minds of many filmmakers. Debates raged over the importance of final cut—that ability to have the final say over the cut of your film—and test screenings. Directors like Todd Phillips told me that "Testing a movie in general is crucial. I always find it amazing when directors—outside of Steven Spielberg—just say, 'Here's the movie; take it or leave it.' I just find it astounding, because ultimately you really don't know what you have until you put it up there." As for final cut, Brett Ratner asked rhetorically, "Why do I need final cut? Final cut is for artistes quote unquote, directors whose movies don't make a lot of money." On the other side of the fence was a filmmaker like Karyn Kusama, who in the midst of editing her first big studio film told me she'd likely never do another film of that kind without final cut. "I've realized I'm a strong-minded director with a very clear sense of what I want to do, and I just want to be left alone to do it," she said.

As I talked to the filmmakers, I repeatedly asked myself, "What defines them? What qualities does such a diverse group share?" You first have to look at the time that has produced them. This is the first group of filmmakers to make films in the wake of Quentin Tarantino. Make no mistake, the long shadow of the famed former video-store clerk hangs over many whose stories are told here. As Joe Carnahan says, "Tarantino moved over the entire independent film scene like the fucking Hindenburg."

Like Tarantino, these men and women grew up with super eight cameras, cable television, and VCRs. For the first time we have a generation of moviemakers who did not need to leave their homes to study the greats of the past. In fact, this may be the first filmmaking generation whose greatest influence wasn't the world around them so much as the world they saw in their living room on TV. David Gordon Green recalls the opening of the second Blockbuster video store in the nation just blocks away from him in Texas. "I remember a sign when they were first opening it saying 10,000 VIDEOS and I thought, whoa that's going to be trouble." Video literally changed these budding filmmakers' lives. If the filmmakers of the 1970s had Vietnam and the civil rights movement shaping their ethos, today's moviemaker is more likely to be shaped by the society reflected to him in pop entertainment. It's no surprise that perhaps the most dominant filmmaker in the young lives of these filmmakers was Steven Spielberg, the man who seemed to control Hollywood in the 1980s.

This is a group that has lived through the rise and commodification of the independent film. Is such a seeming oxymoron possible? It would appear so when the term "indie" needs be redefined every year or two to the point where we now cast a cynical eye on the new independent feature released on 500 screens by a branch of one of the largest studio conglomerates in the world. But that does not mean there is no independence left. The filmmakers here look not just to Tarantino but to men like Steven Soderbergh and John Sayles for inspiration, two directors who have perfected the art of operating within the studio system without becoming slaves to it.

One of the keys to negotiating this uneasy truce between commerce and art lies in technology. And it may be the burgeoning filmmaking technologies that will truly change the face of the filmmaker of tomorrow. No longer is filmmaking a forum for the few. The speed, ease, and affordability of digital video may have imploded the filmmaking world as we knew it. The filmmakers in this book represent the beginning of this shift. They are the last to be reared solely on celluloid and the first to enjoy the flexibility of the digital world. Nowhere is that reflected more clearly than in the story of Kerry Conran, an unassuming CalArts computer maven who began creating miraculous worlds in the comfort of his own apartment. It is not just the technology available to the makers of film that has made a difference to the directors of today. In an altogether different way, the advent of the Internet is surely one of the key factors in the career of Richard Kelly, whose *Donnie Darko* was rescued from box-office oblivion thanks to a fervent online following.

Like Kerry Conran, virtually all of the filmmakers in this book charted their own unique paths to successful careers. Of course, there is Kevin Smith famously cobbling together a modest budget for *Clerks* on maxed-out credit cards, but there are also people like Richard Kelly spending more than $40,000 on an ambitious short film, and a playwright, Neil LaBute, with no film experience whatsoever, creating one of the most provocative debuts in the modern era of the medium.

While talking to these filmmakers, I quickly realized that their stories—their journeys from wide-eyed adolescents to celluloid power players—were as compelling and illuminating as many of their films. Often their moviemaking dreams seemed almost too far out of the realm of possibility to even say aloud. "Daring to think that I could ever make films in Hollywood was beyond even a fantasy," Kerry Conran told me. When asked how his parents reacted to the news that he wanted to make movies, Kevin Smith said, "It was as if I'd said to them, 'I'm going to go discover the nineteenth dimension.' It was a foreign fucking notion to them. They were like, 'OK. Good luck with that. We support you, but if it doesn't work out, go get a real job.'"

My goal for the group of directors I chose to talk to for this book was simple: to bring together a group of filmmakers who represent the breadth of talent and diverse voices making films for American audiences today. That meant filmmakers who have specialized in comedy, those who have specialized in drama, and those whose specialty has been in having no specialty. Perhaps the greatest testament to the breadth of talent that exists today is that twenty-two more filmmakers could have been added to this book without any diminishment of talent.

I had no hard and fast criteria for the filmmakers in this book other than talent and significant and promising contributions to American filmmaking. No arbitrary age requirement was determined, no quotas were given. If a book like this were done thirty, twenty, or even ten years ago, the lack of diversity would have been striking. Even today, the reality remains that Hollywood filmmaking is still dominated by one gender and race. However, the playing field today is undeniably shifting and will, no doubt, continue to do so, though there is still a ways to go. Karyn Kusama reflected on how, as a female director, often she was treated as something special, an anomaly, after her first film, *Girlfight*: "I don't want to be considered, like, the miracle baby."

I was continually surprised by the generosity and candor of my subjects. Access and time are the greatest assets an interviewer can receive. All the filmmakers in this book were extremely generous with their time, some speaking with me on as many as four or five occasions. And in an industry where honest communication sometimes seems hamstrung by publicists, I was pleased by how many of these filmmakers spoke with disarming honesty. I remember being taken by surprise as Patty Jenkins revealed to me that, on the eve of filming her breakthrough movie, *Monster*, she was on the brink of death because of a freak accident. I have a feeling that Trey Parker would have told a chimpanzee how much he and partner Matt Stone "fucking hate actors" the afternoon we spoke. I just happened to be the one chatting him up that day. I recall a wide-ranging conversation with F. Gary Gray where I found him interviewing me almost as much as I was him. Halfway through our afternoon on the phone, he admitted he was extremely nervous, having never spoken in such depth to a writer about his career. Only weeks after his second film had left movie theaters, I found myself in a coffee shop with Dylan Kidd, dissecting what had gone wrong on his sophomore effort, *P.S.*, after everything had gone right with his first, *Roger Dodger*. I met Michel Gondry at a SoHo restaurant for lunch as he was taking a break from editing his third film. He admitted to being fearful about what his still-in-progress work would turn out to be, this only months after his *Eternal Sunshine of the Spotless Mind* had been named one of the best films of the year by virtually every major film critic and institution.

Fear, in fact, was a recurring theme in my talks with many of the filmmakers: fear of temptation, fear of money, fear of failure. Kevin Smith told me that he thought he might have been kicked out of the moviemaking club because of the disappointing returns of *Mallrats*. Luke Greenfield predicted that fear would be the overriding theme of his career. Fear was perhaps rivaled only by feelings of self-doubt. Perhaps it is the nature of the business to always believe someone more talented and driven is out there gunning for your job, but the men and women making movies today seem to doubt themselves at every moment. Michel Gondry has yet to be satisfied with any of his film work. F. Gary Gray says he dusts off his résumé every time he sees the first cut of one of his films. It goes beyond doubt for Trey Parker and Matt Stone; it's more about misery, as they told me how every moment of making movies is excruciatingly painful for them. Filmmaking, as if it were a surprise, is not a business for the weak.

Despite the pain and self-doubt and borderline paranoia, each of these filmmakers holds an astounding measure of optimism and self-confidence. Their trepidation about making movies is rivaled only by their singular belief at times that they are truly meant to be making films. Many are resolute that this is their one true destiny.

The first films of many I spoke with stand as testament to their belief that their stories, however uncommercial they may have seemed, demanded to be told. If there is a lesson to be learned from this group, it is perhaps to tell the story you want to tell however you can tell it. You will find no release slate for a major studio that includes such seemingly commercially averse properties as *Donnie Darko*, *Monster*, and *George Washington*. But each found its way to the screen thanks to a vision that could not be compromised.

It is hard to believe sometimes that filmmaking as we know it is less than a century old—an extraordinary art form still in its infancy. The filmmakers here are aware of the past, hopeful of the present, and a little wary of the future. After all, just as the moviemakers of today are assuming the mantle of the last generation, there are always others rising to take their place. As Karyn Kusama says, "There're always new, young mavericks around the corner."

Josh Horowitz
July 2005

# JOE CARNAHAN

"I decided I didn't want to turn out like one of these guys at Starbucks, sitting there talking about what kind of movie they're going to make."

## SELECTED CREDITS

*Blood, Guts, Bullets and Octane* (1998)–writer/director
*Narc* (2002)–writer/director

Joe Carnahan announces how audacious a filmmaker he is in the opening moments of his gritty 2002 crime drama, *Narc*. A high-speed chase between an undercover cop and his prey leaves you breathless. All bets are off by the time the sequence concludes with a pregnant woman shot and the hero screaming from the gut. Carnahan knew there was only one way to achieve what he wanted: Give a stuntman a camera and have him haul ass after his two actors. Those opening minutes set a tone for a film that recalls the danger and rawness of Friedkin's *The French Connection* and Lumet's *Serpico*. But this was 2002, and no one was making movies like that anymore. No one except for Joe Carnahan, a former promotions producer for a Sacramento TV affiliate who managed to cobble together a career by using the tools around him and never giving up. *Narc*, as he's quick to point out, was his sixteenth script. In the wake of the low-budget film, Carnahan found himself sought after for projects by the likes of Tom Cruise and Harrison Ford. Ford was said to have called *Narc* the best film he had ever seen.

---

*Where did you grow up?*
JC: I grew up in Michigan. I lived for a time briefly in Utah, and then in Michigan.

*Your dad was in the Air Force, and he also had a grocery store?*
JC: Yeah. He had a small grocery store.

*When did you realize your family wasn't well off financially?*
JC: We lost our house and we moved out to California. The bank basically took it. I'll never forget my mother one Christmas said, "Instead of having presents under the tree, why don't we cut pictures out of catalogues of things we like?" And I remember my brother and I laughing at that suggestion. I didn't realize until I was much older how hand-to-mouth it really was. My dad I think in his best year was making almost $19,000 a year. I'll never forget to this day being in this really small house and the Realtor actually telling my parents, "You

guys are poor." He literally said that. He was looking over our credit report. How my dad didn't kill him, I don't know.

*That's got to hit you hard as a kid.*
JC: Oh, yeah. We weren't below the poverty line or anything, but we certainly were lower middle class.

*What early film experiences resonate with you today?*
JC: Nothing really knocked me on my ass like *Raiders of the Lost Ark*. I'll never have an experience like that in a movie again. I was just so thoroughly swept up. It was the first time where I realized I was being manipulated by a movie. I saw it in a little theater in Mt. Pleasant, Michigan. And I remember *Star Wars* specifically. I remember in '97 I was seeing the new release, and it was a brand-new print. I was sitting there at the end in that trench scene and he goes, "Use the force," and I swear to God the hair on my arms stood up. I'm like eight years old again. It was that kind of moment.

*What were the first shorts you had an opportunity to shoot?*
JC: We had a great super eight camera and I shot a bunch of shorts on that. I shot a Sergio Leone kind of thing called *Noose*. I did a bank-robbery movie with some buddies of mine because I had an old '77 Camaro that looked like a getaway car. We did all kinds of shit like that, and I shot it on this super eight with a wide-angle attachment because I just was in love with the way it looked. I remember sitting in my bathroom at my mom and dad's house during the 1988 NBA finals cutting my films. It was great. I was very contemptuous of video.

*You went to San Francisco State? Is that where your film tastes began to expand?*
JC: That's where I really became aware of the avant-garde, Kenneth Anger, Stan Brakhage, Maya Deren, stuff that was really off kilter to me because I considered myself, and still do, as having reasonably commercial tastes. I remember looking at *Persona* for the first time, and it really knocked me on my ass and I couldn't figure out why.

Some of the images really haunted me. I was kind of picking my favorites and watching everything I could, just developing different tastes in movies.

*Were there any moments where you became especially resolute about pursuing filmmaking as your career?*
JC: I was working myself through school, doing a lot of manual labor and working for a moving company. I worked for a deli supplier for like a year. It was just brutal. I'll never forget the conversation I had with the owner taking me through this warehouse with all this provolone and these big wedges of salami and him telling me, "Film you could do as a hobby; this you could do for your life." I'm thinking, "Oh my God!"

*If there's anything that's going to motivate you to make films . . .*
JC: We all look for little catalysts, and that was kind of a little signpost, "Dead End Ahead."

*When did you start to write?*
JC: I started actively writing in college. To be honest with you, I didn't know how to write a screenplay so I took *Silver Bullet*, which is a published shooting script, and wrote it like that. I had no idea what I was doing. It was unreadable. I'll never forget sending a script to Shane Black, who at the time was probably twenty-five and he'd written *Lethal Weapon*, and getting a letter back from him. He could have really dashed the hopes of this impressionable kid. He took the time to read it, so that was huge. I just thought that was such an amazing thing for him to do.

*What did you say to him?*
JC: I was like, "Can I use your name to get an agent?" I was just a dumb kid. I didn't know any better. He said, "I'll do my best for you." But his hands were really tied. The fact that he was even willing to take time out was such a huge thing for me. I always tell people that *Narc* was the sixteenth script that I'd written. You have to really go through that to appreciate it. It was a ton of stuff that will never get

made! I remember writing three scripts in a ten-month period. I was working a warehouse job, and I would go in at five in the afternoon, get off at five in the morning, and come back and write until I had to work again. I was just seized by this kind of paralyzing fear that that's where I was going to be for the rest of my life. I didn't want to end up there under any circumstances.

*How were the films you were making in school received?*
JC: Some were kind of head-scratchers. I did a thing called *Wired to Blow* about a conversation between a prison psychologist and a mass murderer who had targeted women. When I look back on that now, it's really deeply disturbing some of the stuff that's coming out of this guy's mouth, how misogynistic it is. I remember screening that and making some enemies out of the women in that class. (laughs)

*When you graduated, what were you thinking about your future?*
JC: I thought, "I have got to transition out of moving dressers and humping refrigerators. I have got to stop doing that and really take myself seriously." So I go to work for this guy named Gary Jones and you know there's, like, a handful of people in your life who you say, "OK, if I have an enemy list, this guy's on it." So I go to work for him and he's a Jet Ski salesman and he wanted to get into video duplication and commercials. Basically what he's doing is soft-core porn out of the back of this place. At night he's bringing strippers over. I just had nothing but contempt for this guy. I thought he was a jack-off and a punk. Gary had a habit of firing guys on a Friday so they wouldn't roll over into the next pay period. So he calls me into his office around four thirty and cans me, and I went after him. I had to be taken out of there forcibly. I was just livid because at the time my wife was five months pregnant and I thought, I'm done. So I go home and I sit there and I'm spinning. I literally sit down and I remember there was a TV station in town that did all their own on-air promotions. So on a lark I said, "To hell with it," and I sat down for an hour and wrote three of them. I take these down to the station and I put them in a manila envelope to the attention of the promotions director. I got the gig, and

that began what I still consider the best day-to-day kind of time-clock job I ever had.

*And it was because of the access to the equipment there that you were able to make a small film of your own?*
JC: Yeah, and by then I'd made a lot of professional contacts. I knew people at the TV stations in Sacramento. I'd done favors for them. I'd written short scripts for them, and I knew there was going to come a time where I was going to call on all these markers. And I'd read Robert Rodriguez's book [*Rebel Without a Crew*]. He kind of demystified a lot of it. I took from that, how to do it quickly and inexpensively.

*Is it true that* Blood, Guts, Bullets and Octane *started as a play?*
JC: Yeah, it was called *Filibuster*. It was about the kidnapping of a congressman, and I thought, It's not working as a one-act. It doesn't have legs but these characters are really fascinating. I started shooting it. I just didn't want to wait anymore. I had, like, thirty really good pages and I thought, "What the hell, I don't know where it's going. Let's just go and we'll figure this out." It was thirteen days over six months we shot that film. I decided I didn't want to turn out like one of these guys at Starbucks, sitting there talking about what kind of movie they're going to make. It's in their head and it's never going to get out. I was twenty-six and I was like, "OK, I want to go, man." It was important for me to do it, because it was going to keep my skills sharp and it was better than just sitting with my thumb up my ass waiting for a break to come.

*And it cost just $7,300 to make?*
JC: Yeah. That's what it wound up being. At the time it was like, "Guys, let's just have some fun." We weren't looking to launch careers. I was looking at it like, "OK, I'm done doing shorts. I just want to see if I can hold a three-act narrative together." And I'm using myself and a lot of amateur actors. You're not going to find any method-trained actors in it. (laughs) No one had read *An Actor Prepares*.

*A lot of comparisons were made to Tarantino's style when people looked at it.*
JC: It became very easy to say it's just a fucking Tarantino knockoff and that's all it is. I look at that film and I see a lot of my personal life in there, the relationship between this old man and this infirm, invalid woman and this whole sacrificing-at-all-costs stuff. I don't look at the aspects of it that are kind of crime fiction. Would I make that film again? Hell, no. Nor would I make any of the short films I've made. It's either you evolve or you don't. At the time Tarantino moved over the entire independent film scene like the fucking Hindenburg. I take nothing away from Quentin. I'm a huge fan! But I thought this idea that he'd somehow invented sliced white bread, it didn't hold. You were really discounting the work of John Woo and Sam Peckinpah and Elmore Leonard, a lot of the stuff that influenced him.

*What was the film about if it wasn't the crime elements for you?*
JC: Once the hipster shit was stripped away, you had a story about a guy who was doing extraordinary things to save his dying wife. That's really what it was. It's very important to me and, if anything, that's the part that's most ignored. It's funny, I see the Danny Woo character in Ray's character in *Narc*, that the ends do justify the means. Sometimes you have to do horrible shit to see a right done. I'm absolutely drawn to that. The stuff I'm working on traffics in that vein I think because maybe I see myself in a lot of ways like that. I consider myself a relatively decent guy and a polite guy and I treat everybody the same and I'm not an asshole, but there's a part of me that's incredibly mercenary. But I think it's all in the justification of the greater good.

*What was the turning point for* Blood, Guts? *Before Sundance, how did it gain momentum?*
JC: We went to the Independent Feature Film Market which is a meat market. But Amy Taubin in *The Village Voice* decided to champion the movie and literally everything changed overnight. And then there was this whole hustle to get this thing ready for its Sundance premiere.

*How much were you working on it up until Sundance?*
JC: Eighteen hours a day at some stretches, just brutalizing ourselves to get this thing done. I remember going to Seattle and they had done an optical—I think it was the sniper rifle scope POV—and I looked at it and thought it was one of the worst optical effects I'd ever seen. I remember going outside in front of this lab and pulling a signpost out of the ground and throwing it in the street. Once it went to Sundance, I had a bad screening and then at the Holiday Village Cinema, it was a bunch of snowboard kids and they loved it. Then once I got the film in decent shape I went on to Berlin, went to Edinburgh, went to Tokyo. It was great. I got to see most of Europe and Japan and Asia on a little $7,300 nothing investment.

*Your follow-up was* Narc. *Was that a script that was ever shopped around as something for someone else to direct?*
JC: Mark Pellington was a name that they were mentioning seriously at one point to direct, and I was just not having it. I was not going to allow that thing to go out without me directing. At the time, it was functioning as a tremendous writing sample. I was getting all these tremendous writing jobs off of it.

*But you still couldn't get* Narc *off the ground for you to direct?*
JC: For three years it was, "Nah, we're not interested." I was like, Jesus, I cannot get this thing afloat at all! But I was just bound and determined that I was going to do that film come hell or high water. If I had to do it for five hundred grand, if I had to do it for fifty grand, I was going to make that movie.

*I know the turning point came when Ray Liotta signed on. Did you guys connect on the material right off the bat?*
JC: Almost immediately. Because I saw in Ray this willingness to allow himself to be kind of reinvented and for me to mess with his physical appearance. I like to take an image of something and just stand it on its ear. I don't see Ray when I see that movie. I see that character. I always remember watching the monitor while Ray is sitting in the

car, talking about his wife. To watch something you've written conveyed so effortlessly and so beautifully and so sublimely by a guy that talented is just a treasure! You feel this kind of lump in your throat as you're watching him do this and you're just thinking, "My God, man, I'm literally watching a home run in slow motion." That's what it felt like.

*There seem to be influences from William Friedkin's work and Errol Morris's* The Thin Blue Line *in the film.*
JC: Oh, absolutely. I was a huge fan of *The Thin Blue Line*. It's a much bigger trendsetter than it's remembered for. All those TV reenactment docudrama things owe a huge debt to that movie. I had always been a big fan of the cop film. I'd watched *Serpico* and obviously Friedkin's stuff. They were inspired by the French New Wave and this kind of documentary style of capturing things. I just kind of wrote this script in the spirit of that. I also had a lot of friends that were cops, and one of my friends—one that was in a lot of my short films—is a raging heroin addict. He was a snitch for this undercover narcotics cop and, for whatever reason, I was granted kind of this fly-on-the-wall status when I would hang out with these guys. They would talk about any number of things in front of me, a lot of which wound up in the film.

*Did the prevalence of television cop shows influence you at all?*
JC: I thought that TV had effectively killed what I considered to be this classic genre. *NYPD Blue* had come out, and I thought it was incredibly by the numbers. If you ask anybody during the time we were making *Narc*, I kept saying, "We cannot make fucking *Law & Order*!" Because when the script was making the rounds, I was hearing, "Oh this is fucking *Cagney & Lacey*. Who gives a shit about this stuff? Nobody cares about a cop film." It was rejected out of hand by everybody.

*The film has an accomplished look despite the small budget. How much did you have?*
JC: If we had $3 million to make that film, I'd eat my hat, man. The crew was constantly being told there was no money and they were

going to shut the film down. It created this powerful sense of dread and angst that if you're shooting a romantic comedy you're fucked, but the fact that we were doing this kind of heavy-duty melodrama, it worked beautifully. I would never want that kind of dread hanging over a project, but it actually pervaded the entire film and I think really worked well.

*The money in fact nearly ran out at one point, didn't it?*
JC: I remember walking on the set and hearing the production manager say to the crew, "I don't know when you're going to be paid or if you're ever going to be paid again." Rounding the corner and seeing the entire crew standing there, what do you do in that moment? You really have to find your feet in that moment, because they are definitely put to the fire. So I was really straight with them. I was like, "Listen, I've got a wife and children and the family and bills to pay and if this shit continues, if we don't have money by the end of today, I'll walk off this film." And for whatever it was worth I think being totally honest with them in that moment in some way galvanized us and we carried through.

*Having to lead in those conditions with seasoned pros like Liotta and Jason Patric, was there ever tension? I've heard you and Jason had some conflicts.*
JC: We had plenty of tête-à-têtes. Literally that same morning I heard that announcement I got into a major screaming match with him, thinking, "OK, I'm going to hit this guy." It was that kind of shit and then we're drinking beers together by the end of the night.

*What got you so enraged at the time?*
JC: My opinion at the time was not everybody was doing their homework. Not everybody was prepared to do what we needed to do. And I felt he was reacting from a place that was trying to cover that, trying to mask the fact that his level of preparedness was not where it needed to be.

*So he was relying on his natural talents instead of knowing the material?*
JC: Or using diversionary tactics to kind of conceal what it really was, which was like, "Come on, kid, you don't know your lines." And again taking nothing from Jason, because I thought he was extraordinary and the guy does more with just a look in his eyes than most of this younger generation of actors can do with a fucking three-hour movie.

*The chase scene that opens the film really sets the tone.*
JC: I hadn't seen what I considered to be a really great foot chase. *To Live and Die in L.A.* had a really interesting one. I thought, You know what, let's give it a shot, man. Let's just shoot for the moon and see what happens. I wanted the immediacy and the rush to kind of just take people's breath away and just rocket them into that world. I really wanted the audience to feel the sensation of literally hunting someone down with the intention of either apprehending them or killing them.

*Does* Narc *feel like a personal film to you? Do you see yourself in it?*
JC: It's funny, I look at *Narc* and I see the kind of disintegration of my marriage. They're always fighting and you know cop work, like in filmmaking, you're taken away for large periods of time and you obsess over your work and things get left by the wayside. It's kind of like, Goddamn I don't want to see something that the director doesn't personalize in some way. I look at *Punch Drunk Love* and I think, Damn, I want to believe that this guy was in love like that at some point in his life, because it moves me in a way that I see myself in that. I think that's what all great films do for us. They come down to two very simple things: human beings and human behavior. At least, the ones that I'm really intrigued and interested by. I don't need to see fucking spaceships blow up.

*When you look at the filmmakers out there today, is there one in particular to emulate?*
JC: To me, the career to have is Soderbergh's. Soderbergh is that throwback to kind of that early '70s filmmaker that was really iconoclastic

and truly maverick in the way they made movies. He makes *Ocean's Eleven* and then goes on to make *Full Frontal* for $2 million. I have great admiration for those types of choices because they don't adhere to conventional wisdom. Unfortunately you wind up with the generation of filmmakers we have now. They're certainly not setting the world ablaze with personal vision. We're becoming more and more commercial, more driven by the opening weekend. It's a bunch of fucking nonsense, because those are not the movies that we're going to remember in twenty or twenty-five years, nor are we going to give a shit about the people who make them. There're so many directors kind of dabbling here and there. And you go back to Scorsese and he just made movies, man. He wasn't developing fucking TV!

*Since* Narc *you were attached to two very high-profile projects starring Harrison Ford and Tom Cruise respectively. Because your participation with both fell through, have you been concerned that perhaps there might be a perception that Joe Carnahan isn't ready for that level of filmmaking?*

JC: No. If anything, I've gotten this amazing street cred and it's not anything that I'm looking for. But I don't think that perception's out there. If it is, do I give a shit? Not really, because I know I was perfectly willing and able under circumstances that were obviously beneficial to me to execute both those films. I'm not saying that I'm any better than anybody else. I have my own personal demons and my own kind of things that I have to answer to internally and I also have two small children and if I don't love it every morning when I wake up and every night when I go to bed, I'm wasting my time. I'm taking time away from my kids and [that is what] really is going to mean something to me in fifty years when I can't get a film made because I'm too old or dead. I'm not going to be known as the dad who was never here or never around. I refuse to be that guy! If that winds up costing me professionally, I'm willing to pay that price.

## THE DIRECTOR'S TAKE
## JOE CARNAHAN

*What is the first film you ever saw?*
The Love Bug

*What is your favorite film of all time?*
Raiders of the Lost Ark and Yojimbo

*What's your favorite line in a film?*
"Isn't that just like a Dago, brings a knife to a gunfight."—*The Untouchables*

*What movie made you realize that film was an art?*
Raging Bull

*What movie do you consider your guilty pleasure?*
American Pimp

*Who is your favorite movie character of all time?*
Cool Hand Luke

*What's your favorite movie snack food?*
Popcorn soaked in butter

*Who is your favorite director of all time?*
Akira Kurosawa

*Who is the most impressive filmmaker working today?*
Paul Thomas Anderson

*What quality do the best directors share?*
Great humanity

*Who is your favorite actor or actress of all time?*
Paul Newman

*Who is your favorite actor or actress of today?*
Meryl Streep

*Who would you cast as yourself in a film about your life?*
Myself

*If you could remake one movie, what would it be?*
Citizen Kane

*What is your best quality as a director?*
Sense of humor

*Finish this sentence: I'll never direct a movie with . . .*
more special effects than dialogue.

*Finish this sentence: The perfect movie is . . .*
inspiring, consciousness-shifting.

*What will they be saying about your work fifty years from now?*
"Joe who?"

*What piece of advice do you have for aspiring filmmakers?*
Hustle your ass off and, to quote current San Diego Chargers coach
Marty Schottenheimer, "Refuse to be blocked."

*What are you as passionate about as moviemaking?*
My kids

# KERRY CONRAN

"We've finally come to a time in our history where you can create what you see in your imagination, what you dream. To have that as an opportunity is very interesting."

## SELECTED CREDITS

*Sky Captain and the World of Tomorrow* (2004)–writer/director

Kerry Conran, a seemingly shy, self-effacing Michigan native, threw down the gauntlet as few filmmakers ever have with his first film, *Sky Captain and the World of Tomorrow*. Blending cutting-edge technologies with traditional filmmaking techniques so seamlessly, it's no wonder the project had been labored on for more than a decade. Of course, Hollywood wasn't aware of it being in production. In fact, only a handful of people were. That's because it was all being created in Conran's apartment on his home computers. Eventually the ambitious fantasy throwback to *Flash Gordon* serials became too big to live just there. It was brought to the screen in 2004 starring Jude Law and Gwyneth Paltrow. Conran's imagination and technical savvy may do nothing less than revolutionize and democratize the way films are made for decades to come. It almost sounds like another filmmaker who once dreamed impossible dreams of galaxies far, far away.

---

*Could you tell me a little about where you grew up?*
KC: I was born in Flint, Michigan, and I lived in some of the surrounding communities as I grew up. When I was growing up, Flint was almost like a steel town in the sense that it was built and founded on the auto industry. During the time I was growing up, it was a pretty flourishing town. The auto industry was doing fine and it was very "Americana." It was probably like any other picturesque place you could grow up in. On the one hand, it was a very unremarkable childhood. My mom was an artist and a painter and my father wrote. So they kind of encouraged our imaginations and creative sides, which was perhaps the only unusual thing. In that sort of city you're usually being honed for the auto industry. To think of anything outside of that wasn't blasphemous, but uncommon.

*Your dad worked in the auto industry?*
KC: Yes, in fact, he did.

*What sort of writing did he do?*
KC: Just smaller short-story kinds of things. He would work with me,

encouraging me, helping me, from a very early age. I think I was in first or second grade when I wrote a little play that we performed at the school and it was certainly something he helped me put together.

*What was the first-grade opus of Kerry Conran all about?*
KC: It was the trial for Goldilocks and the three bears. She was being held accountable for breaking and entering. It was a continuation that I don't think had ever been visited. (laughs) A strange topic for a first-grader.

*You're the middle child of three, and in fact your brother would later be the production designer on your film. Do you think you had any of the clichéd characteristics of the middle child?*
KC: Although I've grown to be more introverted, I wasn't that way growing up. Unbelievably, in high school I was actually the class clown. I was a bit more demanding of attention. Maybe that is the trait of a middle child. My brother and sister were happy to yield the stage to me.

*It's very interesting that you say you were the class clown, because many people now call you introverted and even shy. What happened? Did you really change that much?*
KC: I did go through this sort of metamorphosis when I left high school, and I think it's because I got a little bit more serious about really trying to leave Flint. I had always toyed with the idea of making films when I grew up, but it was a very sobering thought that I knew no one. Daring to think that I could ever make films in Hollywood was beyond even a fantasy. So I decided it was really going to take some effort and motivation on my part. Literally the first summer I was out of school, I spoke to no one. I stayed in my room and started writing and thinking, sort of trying to figure things out for myself. I would say that some phenomenon did happen that made me shut off the rest of the world a little bit more later in life than I did growing up. When I left Flint, and this is the strange thing, that memory is frozen in time for me in a way. I have a little bit of a Peter Pan complex in that I don't feel any different. I really don't feel like a proper, functioning adult

member of society yet. I still feel like I'm going through an extended childhood in a way.

*You're just playing the part of an adult?*
KC: Exactly, and that's why it's hard when people actually take me seriously now. When you get in a room with adults and they're talking about giant robots, it's a surreal experience.

*What do you think you were connecting with early on in the movies you saw?*
KC: I think it was a channel directly to what you imagine as a child when you're running around with towels on, pretending you can fly. In the case of *Godzilla* or *King Kong*, it was the sheer spectacle. The scope of it was maybe even a little bit bigger than your own imagination.

*By my math you would have been about twelve years old when* Star Wars *came out. I would guess that it had an impact on you?*
KC: I remember that vividly. I remember getting in the car and pretending you were in a spaceship. It was such an experience that it followed you all the way home and maybe for the rest of your life for those that wanted to follow in its footsteps. I would say, yeah, it was a huge influence.

*When did you first get your hands on a film camera?*
KC: It was probably around ten, eleven, or twelve years old. I started off doing stop-motion animation. And that's actually what I would say was the other gigantic influence, the films of Ray Harryhausen. Eventually I started to do short films with friends and family. Probably the longest film I made was ten minutes long. I was about fifteen or so when I did that, and I spent probably a year or two on it. That was eventually the film I used to get into CalArts, actually.

*How did you end up at CalArts?*
KC: It was a small arts school and, coming from a smaller town, that had an immediate appeal to me over the giant universities. It also en-

couraged experimentation, which was interesting to me. I had never even traveled outside of Michigan to that point, and I was sort of deposited there without a car. I was suddenly exposed to all these artists and film students.

*Your thesis film is notable for its ambition. Tell me about* That Darn Bear.

KC: It's appallingly embarrassing to speak about now. I spent almost three whole years working on it. I saw an opportunity to work with some of the animators [at CalArts] to make a film that combined live action and animation not unlike *The Incredible Mr. Limpet*, but in a way that hadn't been done before—to make it really interactive, to make this animated character physically interact with human beings in a live world. That was sort of the impetus for it.

*Unfortunately Robert Zemeckis had a similar idea at that time with* Who Framed Roger Rabbit?

KC: Yeah, and it was a year into *That Darn Bear* that I was just starting to hear about it. Obviously Zemeckis had really taken this well beyond what I could do on no money. I couldn't even dream to compete with what he had done. When it came time to do the animation, the expense was growing and my desire to finish it was diminished because I'd already seen a polished professional version of what I was trying to do. I never finished the film.

*Coming out of school, did it seem you were any closer to realizing your dreams?*

KC: It seemed clear that the idea of having a film financed was still every bit as distant as it was when I was growing up in Flint. Even though I'd gotten much closer and I'd met some people, it was almost impossible to get anyone to take a chance on you. It was around that time that, for the second time in my life, I decided to drop out of existence. I realized I would never get an opportunity to do [a film] unless I made one for myself. So that's when I started looking at the emerging computer technology and how it could be used. And it was not unlike the same spirit that interested me in making *That Darn Bear*. It was: How do you integrate the computer technology with a live-action film but for a different purpose—to make it look like a real film but ultimately never leave your room? My goal was never to leave my apartment and feel like I'd traveled across the globe, and I thought it was possible.

*When was the first inkling for* Sky Captain *born?*
KC: Around 1990, when I was just leaving school. I wrote a spec for an animated Saturday-morning cartoon that I actually took to Hanna-Barbera, who promptly told me they don't take outside material. It was initially supposed to be a serial about a pilot and a reporter and they were pitted against a scientist who manned a giant robot. And the idea, not unlike the film, was to have it end with a cliffhanger each Saturday morning. So it really began there and was later sort of folded into a live-action version of it and expanded greatly and modified.

*You were working on the short that became* Sky Captain *essentially in isolation for years. How were you making a living?*
KC: By the time I'd graduated from school, I'd gotten a decent working knowledge of what you could do with the Mac. I had written a few little things for it, and somehow word got out that I was doing quirky nonintuitive things with the computer that filled certain gaps. I had gotten a phone call to write a piece of animation software. Instead of being paid, I asked to keep the equipment that had to be purchased to do it, always with a mind of trying to make this short film of mine. I was really on life support. I had just enough money to survive. That also contributed to me dropping out of society. I just dedicated every waking hour I had to working on the short.

*Can you explain to me what the goal was? What were you trying to accomplish with the film you were creating in your computer?*
KC: I simply sat down and thought about the images I wanted to create and the story that I wanted to tell, and I looked at films. One of

the films I studied and tore apart was *The Third Man*, and I would look at not just the composition of the frame but what made it up. I would look at a closeup of Joseph Cotten and I'd realize that the background was a wall that had a splash of light and I thought, "Well, I can create that fairly easily." I can mimic that. Then I would look at an exterior view and it would be a city and I thought, "How would you create that?" I started looking at archival photos and I thought, as long as you had some sort of depth in front of the blue screen, you could make it look like people were walking in front of this photograph. Then I realized if I could put people in photos, then the sky was the limit. I literally could do anything. That was really the impetus and creation of this whole notion, which is to treat live action exactly how animation's been done for the last hundred years and use these new tools to facilitate it.

*At one point I understand you considered presenting* Sky Captain *as a sort of "lost film" that you had discovered?*

KC: I never expected anything I'd created to be seen outside of perhaps the Sundance Film Festival. That was the big dream at the time. I knew that, ambitious as I wanted to be, I could never really finish 120 minutes by myself. So I got this idea where I created a fictional character for myself and made him a protégé of Frank Capra. I thought, What if there was this unknown genius who had done things that no one had seen in that era but it was so beyond what anyone had seen? I was going to take photos of Capra and put someone else in it and just doctor still photography almost like *Zelig* or *Forrest Gump*. I thought that's the way I can do it. I can burn up ten minutes just with still frames and audio and pretend the rest of it was lost. I wanted to present this thing not as a hoax, but a completely fictional accounting of a person and a film that never existed and present the entire thing as if it was newly discovered. It was really only when I showed the film to Jon Avnet that I realized that I could actually fund a real version of it instead and I went in that direction. I'll never really know if that was a mistake or the way to go. I really would have loved to have done the other version, I have to say.

*At a certain point during the years you were working on the short, weren't you getting concerned over how long it would take to finish?*
KC: There was a point midway through the whole process that I found myself in the fetal position when I realized what I had gotten myself into. I accepted that doing it on my own would probably be a twenty-year enterprise. That's why I started investigating ways to maybe only have to make actually twenty minutes of footage and supplement it, presenting it a different way. My brother finally pulled it from my grasp and said, "You should show it." If he had not encouraged me to show it to Marsha Oglesby, who later showed it to Jon, I don't know what would have happened. There's every chance I'd still be working on it right now.

*Marsha was a producer and a family friend. Jon Avnet, of course, had directed many films, including* Fried Green Tomatoes. *After refusing to show what you'd been working on to virtually anyone, you must have been nervous to show the few minutes you had completed to a genuinely successful filmmaker.*
KC: I was curious about how he was going to respond to it, but I almost didn't care. I never expected anyone to give me a chance or to help me. If something came from it, that would be great. If nothing came from it, that would be fine too. I could go home and continue to work. And if it took me forever, it took me forever.

*When you showed him what you had, what did he say?*
KC: Clearly it made an impression on him. He wanted to see it again. Then he asked me, "What is it? Is it real?" I think he thought it was newsreel footage I had doctored. Then I sort of explained to him my idea behind it, that it was a method to make a film that was a little bit different. It was sort of reverse-engineering the way films had been made up to that point, with an eye towards being ambitious but economical. Just the business side of him probably made the lights go on. I think he saw that if we could create something for that little money— at the time we were talking about maybe no more than $5 million to make it—and have it nearly be competitive with mainstream films,

then that really was something new and potentially revolutionary. Our exact conversation afterwards was, he asked, "What do you want?" and I said, "I want to finish my film." And he said, "I think we can do that."

*There were several key changes to the film from how you initially conceived it. One was the decision to go from black-and-white to color.*
KC: Every scene existed in black-and-white first, and we kind of colored on top of that. It was conceived as a black-and-white film. By the time [executive producer] Aurelio De Laurentiis got involved, it wasn't even a question. (laughs) It was, I won't give you money. Either make your movie or not, but it will be color. At one point in time it was maybe only for the foreign release will we have to go color. Then there was talk of maybe we can release a black-and-white version in New York and L.A. Needless to say, none of that ever happened.

*How did casting the film take shape?*
KC: Honestly, discussing names, be it Gwyneth's or Jude's, just seemed absurd to me. It seemed to me so far-fetched that anybody would really want to be in this film. It was like, "Why are we even wasting time talking about these absurdities? Let's start interviewing unknowns and just get it over with."

*Using unknowns was, in fact, your plan for casting from the start.*
KC: I thought if you saw a recognizable face, you would be removed from the film. As the film got more ambitious, the financing of it was more predicated on Gwyneth Paltrow's and Jude Law's names attached to it. I understood [this] from a practical sense. My interest was to get the film made. I do think that all of these things changed and affected the film that I'd originally started. By the same token, I can't say I have any bad feelings about any of it. It's just a part of the process.

*Tell me about your experience of working with actors in your film. I assume you had never worked with actors that much?*
KC: I had very little experience other than directing actors in student films, and those were mainly friends. Student actors and that sort of

thing. To go immediately to a couple Oscar winners—Gwyneth and Angelina—and Jude, who's comparably accomplished, the strange thing was, it all seemed so surreal at a certain point, it didn't affect me anymore. The thing that I had to get over was probably with Gwyneth more than anyone else. We would be shooting a scene, and I would know that it's not exactly how I wanted it, and in my own mind I'm having this wrestling match of, "Who am I to go out there and tell Gwyneth Paltrow to do it another way?" That was the biggest struggle I had—to have enough confidence to give them my opinion. What I learned, especially from Gwyneth, was that she would have been terribly upset in fact if I *didn't* do that. That was probably the greatest lesson that I learned.

*What was that first morning of the shoot like for you?*
KC: That was probably the single most traumatic moment on the entire film for me. I just kind of woke up and realized, "What in God's name have I gotten myself into?" It was basically walking into that soundstage and strangely everything was just kind of barren. You walk in and see Jude Law and Gwyneth Paltrow dressed up as these characters that you wrote, sitting in this blue-screen environment and it was like, "How have they agreed to do this movie based on some goofy idea I had?" But mainly it was just all these people—veterans who had been making movies and had worked on *Star Wars*—they all turned to me at the same time and I was The Guy. I could either turn and run away or finish what I'd gotten myself into. Once we'd shot the first couple of scenes, I knew everything was going to be OK. I can't say I ever relished being in the limelight or being the guy that everyone was looking to.

*What are your thoughts on whether subtlety and nuance of performance is lost when a film utilizes as much blue-screen work as yours employed?*
KC: I don't buy the concept that necessarily you compromise performance. I will agree that it does require a lot more prep and planning and thought on the part of both the filmmakers and the actors, but there's no reason you can't get really solid performances. You can't be-

gin to compare the experience to traditional filmmaking, and that's part of the mistake. It's more analogous to theatre.

*Do you think your career will revolve around fantasy and sci-fi, or do you anticipate that you'll experiment in other genres?*
KC: I hope so. I am more drawn to spectacle and things that are more experimental in nature. For me, the filmmaker who has made films that have continued to reinvent themselves is Robert Zemeckis.

*He seems like the most logical parallel for you as you begin your career.*
KC: He is the guy who I would most pattern myself after.

*It seems that both of you have that dual interest in creating interesting stories and an almost entrepreneurial approach to experimenting with new filmmaking techniques.*
KC: To a tee. He is who I probably most feel a kinship with, both on the scale that he operates and just in the invention that goes into everything he does. There's always going to be something interesting, whether he succeeds or not.

*Your next project, Edgar Rice Burroughs's* John Carter of Mars, *is another ambitious fantasy. It's also a film that has a storied past.*
KC: Over the last seventy years they've tried to make this film. There were early tests for it by Bob Clampett from Disney. This was originally supposed to be the first animated film before *Snow White*. Ray Harryhausen was another person who was looking into doing it and was overwhelmed by the technical challenge that it represented. More recently, I think John McTiernan and Tom Cruise were attempting to do it. It's kind of like *Lord of the Rings* in that for many years people have been trying to bring it to life. That's probably what intrigued me the most: Can I do something that no one has been able to do for the last seventy years? It's the father of modern sci-fi in a way. Without *John Carter*, you likely wouldn't have had *Flash Gordon* or *Buck Rogers*, *Star Wars*, and *Lord of the Rings*. It's an intriguing thing to bring [to the screen] this seminal work that has largely been forgotten.

*With* John Carter, *is there a goal as to what technological boundaries you'd like to push?*
KC: I think the goal is to try to bring things to the screen that you've never seen before. I like to present things that are new and fresh, which is really difficult to do in this day and age. A lot of it falls on using all the tools that are available right now in creative ways and applying them in ways that you haven't seen before. For instance, in the use of live sets and miniatures. Film is such a rich medium that isn't just limited to filming live actors in front of a set. There's so much more that we can do, that we've yet to scratch the surface. We've finally come to a time in our history where you can create what you see in your imagination, what you dream. To have that as an opportunity is very interesting.

*And that's what you want to be, the dream-maker, the guy that can actually translate the stuff in our heads to the big screen?*
KC: That's right. Yeah.

*As you look to the future, what do you envision for yourself?*
KC: There is a group of us that made *World of Tomorrow* who are now embarking on this project I think we'd like to form. The nearest I can compare it to is sort of a live-action Pixar production company—one that's all-encompassing but would principally deal with live action. The idea would be to utilize the technologies available to create very interesting, novel films that might be of a more independent nature, and also to give a chance to other filmmakers. If we can tear these budgets down, we might be able to produce films that give other people chances, but to use some of these techniques would allow them to dream a little bigger.

## THE DIRECTOR'S TAKE
## KERRY CONRAN

*What is the first film you ever saw?*
*Snow White and the Seven Dwarfs*

*What is your favorite film of all time?*
*King Kong* (1933)

*What's your favorite line in a film?*
"You're gonna need a bigger boat."—*Jaws*

*What movie made you realize that film was an art?*
*The Third Man*

*What movie do you consider your guilty pleasure?*
*1941*

*Who is your favorite movie character of all time?*
James Bond

*What's your favorite movie snack food?*
Red Vines

*Who is your favorite director of all time?*
Steven Spielberg

*Who is the most impressive filmmaker working today?*
Brad Bird

*What quality do the best directors share?*
The best directors have a personal and unique point of view and know
how to capture it.

*Who is your favorite actor or actress of all time?*
Cary Grant

*Who is your favorite actor or actress of today?*
Jude Law and Gwyneth Paltrow, of course.

*Who would you cast as yourself in a film about your life?*
Chris Farley

*If you could remake one movie, what would it be?*
Metropolis

*What is your best quality as a director?*
Patience

*What is your greatest weakness as a director?*
Interminable politeness

*Finish this sentence: I'll never direct a movie about . . .*
giant robots attacking New York City.

*Finish this sentence: The perfect movie is . . .*
one that makes you forget you are watching a movie.

*What will they be saying about your work fifty years from now?*
Perhaps, simply that I was an inventive storyteller and that my films
were uniquely my own.

*What piece of advice do you have for aspiring filmmakers?*
Take advantage of the amazing tools available to filmmakers today.
Anyone can make a film with a home computer and a DV camera.
The trick is to believe in the story you want to tell and never give up
until you realize it. And don't be afraid to dream big.

*What are you as passionate about as moviemaking?*
Honestly, there is nothing that comes close to making films for me.
It's all I ever wanted to do my entire life. It is difficult to top seeing a
dream come true.

# JON FAVREAU

"I've always wanted to call the shots because I
would rather fail than not have a chance to
figure it out on my own."

## SELECTED CREDITS

*Swingers* (1996)–writer
*Made* (2001)–writer/director
*Elf* (2003)–director
*Zathura* (2005)–director

**I**f Jon Favreau had a filmmaking mantra, he might paraphrase *The Godfather Part II*: Jon Favreau always made money for his partners. At least, that's been the plan. A savvy filmmaker, Favreau learned early on that creating profitable films meant getting the opportunity to make more films, and on a larger scale. He created filmmaking opportunities for himself after penning *Swingers*, a script that ironically was meant to launch his acting career. In fact, he was typecast in front of the camera. And so he's made every effort to not duplicate that fate behind it, helming a hard-edged R-rated comedy and PG family film back to back in his first two efforts as a director. With *Elf*, the Queens kid swung for the fences, trying to create a brand-new holiday classic from scratch. He actually did it too.

———————————

*I understand both of your parents were teachers?*
JF: My mother was a teacher before I was born, but she gave it up to raise me. My dad worked with emotionally handicapped kids. He really loved his work. That was a big thing, that he loved his job, and the idea to not love what you do was not really in the cards for me.

*What are your earliest memories of going to the movies?*
JF: My folks split up when I was about seven. I remember a lot of times when I would go with my dad, a movie would be the thing to do. I think that's pretty common. What else are you going to do? (laughs) There's something very special about seeing your dad laughing at the farting scene in *Blazing Saddles*. That's why Mel Brooks is one of my favorites—because it was something where I would genuinely laugh at it and [my dad] would laugh at it.

*Any early fantasies of being in the movies?*
JF: Sure! I was always in school plays as long as I could remember. I even made a black-and-white super eight monster movie with my father when I was in grade school. I guess he was my cinematographer. I wrote it and directed it and starred in it. We shot that in College Point, the neighborhood that he lived in, in Queens. It doesn't really

stand the test of time. It was me running around with torn-up cloth-ing, chasing people around Flushing Meadow Park.

*Where did you go to school?*
JF: I went to Queens College. I spent a lot of time around Washing-ton Square Park and the NYU campus. It was heavy-duty geek time for me. I was playing Dungeons & Dragons a lot, not knowing that those skills that you learn playing those games would help me in my acting and directing later. All the negative things that I did in my life, all the doodling in my notebook as an artist . . . all helped me. It was that sort of amalgam of skills that came together in very strange places but all seem to sort of tie together now in what I do as a filmmaker.

*Somehow you ended up working on Wall Street?*
JF: My friend's father had hired me away from college to work with him at Bear Stearns. I worked there for a year, getting, like, twenty grand a year, which was a lot of money. I finally gave my two weeks' notice. I didn't even want to make it to the Christmas bonus, which is a big thing on Wall Street. By 1988 I took the money and I bought a Harley. I went to Sturgis, South Dakota, for a Harley rally that August. My girlfriend at the time was in L.A., and I drove all the way from Sturgis to L.A. to meet her. I rode back alone and I passed through Chicago and I visited my friend Brian. He was in the Second City training center, and I went to watch him perform. There was his group and then there was a more experienced group. And that more experienced group was Chris Farley and Mike Myers and Tim Mead-ows and all these people who were great. And I remember they inter-viewed me onstage for one of the improv games. It blew my mind. I was like, "Oh my God, this is the best, better than standup, better than written plays, better than movies, this is great!" So I call my dad and I said, "I think I really want to do this." He said, "You're twenty-two years old; you're young enough that if you screw up, you could still change course again," and he gave me his blessing. So I moved out to Chicago and I started bartending and washing dishes at Second City. And all the things I was told I couldn't do, I was doing. I was au-

ditioning and I started a small graphic-design company and I was making a living acting in commercials and doing dinner theater. It was a very, very happy time for me.

*When you were in Chicago and performing at Second City, what was the dream?*
JF: Dreamwise, you work at Second City and you finally make it to the main stage. Lorne Michaels hears about you, you get hired for *SNL*, and then maybe you get on a sitcom or maybe you do some comic movies. Then you esteem yourself as an actor and you get some clout and you're able to get movies made and then you start writing and directing your own stuff, doing what Woody Allen does.

*So even at that point, the dream of all dreams was to direct?*
JF: Being Woody Allen. Directing your own shit, yeah. Being The Guy. Breaking ground.

*You wanted to be the creative force.*
JF: I've always wanted to call the shots because I would rather fail than not have a chance to figure it out on my own. I'm a very lazy person by nature. I have to be really engaged, and then I go straight from lazy to obsessive. I couldn't study chemistry, but I could memorize all the books for Dungeons & Dragons. It was ridiculous. The trick is to find what I like to do.

*How did* Rudy *come about?*
JF: I can't get hired by Second City. I've been there for close to four years. I had missed the first audition because I had done *The Untouchables* pilot. I was like a boxing referee or something. They said, "You really should come in," so I came in for the callback. I didn't know it at the time, but I nailed it and had gotten the part. They had looked in New York, Los Angeles, and Chicago. That was like the dream come true for somebody in Chicago. I remember walking around and my life feeling like a dream because not only did I get the part, but I had to be in South Bend, Indiana, less than forty-eight

hours later. And they don't fly you from Chicago. They sent me in a limo. (laughs) Very bizarre.

*When you got to South Bend, what was your attitude?*
JF: I just wanted to absorb everything. I did not leave the set. I went every day when I wasn't even on. I had snuck onto sets of films in New York with friends just to be around it. I had done extra work in Chicago, not to be discovered, just to be working towards that special spot on the set where the lights were all pointed, just to watch them.

*Do you remember any of those sets in particular?*
JF: Sure. A big one was *Hoffa*. During the riots, there were sixteen hundred extras. And it was a night shoot, so you were there from dusk till dawn every day in the cold. You'd show up and they'd put the shit in your hair to grease you up and they'd put you in the clothes. They'd make sure they weren't seeing the same people, and they'd stage you so that you'd run and they'd have all different groups. Well, I was the worst, because I would *always* go out there, whatever group they'd call, because I always wanted to be out there.

*So there are five different Jon Favreaus in the film?*
JF: Yes! You'd see me running one way with an ax handle, and then you'd see me running the other way with a shovel. I was all over the place—not good for editing, but good for me. Then of course Nicholson would come out and do his speech and I'd be, like, "Holy shit!" I'd listen to Nicholson and watch him do his thing.

*On* Rudy, *what did you observe about the way the director, David Anspaugh, ran his set?*
JF: He was the best. He's the one I still think about as a definitive experience with a director. My first day working, they were shooting me doing something comedic. I think it was a cutaway reaction–type shot and Anspaugh came up to me to and asked if I was wearing a wireless mike. I was like, yeah. He reached around to my pack and he flipped the switch off so now the people with headphones couldn't hear what

he was saying to me. Then he said, "Do you mind if I tell you you're going a little bit big?" And from that day on, I was just like, "This guy's the fucking best."

*That small gesture of turning the mike off so other people didn't hear . . .*
JF: He allowed me to keep my dignity and he was looking out for me so that I wasn't going to look like an asshole. He was going to be my barometer. And when you have a director like that, you can give yourself completely over to them. It's a wonderful, free feeling as a performer, and I try to create that now for my people.

*After* Rudy, *what were the events that led you to create* Swingers?
JF: I decided to travel out to L.A. for pilot season. I ended up moving out there, and my girlfriend didn't follow. She ended up living with another dude who I knew, and that broke my heart. I have issues from my mother dying when I was young, so I always took breakups really hard. I think it tapped into unresolved stuff. I was couch-surfing. It just sucked. I had nothing going on. That whole psychological state spoke to the character that I presented myself as in *Swingers*. I just wrote *Swingers* to make my friends laugh. I got a piece of software from my dad, Final Draft, for Christmas, and just started tapping away at it, and it was amazing how much it looked like a screenplay. Next thing you know, I've got eight to ten pages, twenty pages. You're showing it to people, and they're laughing. So I wrote the whole thing.

*Did the script attract any industry attention?*
JF: My agent sent it out, and people wanted to buy it. I was like, "Holy shit, what a great way to get my acting career going." So I took a meeting with this first-time director, and all his notes were to make it more badass. Put more of it in Vegas, more shit with the gun, more this, more that. And Vince's dialogue was annoying to him. I said, "Why don't you at least do a reading with the people that I had in mind?" and I thought maybe he'd remember one of them and cast them. We did the reading and it was great! My agent was like, "You should just

do this. We'll find the money somewhere." I was like, "Shit, that's pretty cool that she would say that and turn the money down." So we pulled it off the table and we set out to making it.

*You went to Sundance at one point before you had filmed it.*
JF: I was out there with Jason Priestley, who was attached. He was going to play Sue, and it was going to be me and Vince and him. Me and Vince had gone out and celebrated. We thought it was done. We've got Jason Priestley, and now the money's going to come. There were millions of stories about the "almost" of *Swingers*, but what it finally came down to was Doug Liman.

*Liman initially was simply helping you prepare as you pitched yourself as the director for the project.*
JF: He was the guy I was sort of going to so that I didn't sound like an idiot in meetings. I had auditioned for a part that Dave Chappelle ended up playing in his first movie, called *Getting In*. Finally, he was getting so involved with *Swingers* that he was like, "Look, I can get the money together." At first he was talking about codirecting and right before we started shooting, it turned into him directing [alone].

*How exactly did it go to him directing it himself from the two of you collaborating?*
JF: Right before we went into production he said, "Look, you'll still be creatively involved." The way he presented it was I'd run post- and preproduction and he'd be on the set running the show. We'd be partners and we put that all in the contract so I had approvals over everything. It was very much him with the camera and me with the actors. Because it was such a small crew, it was a good marriage because there was a lot of responsibility to go around. I was in the editing room every day, and that process was good. It got contentious at times, but nothing outside the norms of a creative relationship. After things were successful, everybody had issues with everybody but that's like every success story.

*What was the visual approach you and Doug took to the film?*
JF: My whole thing was get the money and shoot it as cheap as you can. It was really Doug's idea to use this documentary cinema vérité approach. His whole approach was, "Don't make *Party Girl* with half as much money, make *Clerks* with ten times as much money." He was taking all these chances. Of course, to us at the time it looked like he was kind of flying by the seat of his pants, but ultimately the movie looked really good and we couldn't have gotten that kind of energy or authenticity if we had done it the way I was planning to do it.

*During shooting, was there tension about the way he was directing?*
JF: During shooting, it was just a little half-assed. We'd sneak onto the golf course with his camera in the bag. It just seems like he doesn't know as much as he does when you're working with him, so it's a little disconcerting. There's a whole air of chaos around the way he does things, which has really served him well since. He definitely has an unconventional way of running his sets, and a lot of people are confused about the way that he does things. But the movies are good so that goes a long way. Trusting that makes you put up with that shit, but we didn't know that then. He cared about the movie and busted his ass on it.

*Did you find that immediately you were viable, as a writer, from* Swingers?
JF: Yeah, I was totally on the radar as a writer, but not so much as an actor. And it was strange, because I'd never really thought of this as a calling card for my writing. It was a great role that I was creating for myself but, you know, surprise, surprise.

*Meanwhile, your buddy Vince . . .*
JF: He totally popped off the movie. Part of it is that when you're playing the type of role you're playing in *Swingers*, people assume you're just playing yourself. They don't see your chops as an actor. The other thing is that Vince just totally fits the mold of what Hollywood is so hungry for in a movie star. He's got the look, the name, the talent.

*Weren't you working on a sequel after you filmed* Swingers?

JF: Yes, I wrote a sequel because I was so frustrated in the editing room when people were telling me a character wouldn't say that. I was like, "Shit, I'll write a whole movie about what these people would and wouldn't say and do. It was *Swingers: Part Two* and it was half flashback to Mike's childhood, like in *Godfather,* and then the other half was what happened the next year. I ended up writing a western too after that, *Marshal of Revelation,* about a Hasidic Jewish gun-fighter. (laughs) Miramax was ready to step up and do it. Harvey Weinstein was like, "Here's a million dollars; let's do it." And then that turned into a half million by the next phone call. But that wasn't the thing that scared me. The thing that scared me was not having final cut, because I saw the pressure that they had applied to other film-makers. And that was very scary, because the film had a very dark ending and I don't think it was inherently a commercial property.

*In this period, were you offered any films to direct?*

JF: The two I remember were *American Pie* and *A Night at the Roxbury. American Pie* didn't seem like a good follow-up for me at the time. I think the guys who did it did a great job. It was very successful, so it worked out for everybody.

*Instead you gained experience as a director first in television.*

JF: I wrote a pilot on spec and then I ended up using that leverage to get me to shoot the pilot and direct the pilot. Directing for TV put me in the position where I was responsible and accountable. The stakes weren't nearly as high. Unfortunately, nowadays you come out of film school and everybody's looking at that first project and judging your ability by that. That wasn't how it used to be. Steven Soderbergh worked in movies a long time before people started calling him a new young filmmaker. Now if you're not red hot out of the box, people are going to label you as you don't know what you're doing. There just aren't any more journeyman filmmakers. You've got to be great off the bat like Tarantino, or you're in trouble.

*How did* Made *emerge as the movie to make your feature directing debut on?*
JF: Vince and I were banging around, trying to get *Marshal* set up, and we had a lot of near misses with Miramax and other investors and, ultimately, it just wasn't happening. It was like, shit, if we just had something more contemporary, a little more of a genre film, we could get it made easily. So it became about writing a piece of material, and when I was on *The Replacements*, I wrote it. There's a lot of downtime when you're an actor.

*With* Made *it seems like you were combining your love of mob films with the sort of characters you are more familiar with.*
JF: Very much so. What appealed to me was, "How do you make the genre movie but not lose the reality of it?" Because if you lose the reality and the characters are not relatable, you're taking a lot out of the equation that I'm good at. I mean, I love Tarantino's films and I love Scorsese's movies, but in both cases I don't feel like that could be me up there. I feel like I'm watching another world of people. What I tried to do with *Made* was create people on such a low level that you could see yourself in that position. It was like the Rosencrantz and Guildenstern of the Mafia.

*I know it was very important to you to get final cut on* Made.
JF: Yeah. The way it worked is Vince said, "I'm going to star in this movie, and Jon and I are going to produce it together. Jon's going to direct it and Jon's writing it, and we're going to make it for the amount of money that Artisan said, which is five million." I would not do the deal until they gave me final cut.

*How important are rehearsals to you?*
JF: I always rehearse. Rehearsal is really an opportunity for the actors to voice whatever concerns they have. I'll usually adjust the language to fit the actor because I want it to be authentic to them. This isn't to say we're free-associating on the set. The beats are always very clearly defined, and I'm always very true to the material that's on the page.

*Why* Elf?

JF: I wanted to do a Christmas movie. I had been offered *Surviving Christmas*, and I opted not to pursue that one any further. And then this one came along and I thought it really plays into my sensibilities. I thought the one thing about Will Ferrell that I had not seen him do a lot of was show his heart as a person and as a performer. In developing the script, although it was edgy and irreverent at times, I wanted to keep it a PG movie, not a PG-13 movie that made fun of Christmas.

*What films did you look at for inspiration?*

JF: We watched *Tootsie*. We looked at the movies that were quote un-quote one-concept, one-joke movies, and saw which ones worked and which ones didn't and why. *Big* was very much a Rosetta stone for us. The thing that made *Elf* not just a one-joke extended skit is we really gave the character an arc and a story and things change over the course of it. We weren't just a series of jokes strung together. We tried to make it something that had a little bit of a message to it, and people responded.

*I appreciated the retro techniques you used in the North Pole scenes.*

JF: It was all stop-motion and forced-perspective. Everything was done the old-fashioned way there. I think the CG stuff looks dated a few years later. By using analog technology and stop-motion, at worst it's going to seem charming and nostalgic. At best it's going to look just as good. And that look never changes, no matter how sophisticated the audience gets.

*Zathura is an epic fantasy adventure on a much larger scale than* Elf.

JF: With this one, it's fun for me to explore special effects further. It's twice the budget *Elf* was. This is like me trying to tell a story visually and learning and taking a step in that direction just to round myself out as a filmmaker. It's very fun for me.

*What about the story drew you in?*

JF: The guy who wrote it, David Koepp, recently went through a divorce and he has two sons, and so the dialogue and the way he presents the kids is very real. It's in going through these adventures that the kids learn to become self-reliant and grow up. It becomes this coming-of-age thing for them.

*It sounds like old Spielberg territory.*
JF: When I read it, I was like, "Shit, that's what Spielberg would do." He would take a very mundane family relationship that people could relate to and set it as the backdrop of this extraordinary world and set of circumstances, like an alien arriving or *Close Encounters* or *Jaws*, even. If you look at the family scenes in *Jaws*, they're very real. So that was the challenge of this one: to keep the story real. If you have the heart and care emotionally about these characters, it's going to make it that much funnier and scarier and more exciting.

*You've said before that you think directing suits you because you're both decisive and obsessive.*
JF: Yeah. (laughs)

*Do you believe those are two important traits for a director?*
JF: Yeah, those are two good qualities, but it gets in the way of other things. What I've found is, if you have good people around you, you actually have to make very few decisions, because if a production designer comes to you and says, "Should the room be this color or this color?" you say, "Which one do you like?" They say, "Well, I like this one, but this one might look better on film." So then you pull your DP over and say, "Which one do *you* like?" Sometimes, unfortunately, what happens though is that every decision you make becomes like a Solomon, cut-the-baby-in-half decision.

*Having worked with directors I'd imagine you had disagreements with, what techniques have you avoided as a director?*
JF: I don't "handle" people. It's so much easier to manipulate actors than to really have an earnest discussion with them. It's very easy to say whatever's going to appease them and then turn around and do whatever you want to do. It's difficult to be forthright with people, be-

cause the job does not lend itself to that. (laughs) But I know that, as an actor, I appreciate it so much and I feel so much commitment to a director that's up-front with me. The trick is to create a stillness amidst the chaos, to be really able to discuss and discover what the scene is. Joel Schumacher used to do a thing where he always would turn to the actor when he was done and say, "Do you want to try another one for you?" He always found the time for anybody to do that, and I do that too. I learned that from him. I think it's all about making the actors understand that you are dialed-in to them. On *Zathura* I was working with two stars who were seven and twelve, and I really would discuss things like intention, subtext within the scene, overall arc during the movie. . . . I just think it's a good part of the process.

*What do you feel are the biggest challenges for you personally as a filmmaker?*
JF: I'm a very lazy person by nature, and if I'm not doing something I can be obsessive about, you're not going to get the most out of me. So the thing is for me to find movies that I can latch on to. I think the biggest challenge for any filmmaker unfortunately—or fortunately— is to learn how to make money for the people that are putting up the money, and that means don't spend more on a movie than it probably will make. Make sure somebody's going to turn a profit, whether you're making a $200,000 digital film or a $100 million action movie.

*But at the same time, your business isn't to predict box-office results.*
JF: It is though, because that's what gives you creative freedom. If I spend $35 million on *Elf* and it makes $170 million, that gives me so much creative freedom the next time out.

*Your first three films all turned a tidy profit. What happens when inevitably one of your films fails at the box office?*
JF: I will have enough of a track record by then that they'll know that it's an anomaly. They say Hyman Roth always made money for his partners. It sounds silly, but truer words were never spoken. Right now I'm making two PG movies in a row because that allows me to

spend the kind of money, build the kind of sets, and learn about visual effects and computer-generated effects and marketing and releasing a movie wide and hitting a wide audience. That's a lot of fun for me after working on very small movies. It's very nice to be able to see a movie hit the whole culture at once. It was very fun with *Elf*, seeing that happen. Probably after this one, I'll want to try something a little different. But I'll tell you this: If I'm making a movie for forty-year-old parents of small children, I'm probably not going to spend as much money as I would if I was doing a PG movie for kids. It's understanding the nature of the beast. Directing, you get one turn every year or two, and you've got to make enough money to live on; you've got to make an impression and you've got to do something you're going to be proud of, because you don't get that many posters on your wall when you die.

## THE DIRECTOR'S TAKE
## JON FAVREAU

*What is the first film you ever saw?*
*Chitty Chitty Bang Bang*

*What is your favorite film of all time?*
*The Godfather*

*What's your favorite line in a film?*
"If they move, kill 'em." —*The Wild Bunch*

*What movie made you realize that film was an art?*
It is?

*What movie do you consider your guilty pleasure?*
*Blazing Saddles*

*Who is your favorite movie character of all time?*
Bluto Blutarsky

*What's your favorite movie snack food?*
Vince Vaughn turned me on to sprinkling Raisinets into popcorn.

*Who is your favorite director of all time?*
Kurosawa

*Who is the most impressive filmmaker working today?*
The Coen brothers

*What quality do the best directors share?*
Their work is real and entertaining.

*Who is your favorite actor or actress of all time?*
Buster Keaton

*Who is your favorite actor or actress of today?*
Jack Nicholson

*Who would you cast as yourself in a film about your life?*
Me. I already did.

*If you could remake one movie, what would it be?*
Death Race 2000

*What is your best quality as a director?*
I really give a shit.

*What is your greatest weakness as a director?*
I'm lazy.

*Finish this sentence: I'll never direct a movie . . .*
that I don't believe in.

*Finish this sentence: The perfect movie is . . .*
emotionally engaging and original.

*What will they be saying about your work fifty years from now?*
"Who was he?"

*What piece of advice do you have for aspiring filmmakers?*
Make it yourself with what you have. Don't wait for someone else to
give you the green light.

*What are you as passionate about as moviemaking?*
My kids.

# MICHEL GONDRY

"My father said that my naiveté was my strength. I have this kind of optimism, even when things seem undoable."

## SELECTED CREDITS

*Human Nature* (2001)–director
*Eternal Sunshine of the Spotless Mind* (2004)–director
*The Science of Sleep* (2006)–writer/director

"Michel is only looking for one thing: to extract a bit of magic and mystery from things." So says Björk about her frequent music-video collaborator and friend, Michel Gondry. In scores of music videos and just three feature films to his credit, the French-born Gondry is one of the most unique talents working in film today. *Eternal Sunshine of the Spotless Mind*, one of the most celebrated films in years, showed off his ability to bring ingenious camera work, soulful direction of actors, and a unifying vision all to a complex script from the mind of Charlie Kaufman. Finally, his storytelling abilities had caught up with his groundbreaking technical work. Gondry is the rare filmmaker who can make the everyday extraordinary, and it all starts with his wonderfully off-kilter view of the world.

---

*There's a dreamlike quality to much of your work. Do you dream a lot?*
MG: Everybody dreams, I guess, but it's the way you think about them or remember them that's different. I don't remember them a lot, but enough to find what's quirky and interesting. I don't like psychoanalysis too much, and I think what it says about dreams is very dated. I've read so much about neurobiology, which is much more captivating. It's like the difference between astrology and astronomy. Astrology is a bunch of old beliefs. As for astronomy, it's amazing to read a book about black holes. It's good, because I like to compare theory with practicality.

*The film you're working on now is about dreams, isn't it? Can you tell me a little about* The Science of Sleep?
MG: It's like a journal of dreams in parallel with this guy's feelings about a girl he's fallen in love with, and how first he thinks they just have friendship and then he realizes he's in love with her.

*Have you finished filming it?*
MG: Yeah. I'm doing the editing right now.

*How is that going?*
MG: It's going. It's hard to judge it. I really like the way the actors are. I'm not sure about the story in general. It's very weird.

*Your last two films were as much known for Charlie Kaufman's writing as your directing.*
MG: Of course.

*And this is your first solo writing effort.*
MG: Exactly! In my life, I would say there are three major people who have been inspiring and supportive as collaborators: Etienne from my band, Oui Oui; then Björk; and then Charlie Kaufman. And now for the first time I am on my own.

*You've graduated, in a sense.*
MG: Well, I didn't graduate yet. That's the scary thing. I will graduate if it goes somewhere.

*I understand that you tend to doubt yourself a lot?*
MG: Yeah.

*So doing this film essentially on your own without one of these influential collaborators must be all the more frightening.*
MG: I got really scared doing this movie. I get scared all the time, but this one was different.

*Do you feel more pressure because of all of the acclaim you garnered for* Eternal Sunshine?
MG: Oh, yeah. Of course. It's more pressure, but it's not a bad pressure necessarily. A lot of people are excited to work with me. They forgive me a lot more than they would before. And my own paranoia is like, "Is it based on the success of *Eternal Sunshine,* or because they liked it?"

*You were born and raised in Versailles in France?*
MG: Yes.

*What did your parents do for work?*
MG: My mom was a flute teacher. My father was a computer programmer. Before that, he was working in electronics, making speak-

ers and microphones in a small company. He had this crazy hair
and a crew of young women working with him. He looked like
Johnny Hallyday, who was a big star in France. I think the girls
liked him.

*I understand you drew a lot as a child?*
MG: I always drew and I played with LEGO and creative toys like
that. I always liked to make systems and inventions. I have a naive
way, to believe that things can work despite the technology or basic
logic. My father said that my naiveté was my strength. I have this kind
of optimism even when things seem undoable.

*It's interesting you have that optimism to go along with the pessimism
you seem to have in yourself.*
MG: Absolutely. It goes in waves.

*Did you have any experiences with a camera at home?*
MG: Yeah. My father, in the early seventies, bought a super eight
camera, but I didn't do crazy stuff with it. I remember doing a little bit
of animation. I would do stuff with my cousin where we would run
and put the camera on a tripod and take a picture every ten seconds
so we could run like Superman. I wasn't very consistent with it. I did
a lot of flip books and cartoons with my cousin. My interest was animation.

*Did you watch a lot of movies growing up?*
MG: Not more than anyone. I remember we watched a lot of Charlie
Chaplin. I remember every Christmas they would have a festival on
TV of the animator Tex Avery, who I was a big fan of.

*And what did you want to do for a career at that point?*
MG: I wanted to be an illustrator or painter. I didn't think animation
could be a job. It was only when I bought a 16-millimeter camera in
'85 or '86 that I started to realize it was something I enjoyed. I was

never precise about the details. I was very much about the idea and the result. With film, you have to wait until the lab processes it and when you see it, you see it all at once. You see this compilation of moments put together, and I always liked that a lot. That's why I liked animation. You would do a little bit and a little bit and a little bit, and then when you see it together, it's magic.

*Many have compared what you're able to do with a camera to something like magic. Was that something you were ever into?*
MG: Yeah, a little bit. I'm not so agile with my fingers and my hands, and I'm not good at manipulating people. I think magic is about how to condition people's perceptions and mislead them. This I'm not good at.

*Isn't moviemaking all about manipulating an audience in a way?*
MG: Yeah, there is a little bit of that. But I think there's another quality about it, like seeing something different or more unique in everyday life and putting yourself unconsciously in what you're doing and telling stories. That's not manipulation. I went to see a play by Neil LaBute that was manipulative, and it was great, but I realized I could never do anything like that. It's really twisting your emotions and misleading you to make you feel strongly about a character. And that's like magic, and this I don't like to do.

*What do you bring, then, if it's not that skill at manipulating an audience?*
MG: I think I bring a certain degree of naiveté that is not compatible with this way of telling a story. It's like my son: If he wants to lie, he's going to get caught. Something in his eye will be wrong. And I guess I have something like that.

*You went to an art school when you were a teenager?*
MG: Yeah. I went to a school from when I was sixteen to nineteen. I did a lot of drawing and I met friends who were from different parts of France who had a similar way of thinking. We were not the

ones who were the most verbal, but we could draw. I had a creative drive from when I was a kid. It was something that would keep me going. I was always unsure about life and death, and the only way to get me out of that was to think of material projects that I could construct.

*It was around this time that your band Oui Oui began?*
MG: Yeah, exactly. That's why school was good for me. I met people who were in these crossover positions between music and art.

*Were the videos you made for the group the first time you had tried anything like that?*
MG: Yeah, my first animated work with a camera was for my band. It basically was like, I wanted to do animation, so I would do a little story using the music of my band. I did three little videos completely on my own using the music. We didn't even have a recording at the time. And later, after we had a record deal and I did the video, I had to deal with the band, because they were creative, especially Etienne. We collaborated, and in some ways it could be frustrating, because I would like to have had complete control. On the other hand it was good, because it was a rich collaboration. And when I met Björk, I found this collaboration to be great because it makes me grow. I guess they both opened my mind.

*Filmmaking is considered such a collaborative form. Do you feel that collaborating comes more naturally to you now?*
MG: It goes both ways. Sometimes I really enjoy collaborations, and sometimes it's good to do an idea without thinking intellectually too much. In collaborations you have to find a common ground for communication. You tend to work more with your brain than your instinct. Using instinct, you can pull out some ideas that are more surprising. But I think I've learned to be creative in collaborations. Even when an actor comes up with a different perspective, I can find a way to use what he says in a way that would not diminish it.

*When you were starting to do videos for Björk and others, were you start-ing to think about doing a feature of your own?*
MG: No, it was years later. I would never think it would be possible until now. I didn't have the magic to put all those pieces together and tell one story. I still doubt that. At the time I was totally sure I could never do that. And, as well, I didn't read much and I didn't think I could write a story. It was something I never dared to think about.

*Were there close calls before* Human Nature *of landing a feature to di-rect?*
MG: Yeah. I remember I did a trip to Los Angeles and I was trying to do this movie, *I Know What You Did Last Summer*. I showed them my ideas for the suspense and tension and fear and I did not get the job. They did not understand me.

*Was that a big disappointment to you at the time?*
MG: Yeah. I was excited to do it. But I had more feelings about this [other] project that I worked on for a year called *The Green Hornet*. I worked with a great screenwriter, and I had a great time doing that, but the studio kind of let us down.

*What kind of a film was it?*
MG: It was before *The Matrix*, and it had a lot of effects. I don't like the style that is too sleek and too comic-book. I like it more tongue-in-cheek like *Superman III*, for instance when it's a little bit absurd and sweet.

Superman III?
MG: Oh, it's great! And when he fights with himself . . .

*Had you read any of Charlie Kaufman's work before meeting him?*
MG: Yeah. I had read *Being John Malkovich*, and I couldn't believe how quick and easy to read it was. It was complex but unpretentious. He had this quirkiness that I was looking for, but not in a contrived

way. It was coming from a real place. The scripts I was reading were bizarre to be bizarre, like somebody conventional would do something that's bizarre to him—but it's not, really.

*Were you nervous to be working on your first feature once production was under way on* Human Nature?
MG: Yeah, of course. Especially when you start to do rehearsals with the actors and you don't know how exactly to communicate with them. I did this big reading with all the actors at the table, and it was very depressing, because some of it sounded very corny a lot of the time. It was really scary.

*How do you look back on* Human Nature? *It wasn't received very well. Did you have to make compromises?*
MG: I don't think I made compromises. Even when I watch *Eternal Sunshine*, I don't feel it's there yet. Obviously it's better, because it had a good response, but I still can't really enjoy it like I do other films. I don't know if it's because I made it or because it's not as good as what I wanted to see. For me *Human Nature* is a little bit sad, maybe even more so. I don't feel I am watching a story. I don't know.

*Is it the same for your music videos?*
MG: No, it's easier to watch the music videos. I think they are OK. They work.

*So it's possible for you to be satisfied with your work.*
MG: I hope so. I hope I will. It may take some time.

*Did the poor response to* Human Nature *significantly affect how you approached* Eternal Sunshine?
MG: I think I was hurt by the response. I was not ready for it, because when you do a video, people don't come to you when they don't like it. And with a film, everyone becomes a film critic. You go to see a movie and it's part of the process of watching a movie to say what you like and what you don't like. And a lot of people came to me just to say

they didn't like it. I didn't understand why they would talk to me about that. And I got to be a little depressed about it. I went into why these comments upset me, and I wrote it all in a notebook. I learned, for instance, sometimes we make a decision based on a reaction instead of as an objective opinion. For instance, I would sometimes be very reluctant to [use] Spike Jonze's opinions when he would give me advice or comments because I felt he couldn't see that we were different and he wouldn't let me be myself. So I was overly reluctant. I could have used more of what he said to me if I was more relaxed. So I learned a lot of things. On *Eternal Sunshine* I wanted to try different ways. I storyboarded everything in miniature. And I wanted it to be like a play. I wanted there to be more room for the actors. I had forty pages in a notebook of comments like this guy who said *Human Nature* was rotten because of this and that, and [I wondered] why is that? And maybe this is true, and then it was like, "What could I do to make this different?" It's funny how if you just take the time to write down the problems, you can find solutions and maybe apply them.

*Did you use the same practice after* Eternal Sunshine?
MG: I wanted to do my next project in a way that *Eternal Sunshine* had not been successful. I remember the feeling I had when [*Eternal Sunshine*] was finished and I watched it on my own. I didn't like it. I liked some of it, but overall I was happy when it was finished. It's not the actors or the story or anything. It's just me watching something I've done. When I watch my videos, I like it. When I watch my movies, it's painful. Maybe that's the way I'm going to go, or maybe I'll try different things until I like it.

*In* Eternal Sunshine, *virtually all of the effects were done in-camera, as opposed to using CGI. You have Jim Carrey playing a scene with himself by having him literally running to different locations in the same shot. Why?*
MG: It's generally something that's fun. It's exciting. I get this feeling of craft that I had when I did things as a kid and waited for the result. Like, with my cousin we would build a big bridge and a ball that would bounce on a scale and make the bridge explode, and we'd be on

the side and it would go boom. This is something that I really enjoy. Doing stuff in-camera makes no sense in that it could be done so much easier in postproduction. Like this shot where there are two Jim Carreys, it would have been much easier in postproduction. But when it works, there are a lot of little elements that are unexpected. In fact the scene, as complicated as it was, made Jim's performance better because he was so worried about doing it right. He's not thinking about his performance, so he did it better. I think it's hard for an actor working with a blue screen. It's not much fun. I've seen movies done entirely on blue screen, and I couldn't watch them.

*Do you think about the themes that reemerge in your work? Both of your first two films were very honest stories about love, for instance.*
MG: I think about it, but not too much. I think there is a way you put yourself into your work, and it's through every stage.

*How do you put yourself into your work?*
MG: It's all by choosing the projects I do. Next will be the way I meet actors and if we bond with each other and have common ideas and I can identify with them. And then the third step is the way I direct them. I try not to be in their face. All of this adds up to filmmaking that reflects the person making the film. A lot of times it's invisible. It's not something you can really express or put your finger on. But at the end of the day if you are true to yourself, after a bunch of projects, what you are starts to come across.

*Is it a good thing to you for an audience member to recognize a film as your work?*
MG: As long as it's not too much [because of] the form, because I think I try to renew the form and explore different ways. I think the common link should more be in the spirit. I guess it's the way I see the world and who I am. But I don't want you to know too much. I think it's stronger if it comes across without me trying to make it come across.

*Has the way you've worked with actors changed over the years?*
MG: It's a slow process from doing videos, from how you try to communicate with a singer or a band and they don't know what to do with their hand or their body. From the first day I did a video, I knew what I didn't like. I didn't like it when people were portrayed as heroes or stronger than who they are. And I didn't like it when people were diminished and you made fun of them. By trying to be in between those two poles I find my way, I guess.

*What do you look for when you meet with an actor? How do you know when you're clicking?*
MG: Well, for instance when I met Mark Ruffalo for *Eternal Sunshine*, he said to me, "I think I'd like my character to wear a pompadour." I just thought it was sweet, and obviously when you meet the guy, you want to be his friend. He doesn't project this thing that a lot of actors project like they're trying to impress you. He was somebody normal, that was funny and sweet. I guess I find these connections and I thought it would be good. I didn't have to read with him. It's hard sometimes when you read with people. They are so insecure and you cannot judge them. Björk taught me a lot of good things about that. Like, when she interviews people, she always makes them feel very safe. She never puts people in competition when she wants to work with them. She explained to me one time that if you do that, you make people feel very unconfident and then you don't know who they are. She finds qualities in people that they themselves don't even know they have. So I think it was a good example of how not to put people on the spot when you meet them. On the other hand, in America especially, people have a tendency to oversell themselves, so you have to figure out what's true and what's not.

*Do you react to things you see in moviemaking today?*
MG: I try to not work in reaction. I've had that problem where I was like, I don't like that shot or whatever. And then you lose a little bit of your objectivity, because you're reacting to something you don't like

and you build up all your opinions based on that. And then you even make marketing decisions based on that like, "I don't like that, so I'll do the opposite." So I think I'm trying to be a little bit more relaxed and openminded, although it becomes like an ethical problem sometimes, like having guns in movies. I have a gun in my first film, and I regret it a little bit.

*At the same time, you probably don't want to make any hard and fast rules to limit yourself.*
MG: No, but sometimes there is stuff. I don't think I could possibly do a movie about a guy who has no weaknesses. I don't think I would be interested. I would say a lot of movies I don't like show how people are superior to each other. I think it's more interesting to show somebody having to deal with fear, like if there's a confrontation in a train and you say, "I can't believe nobody moved. Nobody said anything." I would be more interested to hear why somebody didn't move. Because in most of the cases, I would not move. I would be petrified in fear, and I would feel really ashamed about it. You always see people in situations in film when they're brave. In a way if you hear about someone being cowardly maybe you can grow from it better.

*Kubrick was so selective with his work that he ended up sadly only making a few films. Are you able to go more quickly from project to project? It seems like you are, with* Science of Sleep.
MG: I learned with music videos that you have to deal with imperfection. When it's done, it's done. You have to deliver it, and there's nothing you can do about it. The only thing is to learn for the next one. I wonder if Kubrick didn't have a bit of obsessive-compulsiveness with his films. But I don't know. My son is so into *A Clockwork Orange*. He blasts Beethoven in his ghetto blaster when he goes to sleep. It's funny.

*Your son lives with you here in New York. Does he influence your work?*
MG: I really care about what he says. Sometimes he gives me ideas. He gave me the most amazing concept last week that I think I should

use. I decided to call my mom every day since he said it. An old lady sat in front of us on the train and I said, "She looks like Grandma." And I was like, "Mom is old now." And he said, "Of course she's old. Old people, the less you go to see them, the faster they grow old." I was like . . . ahhh! And it makes me think of so many things like, "Well, then if you go to see her every day, she's never going to die. She's going to stay young forever. And then, how many times am I going to see my mom until she dies? That's really sad. Maybe it's ten. Maybe it's five. You don't know!"

*It's a great concept, but it's awfully depressing.*
MG: I was doing an interview before I was doing *Science of Sleep*, and I was really depressed. And we were talking about how I always work in loops and I realized it was because I was scared of dying. But it didn't come to me in one chunk. It was a long journey into my thinking. I was thinking, "Yeah, I always have been thinking in cycles, because I think of time and I think I'm going to go into a void."

*Looking at the techniques you've used and the stories you've told in your career, it seems like a high priority for you has always been to do or create something unique. Would you agree?*
MG: I think it's partly true. In a way you want to be an artist. You want people to notice you. Obviously I think, "OK, if I do something completely different, people will notice me." But I learned to play the drums when I was an adolescent because I thought that it would make me special, and I was shy and I looked like a girl. I saw this drummer in this band and I said, "I wish I was like him." And I worked hard to try to impress people with my drumming, so this is not like I was trying to create something unique. It's part of the feeling of wanting to put something out there and be creative. That's why when you hear pop music, for instance, there is a part that needs to be different and groundbreaking and new and a part that makes you feel emotion and quotes something you've experienced before. I think filmmaking is somewhere in between art and industry, because you need to have this kind of response from your viewer. So you can't decide that it's

going to be completely new. What I like is the idea. It keeps me going to keep trying something and seeing if it works. It could be in the editing, the shooting, the writing, whatever.

## MICHEL GONDRY

*What is the first film you ever saw?*
*Le Voyage en ballon*

*What is your favorite film of all time?*
*Back to the Future*

*What movie made you realize that film was an art?*
*The Gold Rush*

*What movie do you consider your guilty pleasure?*
*Stuck on You*

*Who is your favorite movie character?*
George McFly, *Back to the Future*

*What's your favorite movie snack food?*
Bon Bons

*Who is your favorite director of all time?*
Jean Vigo

*Who is the most impressive filmmaker working today?*
Ingmar Bergman

*What quality do the best directors share?*
It's really a combination of so many invisible qualities.

*Who is your favorite actor or actress of all time?*
Michel Simon

*Who is your favorite actor or actress of today?*
Charlotte Gainsbourg

*Who would you cast as yourself in a film about your life?*
John Cameron Mitchell

*What is your best quality as a director?*
Creative chaos and precision

*What is your greatest weakness as a director?*
I won't tell you.

*Finish this sentence: I'll never direct a movie with . . .*
a gun (again).

*Finish this sentence: The perfect movie is . . .*
something that stays with you.

*What will they be saying about your work fifty years from now?*
How could I know?!

*What piece of advice do you have for aspiring filmmakers?*
Number one is finish a project. Number two is start a project.

*What are you as passionate about as moviemaking?*
Trying to tell a story

# F. GARY GRAY

"I made *Friday* and *Set It Off* before I really started to delve into what it meant to be a filmmaker."

### SELECTED CREDITS

*Friday* (1995)–director
*Set It Off* (1996)–director
*The Negotiator* (1998)–director
*A Man Apart* (2003)–director
*The Italian Job* (2003)–director
*Be Cool* (2005)–director

A conversation with F. Gary Gray is filled with laughter. His personality is positively buoyant, which is all the more remarkable, considering his beginnings. Raised in South Central Los Angeles, he is quick to say his background is not exactly the typical one for a successful filmmaker. What he did have was drive and an instinct for seizing upon opportunities when they came his way. And it's not as if filmmaking was a passing fancy for him. It has all been part of a master plan he literally put on paper when he was just a teenager. Since making the leap from music videos, his first film, *Friday*, became a cult comedy phenomenon and his attention to character has elevated films like *Set It Off* and *The Italian Job* beyond the trappings of their genre. When I spoke with him, Gray said he had never before talked so openly and in such depth about his career. It clearly wasn't because he had nothing to say.

---

*You were born in New York. How long were you there?*
FGG: Two weeks. My parents were on a trip from Chicago to New York, and I just happened to decide I wanted to show up in New York. (laughs)

*Were there any early experiences growing up that pointed you in the direction of making films?*
FGG: I don't have a typical filmmaker background. I didn't grow up with a super eight camera or a video camera. I didn't start cutting movies when I was four or five. I actually didn't really start to get into the research of film until I was much older. I decided I wanted to direct a lot earlier than I started to do the research, which is really strange, but it is the case.

*There must have at least been a point early on when you started to comprehend the power of the director behind a film?*
FGG: Honestly, I made films before I learned that. I made *Friday* and *Set It Off* before I really started to delve into what it meant to be a filmmaker and what you bring to a story as a filmmaker. I wish I had

all the stories about how one day I watched *Citizen Kane* and it inspired me, but it's not my story. I grew up in South Central L.A., which is a really bad part of L.A. I had a really good friend who's still my best friend to this day, and we would just hang out. I was probably about twelve or thirteen. I had this uncle, his name is Phil Lewis, who was an aspiring actor. He was doing a play at this local kind of community theater. It couldn't have seated more than a hundred people. This is right in the middle of South Central L.A., and he said, "Listen, I really want you guys to come down and watch this play." Now, where I'm from, if you mentioned that you were going to a play, they'd probably kick the living shit out of you. (laughs) So it took him a year to convince us to go to this play, and the only reason he got us to go is he said, "It's summertime and they have young pretty girls." That's all he had to say. Wham! We're there. (laughs).

*He knew how to sell it to you.*
FGG: Exactly! He knew exactly how to sell it. We went to the show and it was eye-opening for us. It was like a window to a whole other world. Sometimes when you grow up all you really see is the neighborhood. It was good to see black people performing, and it was just a great environment besides the fact there was a bunch of pretty girls who were in the show too. (laughs) He didn't lie. And that sparked my interest.

*Your parents split up when you were young. Did you split your time between your parents, or were you with one more than the other?*
FGG: With my mother more than my father until I moved back to Illinois during high school.

*Illinois must have been some culture shock for you after growing up in South Central.*
FGG: It was definitely a different environment! It wasn't gated. You didn't have armed guards. (laughs) It was one of the top-ten public high schools in the nation. I'm one of six black people in the entire school, like twenty-five hundred kids. There was a freedom there that

I didn't have in the high schools in L.A., and there was a life-skills class I took that taught you how to pretty much lay out your goals and identify what it was exactly you wanted to do. I joined a show there called *Giants in Action*. It was a show that we produced, directed, and edited for local cable access. And I remember all you had to do was bring your student ID and you could check out all this equipment. I'm thinking to myself, "Come on, this is not real. There has to be some sort of hitch. Where's the catch? I show them my ID, they give me $3,000 worth of equipment?" It was the first time I realized that people in privileged environments don't take advantage of what they have. So I take out this equipment and I do a documentary on the Shedd Aquarium. It was the ultimate freedom to me, because I realized that there was no one looking over my shoulder and no one questioning what was going on. And that was the beginning of the end. I was the kid who asked all the questions, almost to the point of annoying people. I produced, I edited, I directed, I did everything. And when I mixed what I learned technically with some of the life-skills courses and just some of the stuff I learned from the streets, I laid out what I wanted to do and how I wanted to do it. I did it very, very thoroughly—time lines and everything. In my original time line I wouldn't have made it to the point of where I am today until I was forty.

*So according to your time line, where should you be today at about thirty-five?*
FGG: Working my way up through the ranks. You have to know that at the time, I couldn't really name any black filmmakers. I don't think even Spike Lee was around. Obviously there were black filmmakers—Gordon Parks and people like that—but I didn't know about that at the time.

*Did making movies seem like an attainable dream to you?*
FGG: The way I was raised and the environment I grew up in, there was no such thing as dreaming. I think it did create an environment where I had tunnel vision, and it was kind of do or die for me. And I think because I was so focused and I didn't put a lot of time into any-

thing else, I think that's a reason why it happened for me. Looking back, it looks kind of retarded, because I had no mentors, no clear examples of successful black filmmakers. It was just something I was interested in. But the one thing that you get from growing up in that type of environment is a certain level of determination and survival. It's something you cannot learn in school.

*But why do you think it was making movies that you were so focused on early?*
FGG: You know, if my uncle had taken me up to the neighborhood clinic and there were a lot of pretty girls up there, maybe I'd be a doctor today. Who knows? But in looking back, it just seems like a natural progression.

*After high school, you moved to L.A. and went to college, right?*
FGG: I went to L.A. City College for three months.

*What happened?*
FGG: You're at that age and you're trying to break into this industry, you're trying to do a bunch of different things. You're trying to PA on sets. You're trying to get extra work on movies. You're trying to do so many different things to get close to it that, actually, I felt like school was getting in the way. Maybe I was impatient. I know you had to get a certain amount of credits to even get near a film class, and I was just like, "No, I just want to learn about film."

*You've spent virtually all of your time since you were in high school just working, learning on the job how to make movies. Do you ever feel like you might have missed out on valuable life experiences that could inform the work?*
FGG: Realistically you miss out on certain experiences that could have been beneficial to me as a filmmaker and storyteller. And I'm very sensitive and aware of that right now. Here I am, thirty-five, and I've accomplished some things. But you know, maybe looking back I should have celebrated a little bit more. There was a point where if

you looked at my schedule and how hard I worked and how long I worked, you could say, "Well, this guy is a robot." And looking back I probably was some form of robot. (laughs) But I had to be, because I wasn't born into this industry. I wasn't related to anyone in this industry. I look at my first five or six pictures as boot camp for me. It's hard enough to make a picture, period! It's even tougher to do it without learning it at college and learning at least the fundamentals of film-making. It's even tougher when you're in the middle of filmmaking and you're learning at the same time. So I had to work twenty hours a day for months and years on end to get a grasp of it as I was doing it. So yeah, there is a part of me that says you did miss something. So now what I'm doing is I'm kind of slowing down to experience a little more of life, not only for my career but just for myself, because I woke up one day and I was thirty. (laughs) I have an impressive résumé, but I definitely sacrificed a lot.

*How did you come to direct a short film of your own?*
FGG: When I was younger I used to say, "I can't just walk in the door and say, 'I'm talented. Hire me.'" I would have to walk into a room and leave a tape that said this is what I'm capable of and if it's good enough, then great; and if it's not, I'll keep working at it. I never called myself a director until I directed. I wanted to be able to justify the ti-tle. When I was working as a cameraman, I made good money and I saved that money to do a short film. It was a really big risk and a gam-ble. You just don't give up that type of position at that age unless you feel like you're on to something. But I looked at it as an investment. And all these motivational books I was reading, they had all these ex-amples of people who weren't afraid to take risks. Maybe it was silly, looking back at it, but it's what I was focused on. And I felt like mak-ing *Divided We Fall* was definitely a step in the right direction.

*What was the film about?*
FGG: *Divided We Fall* was in the *Boyz N the Hood* and *Menace II So-ciety* vein. It really touched on inner-city violence. I knew if I was to give any contribution, I had to look at my own environment and my

own neighborhood and where I grew up and try to effect change, and that's what I was really focused on with that film.

*And how did that film lead you to Ice Cube?*
FGG: I ran out of money and I started to look around for help and I went to Ice Cube's production company. I looked him up and said, "I'm trying to finish this project up. Would you like to help out?" I sat down with him and talked to him about this project and he said, "Yeah, I would." He got a company to donate some money for the production. We developed a relationship, and I started actually doing music videos for him. I would write these concepts that were short films—and I'm talking about with dialogue and action sequences and Steadicams and cranes. I would never pay myself, but I would always put in the director's fee to shoot 35-millimeter instead of 16, to add in an extra Steadicam or to put in an action sequence. I just really went out and used music videos . . .

*. . . as your guerrilla film school?*
FGG: Yeah. And at the time I don't think a lot of people were doing that type of work in music videos. You would see a lot of performance videos, but you wouldn't see stories. I would put together stories with a beginning, middle, and end, and the artists would get something that was original and fresh. So that gave me the ability to walk onto a set and put together what I thought was a really decent story and kind of sharpen my chops technically.

*You were quite young when you started to direct these videos, just twenty-two or twenty-three years old. You must have been one of the youngest people on the set. How do you lead in those circumstances?*
FGG: That's something you have to psychologically work around. I've always kind of looked young too. I have a picture of me on the set with Ice Cube back then, and I look like I'm fifteen years old. As far as being a leader, I was always very clear on what I wanted. If anybody else had any issues with it, then that was really just more their problem than it was mine. I wouldn't let anyone break my stride or my spirit.

As I started to grow, I became aware that some of the stuff I was doing was wrong. And then I started to become aware of my approach and that I had to adjust it.

*What did you need to adjust? Are you talking about technical approaches as a director?*
FGG: Not necessarily the technical stuff, but articulating your vision and motivating your actors instead of getting in there and result-directing, which I did for quite a while, for a few films actually, until I realized there was a different approach you could take as a director that is better for an actor.

*Specifically how were you approaching your actors that was, in retrospect, the wrong approach?*
FGG: (laughs) Specifically, when I was twenty-four, I would say, "Well, in this scene you're supposed to be really mad and you're going to cry and I want you to really cry in it." (laughs) I didn't think I was doing anything wrong. But walking onto *The Negotiator* and working with Kevin Spacey and Sam Jackson, it's a totally different situation. And I don't think until maybe halfway into the film did I realize that I was result-directing professionals. I started to read up on Spielberg and on different directors like Kubrick and Truffaut, and I realized that half the people I respected had problems directing actors.

*So that happened during* The Negotiator? *Were there a lot of conversations with Sam and Kevin about the better way to talk scenes out?*
FGG: No, I would never do that, because I was way too afraid to let on that I didn't know exactly how to do it technically. Kevin was amazing, though. I remember giving him, like, a thumbs-up and thumbs-down and stuff like that. I'm not really embarrassed now, because it's all a part of learning. I really changed, because I started going to acting classes and started to learn what it takes to motivate an actor in their language, not in my language. I've always known exactly what I wanted. I never had a problem with vision. Articulating that vision was my issue.

*What's interesting is that many critics and others have cited from the start your attention to character. And from what you're saying, you were a bit clueless about working with actors in your first few films.*

FGG: Well, even before then I was able to get good performances. It's just that it was a very kind of crude way of doing it. (laughs) I'm really embarrassed about this one. I look back and I laugh, and I hope Jada Pinkett will laugh at this too. In *Set It Off* she's supposed to have an incredibly emotional reaction to her brother dying, and I remember showing her a moment in *Glory* with Denzel Washington's character being whipped, and a tear drops from his eye. I'm showing her another actor in another performance in another movie, and I have no clue that this is just not how you motivate an actor to get there. I've never told that story before because I probably won't work again after that. (laughs)

*Tell me about how your first film,* Friday, *came about.*

FGG: At the time, Matty Rich had done *Straight Out of Brooklyn* and Ice Cube was interested in doing something in that vein. Not in subject matter, but shooting something for seventy-five grand. He said, "We can put together a movie for seventy-five grand in black-and-white, and we'll call it *Friday* and it'll be a movie about the 'hood." And here I am, struggling to finish this short film and I'm like, "Great!" Then it ended up getting a lot bigger than a $75,000 black-and-white movie. It was funny, because it was hard and easy. Hard because it was my first movie and I was obviously trying to figure it out. But when I had read the script, I envisioned all of the characters and all the locations and the neighborhood that I grew up in, and so that made it a lot easier for me. I went and shot it in my neighborhood on the block I grew up on, in my best friend's house and my house.

*So you'd recommend this for aspiring filmmakers—to just shoot their first film on their block?*

FGG: Shoot it on your block. It cuts down on the research and development. (laughs) I'm glad Ice didn't come to me with a project about the moon or something, because I probably wouldn't be standing here today if that was the case.

*The shoot was something like twenty days? Did it feel like it was just sort of flying by?*
FGG: Absolutely. One take, two takes, three if we were feeling really rich. We flew through that thing.

*What was your mind-set through the film? Excited? Terrified?*
FGG: I was definitely excited, but probably more nervous and terrified than excited, because you just don't know what you're doing until you put it together. I didn't know we would end up with a movie that people still watch to this day. I just basically used my instincts to put together what I thought was the funniest version of that script that I could and hope like hell it worked.

*When you got into the edit room, did you feel like you had a good film?*
FGG: No. I was like, "I better start calling the TV stations and get my camera. I better dust off the résumé." (laughs) My first four times, every single time after the first cut, I'm thinking I better dust off my résumé and really think about doing something else.

*You're that hard on yourself?*
FGG: Absolutely. I'm thinking, "How the hell am I going to make this work?" I mean, now sitting where I'm sitting today, it's a totally different process for me, but it was all very new to me.

*The Negotiator was the largest budget ever given to an African American director at the time. The press made a lot of that. Did you?*
FGG: No. I've never spent a lot of time basking in any success. I've always wanted to get the green light and go ahead and immediately focus on what it's going to take to put [a movie] on the screen. Filmmaking is tough. It's hard enough to make a bad movie, let alone a movie that's relatively creative and then, beyond that, a movie people consider good. I use the example of eating a bus. You just don't know where to start. (laughs) You just have to take the first bite and keep going.

*Did you feel like* The Negotiator *did what you wanted it to do, at least in terms of your career?*
FGG: I think so. It definitely illustrated what I was capable of. It kind of launched me.

*It launched you to directing* Nutty Professor II *for a time.*
FGG: Well, for a time. You did do your homework. Ouch!

*The favored euphemism of "creative differences" was mentioned upon your exit from that project. What happened? What was the difference of opinion on the project?*
FGG: The difference in opinion from my perspective was that I didn't have enough time to put it together. It was a lot of special effects. Eddie Murphy had to play a lot of different characters, and I didn't have the prep time to put it together the way I felt was necessary. I didn't want to fail. I was working with Brian Grazer, and this was a great set of people. And if I put together the bad version of *Nutty Professor*, that wouldn't have been good at all.

*What was the appeal of* A Man Apart *for you? It was called* Diablo *back when you were working on it, right?*
FGG: Yeah, it was called *Diablo*. The deal was I wanted to make a movie that was kind of a mix of *Scarface* and *Seven*. It was a much bigger movie than ended up on the screen. It ended up being much different than I originally envisioned.

*The film looked to be a "troubled production." It was delayed a few times.*
FGG: It was a tough production from beginning to end. I look at that film and it's hard for me not to think about what I had originally envisioned. It was something much bigger and cooler. Let me give an example: I didn't direct the last ten minutes of that movie. John Herzfeld did. And that was because I was on *The Italian Job*. I didn't have the chance to do the final mix the way I wanted to. I didn't have a chance to do the final score the way I wanted to. I thought we were

going to do a completely different ending, and the script was much larger. It was the hardest experience I've ever had, and it was probably the best experience I had too, because I learned so much about not only filmmaking but about this industry and the politics. It definitely made me stronger as a professional, as a filmmaker, and as a storyteller.

*You followed it up with a much better received film in* The Italian Job. *I understand you put together a visual mission statement for your crew before starting the film.*
FGG: I wanted everybody on the crew to have a sense of what movie we were making, because I didn't want it to feel like we were making different movies. If you have a lot of different players involved and they're making different movies, it causes a problem. I created a document that made it very clear on every level what movie I was making. You could easily reconcile any disagreements by saying, "Look, this is what I'm doing or thinking." I think that's the reason we experienced a certain amount of success with *The Italian Job*—because I was very clear about what movie I was making, and I think most people felt the same way.

*Do you think that if we talk in ten or twenty years we'll be able to look back at the films and say, "This makes an F. Gary Gray film"? What do you think the common denominator will be?*
FGG: I think they'll probably get crazier as I go. (laughs) I'm starting to feel that you'll probably get something a little crazier. Maybe I'm predicting the future, but hopefully I'll be able to do something different if I'm able to keep it going. Again, this really is boot camp. I've kind of survived boot camp so . . .

*. . . now the real work begins?*
FGG: I think you're going to start seeing some different things from me. Will the next one be The One? Maybe, maybe not. But you're going to start seeing different stuff, I think. (laughs) I'm already starting my mind brewing. Definitely twenty years from now we're going to have a great conversation.

## THE DIRECTOR'S TAKE
### F. GARY GRAY

*What is the first film you ever saw?*
Cooley High

*What is your favorite film of all time?*
The Godfather, Part II and Imitation of Life

*What's your favorite line in a film?*
Moss: What's your name?
Blake: FUCK YOU, that's my name!! You know why, mister? 'Cause
you drove a Hyundai to get here tonight; I drove a eighty-thousand-
dollar BMW. That's my name!!—*Glengarry Glen Ross*

*What movie made you realize that film was an art?*
Fellini Satyricon

*What movie do you consider your guilty pleasure?*
Chopper and Office Space

*What's your favorite movie snack food?*
Popcorn

*Who is your favorite director of all time?*
Fellini

*Who is the most impressive filmmaker working today?*
Alexander Payne

*What quality do the best directors share?*
Being prepared

*Who is your favorite actor or actress of all time?*
Jimmy Stewart and Meryl Streep

*Who is your favorite actor or actress of today?*
Johnny Depp and Charlize Theron

*Who would you cast as yourself in a film about your life?*
Don Cheadle

*If you could remake one movie, what would it be?*
A Man Apart

*What is your best quality as a director?*
I'm still working on that.

*What is your greatest weakness as a director?*
Craft Service

*Finish this sentence: I'll never direct a movie about . . .*
I never say never.

*Finish this sentence: The perfect movie is . . .*
a great script, a great cast, a great studio, great producers, and a great
experience.

*What will they be saying about your work fifty years from now?*
That I wasn't afraid to take risks.

*What piece of advice do you have for aspiring filmmakers?*
On all levels, you must do your homework.

*What are you as passionate about as moviemaking?*
Music

# DAVID GORDON GREEN

"I always like movies about people I recognize. I'm a lot less inspired by a trip to the moon than I am a trip to the grocery store."

## SELECTED CREDITS

*George Washington* (2000)–writer/director
*All the Real Girls* (2003)–writer/director
*Undertow* (2004)–cowriter/director

A t just twenty-five, David Gordon Green's debut feature, *George Washington*, was recognized by Roger Ebert, the *New York Times*, and *Time* magazine as one of the best films of 2000. But who would have thought the maker of films of such lyricism as *All the Real Girls* and *George Washington* grew up loving *Iron Eagle* and *Red Dawn*? There you have the paradox that is Green. He devours all forms of moviemaking, but what he has created in a short period of time is entirely unique—odes to love and humanity and, of all things, the industrial decay of the South. There is poetry in Green's work all too rarely found in American filmmaking today. It is no wonder that he found a mentor early on in a filmmaker as preternaturally gifted and enigmatic as himself—Terrence Malick.

---

*You grew up primarily in Richardson, Texas. Could you tell me about it?*
DGG: It's not so much anymore. It used to be amazing—a bunch of old crazy people and a lot of one-of-a-kind people. It was a good melting pot too. Every ethnicity, religion, economic background was represented. Now it's just been kind of taken over by all the other crap that seems to pollute the nation.

*One of those chains you're alluding to had a big impact on you as a kid, when you were about eleven.*
DGG: Blockbuster?

*Exactly.*
DGG: Yeah! I was the first member of the second Blockbuster, apparently. They had two test shops when they first were getting going. For the longest time I thought I was the first member of Blockbuster ever.

*It's pretty ironic, considering your thoughts on the chain now.*
DGG: Yeah, I wouldn't be caught dead in one now.

*But at the time you must have been excited for the opening.*
DGG: I remember a sign when they were first opening saying 10,000

VIDEOS, and I thought, "Whoa, that's going to be trouble." It was literally three blocks from my house. I was sitting there counting the days until I could get to all these movies I'd never seen besides being edited for TV and that kind of shit.

*Were you ever into escapist entertainment as a kid?*
DGG: I was totally into everything. I always liked *Big Trouble in Little China* and *The Goonies* and I liked a lot of horror movies too. I didn't like things that were kind of overblown. I mean, I wasn't into *Top Gun* but I was totally into *Iron Eagle*.

*That really tells a lot about somebody.*
DGG: I was *totally* into *Iron Eagle*. I saw all three [sic] *Iron Eagles*, and I couldn't make it through *Top Gun*. I don't know. It's probably my knee-jerk reaction when people are all clamoring over something to go find the oddball version of it. Chappy Sinclair? I mean that movie was awesome.

*You wouldn't strike me as a* Predator *fan, but I heard you were.*
DGG: Where would you have heard that? I mean, it's totally true, but I can't remember ever saying that. But, yeah, I love all the old Schwarzenegger movies, from *Commando* to *Predator*. And *Red Dawn* . . . can we talk about that? One of my goals in life is to make a movie called *PG-13* that's about the opening of *Red Dawn*, the first PG-13 movie.

*I've also heard you were a big* Dukes of Hazzard *fan.*
DGG: It had a lot of characters that were familiar to me. I spent a lot of time in my childhood in this town called Longview in East Texas, where a lot of my family and relatives all lived, and it was very much just going out to the country and racing cars and getting drunk and going out on the lake. Those were the surroundings of my youth, so that show kind of brought out all the hee-haw spirit.

*What are your earliest memories of wanting to make movies?*
DGG: I remember taking it very seriously in the sixth grade. We had to write a letter to ourselves in the future. It was this weird little proj-

ect, and I remember writing a letter to myself asking what good movies I'd made lately. (laughs) I was pretty geared from maybe the second grade or third grade. I was always into music and drawing and art of any kind. I remember my parents were always like, "Yeah, you should go be an architect or work in advertising or something." They were trying to think of a more realistic way to kind of gear those instincts, but it didn't really work. I was always playing with a super eight camera, still photographs, and stuff like that. I was making movies when I was fourteen.

*What were those first ones about?*
DGG: I remember the first one was called *Fried Chicken*.

*What was that about?*
DGG: It was about this retarded kid that lived in my neighborhood. People used to make fun of him, so I decided to make a movie about him because I thought he was cool. I don't know why I called it *Fried Chicken*. Then I made another movie called *Black-Eyed Peter* that was about a can of black-eyed peas that was possessed. I was the typical jackass kid trying to be funny and cool in the movies—get your friends and the kids in the neighborhood to come and make assholes out of themselves.

*Where did you go to college?*
DGG: I went to the University of Texas in Austin for a year. After high school, I enlisted in the Marines, and then my mom convinced me to just give a year of college a try, so I went down there to UT.

*Was joining the Marines your idea?*
DGG: I'd always wanted to join the Marines because I figured there were a bunch of jackasses and jarheads over there that needed to be led with some sense of intelligence. I've always been kind of angry about one thing or another. I was just wanting to take some of that leadership away from people that I thought were probably pretty ignorant around the country, meatheads being brainwashed and going through drills.

*And your mom convinced you to reconsider?*
DGG: Yeah, she didn't like the idea of me going. My dad was a Navy guy, so he was all pumped up about it and my grandfather was in the Army. My mom was like, "Let's just try school for a year, and if you don't like it, then join the Marines." So I didn't like it and I was getting kicked out of school and I was getting ready to go back into the Marines, and then my mom saved the day again and found out about this art school in North Carolina.

*Tell me about that school, the North Carolina School of the Arts.*
DGG: It's kind of a little undiscovered thing. It's primarily known as a ballet school. I went there and saw a bunch of dancers hanging out on campus and decided I could be happy. (laughs). And I heard they had this huge, insane 35-millimeter collection that was coming in there. So I got the movie archives, I got the young lovelies prancing about, and it was in North Carolina, which is near the mountains and the beach. It seemed like a beautiful place to shack up for a little bit. I went there and met a lot of amazing people who I make movies with now.

*Including Tim Orr, your cinematographer?*
DGG: Yup. Tim and Richard [Wright], my production designer and my sound mixer; my producer, Lisa Muskat; and probably forty other people I could rattle names off for you.

*It sounds like it was exactly the environment you were looking for.*
DGG: There was just instantly kind of a collaborative energy there. I met people who had common instincts, and they opened my horizons up to foreign influences I had just never been exposed to—Lindsay Anderson and stuff like that. I was just like, "Oh shit, there's a lot of amazing possibilities I never knew existed." I remember the University of Texas right when John Woo had blown up and I was kind of like, "Whatever, that's kind of boring." My taste was to go and watch *M\*A\*S\*H* or *McCabe & Mrs. Miller*.

*Early on, did you ever try your hand at writing a big Hollywood kind of script?*

DGG: I write those all the time. The first script I ever wrote, as far as features are concerned—I was probably nineteen years old—was about a little girl who becomes president, called *P Is for President*. Everything was high-concept commercial. I wrote those all the time. Because my strategy was, let me be a hack Hollywood writer. Let me take that money and do the John Sayles thing. That was the first way I remember strategizing how a middle-class kid would get in the business. It was like, let's see every cheeseball movie that's made over $60 million in the last fifteen years and apply some of that garbage I've learned.

*When did you move out to Los Angeles?*

DGG: The day after I graduated I drove out there. I didn't get an apartment or anything, but I lived under the staircase of a buddy of mine for six months.

*What kind of work did you do?*

DGG: I did every imaginable job. I did a lot of PA work. I was an assistant to this cheeseball B-movie producer. That was amazing. It was shocking to see how movies were packaged. We would put together movies that were presold to foreign territories. So they'd already made 50 percent profit. The movie cost $1 million. They'd finance it based on $1.5 million foreign presale dollars, so then the movie went into production and the producer didn't even have to show up and give a shit about what it ended up like. It was just people who didn't care and were looking to get, you know, Joey Travolta in their next movie. (laughs) It was amazing to see how that process worked and how people spent all day every day putting together crap and pretending they cared about it. I would get so depressed. I was like, if this is what makes sense in Hollywood, let me go home and make a film that no one will ever see. I also worked at NRG, which is this big market-research company. So I would go to test screenings at night and watch how studios would come in and take a director's work and basically make it as mediocre as possible so that the largest number of people would like it.

*The time in L.A. was not a total loss. You used the money you earned there for your first feature,* George Washington.
DGG: During that time in L.A., I went in there basically saying, "I have got to make as much money as I can." I was living for free, never going out, never eating out, never going to a bar, sneaking into movies always. I was working, like, five jobs. I worked as a maid. I worked as a janitor in an insane asylum. That was also during the dot-com boom, and I was gambling on the stock market a lot, so I was a little businessman. I had $30,000 by the time I got fed up and had to go. I needed $42,000 to be able to shoot *George Washington* in anamorphic. For a while I was trying to get Biz Marquee to come be in it. (laughs) I was like, "I just need somebody's name." But I was talking to my friend Tim, showing him the script, and he was like, "If we're going to do it, we really have got to do it the way we would dream of making it. And that means no stars." I needed to raise another twelve grand, so that's when I started writing letters to friends and family saying, "This is not an investment. You will not see your money back. If you donate money to the arts or NPR or your local library or whatever, look at me as your charitable art project for that year." So I ended up putting together about $12,000, most of it coming from people giving three or four hundred dollars. So we got enough to get it in the can and edit it. Nobody got paid on the movie. We ate pizza every day and chicken fingers and lived in the same house.

George Washington *shares a landscape with* All the Real Girls *and to a lesser extent,* Undertow. *What is your preoccupation with industrial decay about? It's not a typical landscape seen in films.*
DGG: I love where man meets Nature and where Nature comes back and takes what's rightfully hers. I don't know. There's something

about the texture of rust and the color of collapsed industry that I've always been infatuated with. There's such a flavor to it. And just living there and knowing what it means to people, it's a very hazardous background to a lot of people's lovely lives.

*Since* George Washington *was so well received, I'd imagine you met with a lot of interesting people intrigued by your work.*
DGG: I have a journal that would knock your socks off. The funniest thing is when I had breakfast with Sean Penn and he made me watch him read my script. He was just sitting there reading it to himself, and I was just sitting there watching him. That was amazing.

*How long did that take?*
DGG: A while, actually. Long enough for it to be uncomfortable and then hilarious and then uncomfortable again and then really funny.

*In virtually everything ever written about you, comparisons are made to Terrence Malick. He produced* Undertow *after getting to know you after seeing* George Washington. *When you finally met him, I'd imagine that was important for you.*
DGG: Getting that first note of, "I like your movie and here's a project idea I've got for us," that was pretty surreal. But there's a little gear that switched when I want back to North Carolina and decided to spend every dime I had. I think it was the sanity switch. I just decided I'm going to invest everything I have. And I haven't been surprised since. It's like you can't shock me anymore, with the good and the bad of it. So I just said, "OK, when am I going to meet him?" and I met him and then was like, "He's a great guy; when am I going to make a movie with him?" He was very inspiring and encouraging.

*A lot of people see his influence in your work from* George Washington *on. Do you?*
DGG: I never really thought about that. *George Washington* was just a reaction to things I loved and hated. In no way do any of the elements

of the story or characters have anything to do with *Days of Heaven*. But once you take on kind of a cinematic style and a lyrical quality, there's not a whole lot of other reference points. People like to be able to put you in a box so they can define you.

*All the Real Girls came from an idea you had been working on with your friend Paul Schneider, who starred in the film.*
DGG: It was something we wrote when we were probably beating our head against a wall because some girl cheated on us or broke our heart or we cheated on them or whatever. I don't identify with a lot of movie love stories. They're always about the good-looking guy and the hot girl and the perfect music and beautiful ending. And it doesn't register as true, so I wanted some aggressive attempt at authenticity. A heartbreak movie from a guy's point of view hadn't been done. I mean, it was great in *Better Off Dead*, but I wanted to make a realistic love story, which there are very few of. *Say Anything*, maybe.

*There's a lot more realism to the romance in the film than we're used to seeing in the movies. There's plenty of awkwardness.*
DGG: That was certainly the hope. It's really scary to make yourself vulnerable, to just put yourself out there saying, "I know I say some goofy shit with girls, and now I'm going to let people watch what I would say or what's said to me regardless of how pretentious or annoying or silly it is."

*What was your budget?*
DGG: Just over $1 million.

*Was there pressure to cast someone other than Paul in the lead role?*
DGG: Yeah, after *George Washington* we had a lot of interest from places about it. We had an offer to set it up with a studio and they wanted to do a $14 million version of it and they wanted me to look at their up-and-comer list, and Paul certainly was not on it. (laughs) But it was kind of a promise I'd made to Paul early in the process.

*Could you imagine shooting something in a studio rather than on location as you have thus far?*
DGG: I don't know. *All the Real Girls* we shot in Paul's hometown. We would shoot outside his ex-girlfriend's house and try to make as much of an emotionally responsive atmosphere on location as possible. I always try to find the most appropriate context or situation for any movie I want to do. There's this Nick Cave book called *And the Ass Saw the Angel* that is this really gothic Southern book, and I really want to do it on soundstages in eastern Europe.

*Do you think that you will always use non-actors to some degree in your films?*
DGG: I hope so. It's always fun and unpredictable, and I like having that degree of uncertainty sometimes. A lot of trained actors have a difficult time improvising. I've certainly been unsuccessful in some instances of trying to make it work or get somebody up there and be themselves. But I'm always up for that challenge to get those really human notes that are a little less designed and a little less off the assembly line.

*Are rehearsals an essential part of the process for you?*
DGG: I can't think of a scenario where a rehearsal wouldn't be beneficial. I just put little stock in the script. I don't even take a script to rehearsals. Script supervisors always quit my movie. They hate me.

*I've heard you'll sometimes talk to an actor during a take?*
DGG: All the time. They hate that, but it's really fun. I'll just yell at them or something. In *Undertow* when Josh Lucas is chasing the pig around, you can hear me laughing. We tried to cover that up with pig squeals, but you can still hear me laughing because it's so funny. I'll ruin takes because I can't hold my laugh. A lot of people just check out compositions and look through lenses and stuff. I don't do that. That's why I need Tim—because I don't need to do that. I just know it's going to work right, so I get right up there with the actors and act vicariously through them.

*Did* Undertow *feel like a natural progression for you? It was more of a genre film than your first two.*

DGG: I knew I needed to do something that wasn't as slow-moving and lyrical as the first two movies. There was a strategy to open my career up to not be doing Southern weepy movies all the time, which is fine, but there're a lot of things besides that.

*Is it true you wanted to film in Germany?*

DGG: Yeah, I wanted to do it in Dresden. Where'd you read that? I love Dresden. It's an amazing kind of dark city, and I wanted to do the second half of the movie in Dresden.

*I assume it was another budgetary consideration to abandon that idea?*

DGG: Well, originally we were going to shoot the movie for $6 million, and then I got into conflicts with the studio and they didn't want to cast who I wanted to, so we agreed to part ways and I was going to make it for a million and a half with freedom.

Undertow *makes it three films in a row of yours that have begun with a scene talking about love.*

DGG: It's never been designed. It's just subconscious or coincidental or something. A moment of love would always seem like the right moment to start the movie. But yeah, I need to stop that. In *George Washington* that scene was totally improvised. In *All the Real Girls* there was a whole first act that we don't see because it was not great. And in *Undertow*, that wasn't supposed to be the first scene. I don't look at scripts or anything like that after I start shooting a movie. And when we edit it, I just see what feels right. After we put it together I was like, "Shit, we did it again."

*Do you want a moviegoer to recognize you as the director in one of your films? So far, your style seems pretty recognizable.*

DGG: No. I don't want to be recognizable. I don't know that I can help it, but I don't want that. Just like any actor, no one wants to be stereotyped or put in a box. I have buddies that make big-budget movies and I go to their sets and they get forty takes sometimes. I've never had *four* in my life except on commercials. If I had every option to get it to where I wanted, to where I predesigned it to be, there'd be a different game in the editing room. The hardest thing on *Undertow* was it'd be like we didn't get the performance I needed and we would need to move on.

*Do you feel at this stage in your career that your ambitions are exceeding the budgets you're being trusted with?*
DGG: Yeah, that's the problem. There're two big-budget movies I really want to make more than anything. There's this demolition derby action comedy, and there's this western about drug addicts in the Old West. It's about the birth of heroin, which is totally grim and dark and awesome as crap but nobody will ever let me make it unless I do certain things like put a nice ending on it. I need to get myself to a point where people trust me with more money and I'm more of a commercial commodity in order to get that done. Or do I find a way to make that a tiny movie rather than the movie I want to make in my head? Do I look at it strategically? I don't know.

*You've said in the past that you wish you were making films back in the seventies. Do you think audiences back then were more in tune with the films you're interested in making?*
DGG: Yeah, audiences I think were open to challenges and now they're conditioned to the flavor of Starbucks. They're conditioned to see a romantic comedy that hits the same notes whether it's a foreign film or a domestic film. People want to know what they're getting into when they go to a movie. If you're advertising a thriller, it better not be funny! That's the dumb thing now. You don't even see scary movies anymore. It's all funny. Scary is now funny.

*Do you worry about losing touch? Many filmmakers of the seventies have been accused of that.*
DGG: That's exactly what happened to all those guys who made amazing movies. I think there's a point in your life as an artist when you're aggressively reacting to the world around you—who you know or what

you know and who you hear—there's a point when you're not listening anymore and you're just Woody Allen. Woody Allen can't have the keen insight to human dialogue that he used to have, because when he goes out, people are all talking about who's sitting next to him. He's not able to be a fly on the wall and kind of pick and choose the funny parts anymore. I think people in their lives become so obsessed with what they do that they lose a little bit of who they are. I don't think it's necessarily running out of good ideas. It's just running out of the soul and patience in making a movie. And that's one of the things I really worry about as far as any sort of consistency in a career goes.

*How do you avoid that?*
DGG: To live as anonymously outside the industry as I can and do all my writing in a way that doesn't have anything to do with Hollywood or movies. And work with people that aren't going to hit me with the burden of politics and the frustration of the industry. When I'm in production, it's kind of an escape and a freedom—an exploration. We're all discovering things. It would be really smart if I would take a couple years off and go join the French Foreign Legion.

*There's always the Marines . . .*
DGG: I'm too old for the Marines now. I just found out, and I'm really upset. I can do the Peace Corps or the French Foreign Legion. I think the more you listen, the more you expose yourself to new elements and new ways of living. People get assistants, and their assistants go do their laundry for them. I mean, how do you find the cool voice of the lady at the Laundromat who's bitching about not getting her quarters out of the machine, you know? You don't know those human obstacles anymore, because you just went and paid someone to go and make your life easier.

*What don't you like to see in films today?*
DGG: I don't like picturing the witty screenwriter. I just really get irritated when I see a writer taking over a performance. In my past I've attacked certain people, and I have no business doing that, because they're successful and they'll make money and people love their movies

and they'll win Oscars. And, shit, I can't watch it. I get criticized for the same thing. I've got a perspective that some people don't agree with. People think I'm pretentious. But I kind of disagree because I just present what people come up with. What I hear, I write it down.

## THE DIRECTOR'S TAKE
## DAVID GORDON GREEN

*What is the first film you ever saw?*
*Young Frankenstein*, at two weeks old

*What is your favorite film of all time?*
*Thunderbolt and Lightfoot* or *The Conversation*

*What's your favorite line in a film?*
Ned Beatty saying "This corn is special" at the end of *Deliverance*

*What movie made you realize that film was an art?*
*Never Cry Wolf*

*What movie do you consider your guilty pleasure?*
*M.A.C. and Me* and *Bad Ronald*

*Who is your favorite movie character of all time?*
Curtis Armstrong's "Booger" from *Revenge of the Nerds*

*What's your favorite movie snack food?*
My fingernails

*Who is your favorite director of all time?*
Frederick Wiseman

*Who is the most impressive filmmaker working today?*
Lukas Moodysson

*What quality do the best directors share?*
Hunger

*Who is your favorite actor or actress of all time?*
Richard Pryor

*Who is your favorite actor or actress of today?*
Michael Shannon or Lily Tomlin

*Who would you cast as yourself in a film about your life?*
Jaime Bell or Chris Elliott

*If you could remake one movie, what would it be?*
H.O.T.S.

*What is your best quality as a director?*
I go to bed early.

*What is your greatest weakness as a director?*
No beard/can't dance

*Finish this sentence: I'll never direct a movie about . . .*
Never say never.

*Finish this sentence: The perfect movie is . . .*
watched at the right time.

*What will they be saying about your work fifty years from now?*
I'm sure the world will have better things to be talking about.

*What piece of advice do you have for aspiring filmmakers?*
Enjoy it.

*What are you as passionate about as moviemaking?*
Tacos

# LUKE GREENFIELD

"I am like the book of fear, and every one of my movies
taps into that emotion."

## SELECTED CREDITS

*The Animal* (2001)–director
*The Girl Next Door* (2004)–director

Luke Greenfield talks so passionately and earnestly about going for "the chill" in his work that it seems like he's still an adolescent dreaming of a career in the movies, instead of actually making them. "The chill" is that moment "where your hair stands up on your arms," Greenfield explains. A worshiper at the church of Spielberg, Greenfield speaks of his "audience" with the great filmmaker as if it were with the pope. His mother must have known something was up, naming her son after one of the most iconic film characters of all time, Cool Hand Luke. Most in the industry agree that Greenfield's potential is far greater than the sum of his filmography's parts. After all, one Rob Schneider film and a *Risky Business* retread doesn't amount to much on paper. But as anyone who witnessed one of Greenfield's "chill moments" in *The Girl Next Door* can attest, the best is surely yet to come.

---

*Where did you spend most of your childhood?*
LG: We moved around a little bit. My parents got divorced when I was four. I lived in Norwalk, Connecticut. I lived there for a bunch of years. I moved to Westport when I was eleven, and then I was there until I was eighteen.

*Did you live at all with your dad? Were you close?*
LG: I visited my father every other weekend. It's not that my father and I aren't close. It's just that my mother and I are unusually close. We're much more best friends. My mom lives for me. She was part of this dream with me. Every time she gets onto the set of my movies, she's always crying.

*Your mom in fact was an aggressive advocate for your career early on, wasn't she?*
LG: When my mom realized I seriously wanted to become a director, she wrote a letter to Steven Spielberg. I was sixteen years old and my mom wrote this letter saying, "My son has wanted to be you since he was ten. It's all he wants to do and I've never seen a kid so passionate

for a dream at such a young age." She said, "We don't know anyone in Hollywood, we don't know how the business works, can you please tell me if my son has what it takes?" With the letter she enclosed two of my super eight movies and a research paper I did on Spielberg. Well, she sent it to Amblin and forgot to include a return address. Even to this day we don't know how it worked out, but somehow, some way Steven read my mom's letter, was touched, watched my little super eight movies, and turned to his assistant and said, "Find this kid." Steven wrote me this heartfelt two-page handwritten letter. It changed my life. I still have it memorized. He wrote in the end, "Your raw beginnings are so similar to my own, I know you'll make it. The next stage for you is film school." And the most important part of that letter is when he gave me advice on how to reach audiences. What he was saying was, "It's the 'truth in the telling' of stories that really reaches people." I remember him saying these great stories can be found in your hometown and your neighborhood. Basically he was saying *Jaws*, *E.T.*, *Poltergeist*, these huge concept movies, what they're really about is how relevant they are to us as people and the relationships and the things we go through. That's why his movies have reached so many billions of people.

*Do you still have the letter?*
LG: I do. I still keep it in the original UPS brown package in a drawer in my desk. He's definitely been a strong influence in my life.

*Much of Spielberg's work has been informed by his parents' divorce. Do you think yours is?*
LG: In Steven's work I always see the themes of divorce, and I don't have that theme at all. My themes are more about fear. For a long time I lived in fear and worried a lot and was afraid of the unknown. The movies I'm writing now are still thematically about fear. That stems completely from childhood and from not having a father figure from the age of four to eleven. If I could go back and do it all again, I would go back to elementary school and get in as many fistfights as I could. I think it would make me more of a courageous person, and I wouldn't

have lived in fear for so many years. It's not fistfighting anymore. Now it's confrontations with studio heads.

*What are the first moviegoing experiences that you remember?*
LG: My most memorable early movie experience was a traumatizing one. I was probably six years old, and I asked my father if we could go see *The Amityville Horror* because I thought it was a ghost movie like *Casper the Friendly Ghost.* My father warned me that it'd be scary, but I assured him that *Casper* didn't scare me. So my father took me to see *The Amityville Horror* when I was six years old. It literally almost killed me.

*No wonder you've been dealing with fear your whole life.*
LG: No kidding! I'll never forget fifteen minutes into that movie I was so traumatized, he had to take me out of the theater. I couldn't sleep for years. Actually, it's funny; I became obsessed with scary movies. I really loved the *Halloween*s and the *Friday the 13th*s. These movies scared the shit out of me, but for some reason I was addicted. One day I really do plan on making a truly terrifying movie.

*How did you come to start making films when you were a kid?*
LG: When my uncle gave me a movie camera, that's when it all kind of began.

*How prolific were you playing around with that camera?*
LG: By the time I graduated high school, I must have made about fifty short films on super eight. All my friends became the actors. I was basically making movies where these ten- and twelve-year-olds were playing adults with guns. And then I started getting much more into story and character. My last film in high school was called *The Prey* and was about forty-five minutes long.

*Were you storyboarding these films?*
LG: I can't draw. That's one of the main reasons that I'm a filmmaker. If I had the natural ability to draw, I would have been an artist. But

what I kind of did was remedial shot lists. On *The Girl Next Door* I called it my "visual design," creating the movie shot-for-shot. But it goes way beyond a typical shot list. It's actually twice the length of the actual script. I go into great detail for myself on exactly how I want to tell the story visually. It's my guide. And it's funny, I still think it stems from fear. I can't imagine being on a set without a game plan.

*I understand USC was an early goal for you?*
LG: I was obsessive about it. It was like USC film school or die. When I was thirteen, I started writing letters to the film school. I would send my super eight movies. So by the time I was eighteen and able to apply to USC, they all knew me.

*When you got there, did you feel a kinship with your fellow students?*
LG: It was shocking because out of the thirty kids accepted to my program, only two of them had ever touched a camera before. They were scholastic people, academics who excelled in grades and had great SAT scores. The actual film program doesn't begin until your junior year. They want you to take their academic courses through sophomore year, which is a complete waste of time. Luckily for me I was so far ahead, technically, because I had shot and edited film. I had a good friend named Matthew Jensen, and he also was from the Steven Spielberg school of making mainstream films—making them connect to people, giving people "the chill" where your hair stands up on your arms at the unforgettable moments. And that's what we went for.

*Was USC an environment that was welcoming for an admirer of Spielberg like yourself?*
LG: I was the enemy. At USC I was the biggest defender of Spielberg. This is in 1990. Basically everyone in film school in my experience are Scorsese fanatics, they're Kubrick fanatics, and they're like, "Fuck you, Spielberg." USC for me was just about the people I met and my own film experiences. I tell this to students: If you really have made a lot of films in high school and you know what you want to do and you've found your voice, go make independent films. Believe me,

USC tried its best, but I really believe the only way you get better is if you keep making films. And USC is all competition. You have thirty kids and only two are picked your final semester to direct what they call the 480 film, and the other kids end up working on your crew. So you can pay $100,000 to go to film school to be a director and wind up just being a boom guy in one of your classmates' student films. It's ridiculous.

*Were you one of the two picked?*
LG: I was, and believe me, it's just luck of the draw. I was very fortunate to have made a 480 film and screen my film at the First Look Festival and sign with a big agency. Jeff Robinov was a hot agent at ICM at the time, and he just picked me right up. I remember him calling me and he said, "I'll make it really clear to you: I want to represent you, and I think you should be directing mainstream studio films and I think I can get you a mainstream studio film based on your short film."

*Did you feel like you had hit the lottery?*
LG: I was so green and so naive. I hardly knew what an agent really was, and here I thought, "I'm on the path." Little did I know there would be pure darkness and horrible times coming to me. My expectations of what was going to happen did not come true at all. Here I was thinking I am a hot young writer/director with a big agent over at ICM, and I'm delivering dailies tapes for Viacom for six dollars an hour plus mileage. My whole life I had been a Spielberg fanatic. I'd wanted to follow the chronology of his career, which is impossible to follow today. I wanted to make my first studio feature film at twenty-two. I knew the key for a director coming out of film school with a short film was to have a script that you're ready to direct. So I wrote a really personal story called *Sticks & Stones*. I did everything I could to set it up. ICM did everything they could, but there was never a close call.

*How long did those lean years last?*
LG: From 1994 to 1999. The most frustrating thing was I hadn't been behind a camera for four or five years, and that was a dreadfully long

time, seeing how I'd been behind a camera ever since I was ten years old. I was freaking out. It was a really depressing, horrible time and I didn't know what to do. I kept saying to my parents, "There's no way to work your way up as a director," and my family kept saying, "That can't be true." They kept lecturing me, that in every industry you can work your way up. We always had this constant argument about why I wasn't trying to be an assistant director, and they wouldn't believe me that an A.D. is not a stepping stone to becoming a director. I'd tried numerous times to get into the music video/commercial world. I would have killed for that. They kept saying in order to get into music videos and commercials, you really should do something on spec. They said, "Go raise five thousand dollars and do a spec commercial music video." I said, "Motherfuckers, I can't even eat! I could *live* off five thousand dollars for a year." It was a really brutal time because everything started falling through.

*This is a long period of time to struggle. Is there a plan B at any point?*
LG: There is no plan B. For survival I was doing data entry at Disney Interactive. It was the most soul-killing job, working in this office in Glendale just punching in numbers. It was brutal. I was in debt and even if I won the lottery, I still wouldn't be happy, because I didn't care about the money. I just wanted to be a movie director. That's all I've wanted to do since I was ten, and when you rip that away from me I don't have anything left.

*Eventually it was your short film,* The Right Hook, *that sort of brought you back?*
LG: *The Right Hook* brought me out of that abyss of darkness. There was a pending actors' strike, and everyone was terrified. *The Right Hook* was done on videotape. And there was no sound mix. It was still a glamorized rough cut. I didn't have a manager. I didn't have an agent. And my plan was I wanted to hold *The Right Hook* and not show it to anyone until I had a feature script ready to direct, and that was going to be *Destiny*. This manger happened to see the film and he went crazy and said, "Luke, if you don't get your short film out there and this strike happens,

good luck. Then your short film is a year or two old." He scared the hell out of me and he said, "Let me just show it to one person." It happened so quickly, it's kind of terrifying. This manager showed it to Greg Silverman at Revolution who loved it and raced it over to Todd Garner, and Garner called me immediately. He says, "Hey, it's Todd Garner. Listen, you're going to direct *The Animal*, so meet me tomorrow." He sent the script to me, and twenty-four hours later I'm in a room with Rob Schneider and Adam Sandler and the writer.

*What happened at the meeting?*

LG: They make a semicircle around me and they start drilling me with questions about my favorite comedies. I started listing them off: *Midnight Run, Flirting with Disaster, Back to the Future, Swingers, Office Space*, and there are these frowns on their faces. They're like, "What the fuck are you talking about?" (laughs) Rob's very intense. He's looking for a certain personality. I just told him if you're looking for a guy who will kill himself and works nonstop, you've found him. The next day at a second meeting I remember him shaking my hand and he says, "You got the job, kid." I'd been waiting so many years and here it was—boom. From a $30,000 short to a $30 million feature.

*Did you celebrate? What did you do after you knew you got the job?*

LG: I'm driving on Bundy, calling my best friend, telling him what happened, and Spike Jonze pulls up next to me in his Mercedes. So I rolled down the window and I signal him to roll down his window. He's like, "What the fuck do you want?" I smile and ask, "Do you know where I can get laid around here?" and Spike looks at me like "What?!" He's like, "Yeah, buddy. Go three lights up and make a right at the sign," and then every light we hit, he's running red lights because he doesn't want to get stuck next to me again. I kind of creeped him out. I raced home and like the typical sap, I cried my eyes out. I finally did it. I have a movie, and I start shooting in six weeks. It's the most crazy time of my life. I'm prepping a movie where I have no control. It was an experience that I had to have, but it was everything backwards of what I thought filmmaking was.

*What do you mean when you say* The Animal *was everything backwards of what you thought filmmaking was?*

LG: *The Animal* didn't have much to do with me. This was a Rob Schneider movie, and I was just a gun for hire. It was my first time directing something that I had nothing to do with creatively. Rob co-wrote the script, and he's very hands-on. I got along really well with Rob, and Rob's tough. He should be directing. I wouldn't even call myself the director on *The Animal*. I was a guy who knew how to tell a story, and that's what they kind of needed, but as far as any creative input, I look at *The Animal* as Rob Schneider's movie through and through.

*What are your memories of the morning of the first shooting day?*

LG: I remember listening to the U2 song "Beautiful Day," and I drive up to the set at five in the morning and there're just trailers and equipment trucks everywhere and I'm just like, wow. When you make short films you feel so alone. And all of a sudden you have a top-of-the-line crew ready to work—it was amazing. I was very comfortable. I've been making films since I was ten years old. I know what to do, and I went into it full steam. I had that entire movie storyboarded. Not that we followed the storyboards. (laughs) I wasn't really allowed to. But I knew exactly the movie I wanted to shoot. I think I immediately proved myself in preproduction and the first day of shooting because I was just so comfortable directing. I told myself I was back in Westport, directing my little short films on a super eight.

*What was your goal for the film, knowing it wasn't really your film in the end?*

LG: I'll be honest with you, my goal of *The Animal* was: don't get fired. Because if I got fired, it was over. It meant I couldn't handle a film with the big boys. It was not a filmmakers' movie. It was extremely frustrating, but I was very fortunate to get that experience so early in my career. *The Girl Next Door* was the exact opposite experience. I was maniacally in control.

*When you got the script for* The Girl Next Door, *it was very different from the kind of film it ended up, wasn't it?*
LG: Oh, yeah. The original script was the tawdriest, a T&A movie with cum shots. It was completely the broadest film that you could possibly imagine, with absolutely no reality to it.

*So what did you respond to?*
LG: I just loved the idea of a kid like me in high school who never had any adventure falling for this incredible girl who takes him on a wild journey to kind of capture all he'd missed out on because he was so focused on getting into college. It was me. All I wanted to do from age ten was get into USC film school, and the Matthew Kidman character in *Girl Next Door*, all he wants to do is get into Georgetown.

*The lessons learned from* The Animal *could have been about control. I would think the lessons were different coming out of* The Girl Next Door.
LG: Love or hate *The Girl Next Door*, every single frame of it is mine. The major lesson I got out of *The Girl Next Door* was [about] the challenges of marketing. That was a huge wake-up call to me, that making a great movie is one thing, but if you don't have the people or the right ideas to market the film, you're dead in the water. So challenge number two is: How do you relay to America and the world the type of film you made? Nowadays when I'm working on my movies, I'm already thinking about the trailer; I'm thinking about the billboard; I'm thinking about what can be used in presentation materials. My whole goal is to share these stories for the world to see. I think *The Girl Next Door* really deserved a lot more recognition and it was a bummer, but lesson learned; move on.

*The irony, of course, is that the film that's so much closer to your heart was virtually ignored by the majority of the moviegoing public. The An-imal did very well. That wasn't the case for* The Girl Next Door.
LG: *The Girl Next Door* opened to $6 million. It bombed beyond belief. Our world in Hollywood was expecting this movie to make $100 million, and it was just crucifying. But it was a different thing than

*The Animal*, because instead of just agents and executives being excited, I've got people like Steven Spielberg calling me, which was much more rewarding.

*Speaking of Spielberg, I know you finally met your boyhood hero.*
LG: It was one of the most incredible days of my life. Steven came into the room, laughing, with a Xerox copy of the letter he'd written me sixteen years ago. He says, "Luke, this is very weird. I saw your movie twice because I loved it, and I had no idea I had written you a letter sixteen years ago." He sat down and he was talking to me as if I was George Lucas. He was looking to me and saying, "What should we do together?" We talked for a long time and I said, "My mom's going to kill me because I didn't tell anyone we were meeting." He looked at my cell phone and says, "Well, let's call her right now." He doesn't tell her who he is. He's like, "Hey, Beth, I really loved your son's movie. There's no question we'll be working together." My mom freaked out, crying hysterically. It was very cute. She was literally sobbing and saying, "You have no idea how much you mean to my son." It all came full circle. It was so surreal.

*Does criticism matter to you? Roger Ebert, for one, really ripped apart*
The Girl Next Door.
LG: He's a fucking idiot. I mean, Roger Ebert watches my film and says, "I feel dirty just watching it"? It just makes me sick. It's like either he's being paid, or he truly is a fucking idiot! I don't really care about the critics, to be honest with you, because the last thing I'm going to do is make movies for critics. What I really care about is making sure the audience loves the film and will remember it. There have been so many great movies that have been killed by critics.

*What are you thinking about when you are on the set? What are your priorities?*
LG: My whole goal on the set is to get as close to what I picture in my head at all times. I have the whole entire movie edited in my head. I have the music. I have everything. So it's the challenge of making sure

I can get everyone into my head, whether it's through the storyboards, whether it's playing music on the set, or just even acting things out. When I'm on the treadmill and I'm running or I'm driving my car and I'm listening to the music of the movie, I get these chills, and I want the world to feel those chills.

*Do you have any shortcomings as a filmmaker that you feel you need to address?*
LG: I wish I had been allowed to shoot music videos and commercials, because I need to learn a hell of a lot more. I haven't been given enough experience. I mean, Spike Jonze and David Fincher have done a thousand music videos and commercials. I was never given the opportunity, so I can only go off my experience, which unfortunately for me has been screenwriting and script development. It helped me in a way, because I've been developing great material, but as far as being a technical director, I really lost out on a lot of experience.

*What do you think your body of work is going to look like in five or ten years?*
LG: I want to make movies that people are never going to forget—the types of movies that made me want to be a filmmaker. I love what people call "dramedies," the films that make you laugh and then get incredibly dramatic and make you feel something. I know in my heart that I'll probably be remembered as a filmmaker for making a film called *Invincible*. It's something very close to my heart, and it's extremely edgy and groundbreaking. I'm going to wait a little until I can do it exactly the way I've wanted to. I've been planning to make this film since I was fourteen, so I'm going to make it right. It'll be more of an experience than a movie.

*What do you think all Luke Greenfield films will share?*
LG: My themes always deal with fear. I am like the book of fear, and every one of my movies taps into that emotion. I think I live in fear of so many things. I'm motivated by fear. As a filmmaker and as a person, I'm going to overcome all my fears when I make *Invincible*.

## THE DIRECTOR'S TAKE
## LUKE GREENFIELD

*What is the first film you ever saw?*
The Spy Who Loved Me

*What is your favorite film of all time?*
One Flew Over the Cuckoo's Nest, Cool Hand Luke, Jaws, Jerry
Maguire, Back to the Future, Out of Sight

*What's your favorite line in a film?*
"You're gonna have to kill me."—*Cool Hand Luke*
"The Chinaman is not the issue here, Dude!"—*The Big Lebowski*

*What movie made you realize that film was an art?*
I'm not sure when I realized it was an art. Axel Foley in the original
*Beverly Hills Cop* had an effect on me, believe it or not.

*What movie do you consider your guilty pleasure?*
The Money Pit, Point Break, Rocky III

*Who is your favorite movie character of all time?*
Randle McMurphy in *One Flew Over the Cuckoo's Nest*
Luke in *Cool Hand Luke*

*What's your favorite movie snack food?*
Candy I steal from the store around the corner

*Who is your favorite director of all time?*
Spielberg

*Who is the most impressive filmmaker working today?*
Spielberg

*What quality do the best directors share?*
The best directors are natural-born storytellers. They can naturally see the story play out in their head. They don't need to con-
centrate or try to force it. It just comes, even when they don't want
it to.

*Who is your favorite actor or actress of all time?*
De Niro, Paul Newman, etc.

*Who is your favorite actor or actress of today?*
Ben Stiller, Tom Cruise, lots of others . . .

*If you could remake one movie, what would it be?*
I don't think I would do a remake, but if they were handing them out,
it would be *The Fountainhead*.

*What is your best quality as a director?*
Making audiences feel "the chill"—when you feel it down your back,
your hair stands up on your arms, and you feel like you can fucking fly.
It's that natural high.

*What is your greatest weakness as a director?*
I'm a pussy.

*Finish this sentence: I'll never direct a movie with . . .*
a story or a script I don't believe in.

*What will they be saying about your work fifty years from now?*
"His movies took you on journeys and when you left the theater, you
felt more alive. It was like an experience rather than just seeing a
movie" or "What the hell was that guy's problem?"

*What piece of advice do you have for aspiring filmmakers?*
Don't let the naysayers get you down and never, ever take "no." Make

the stories that are personal to you. Make the movies that you're will-ing to die for.

*What are you as passionate about as moviemaking?*
Getting a rush out of life, whether it be sex, danger, or some kind of adventure. But to be honest, there's nothing I'm as passionate about as making movies. That's why I have no life.

# JOHN HAMBURG

"I remember getting into arguments with people who were like, 'Oh, you just care about the audience.' And I was like, 'Movies are *for* an audience.'"

TRACEY BENNETT/UNIVERSAL STUDIOS

## SELECTED CREDITS

*Safe Men* (1998)–writer/director
*Meet the Parents* (2000)–cowriter
*Zoolander* (2001)–cowriter
*Along Came Polly* (2004)–writer/director
*Meet the Fockers* (2004)–cowriter

John Hamburg is one of the most potent comic forces making movies today. As a writer he created the "circle of trust" between Ben Stiller and Robert De Niro in *Meet the Parents* and its sequel, *Meet the Fockers*, which quickly became the highest-grossing live-action comedy of all time. Hamburg makes movies for audiences, and he is not ashamed of it. His second directorial effort, *Along Came Polly*, made more in its opening weekend than any other January comedy in history. Raised in New York City by an attorney father and a radio-personality mother, his beginnings were not necessarily humble. But he's proven that an angst-ridden childhood isn't a prerequisite for creating comedy that can resonate with so many.

---

*Your mom has had a radio show on WOR in New York for a very long time.*
JH: She's had a radio show for over twenty-five years. She started it when I was six or seven. My mother was a celebrity in a very weird way. She would get recognized on the street, which was weird because she was on the radio. Anytime we would go out to dinner, someone would come up and they were avid fans who felt like they knew her because of her job.

*You and your sister were referred to often on the radio show. Did you have a heightened characterization on the show?*
JH: I don't know if I did. I certainly know that my movies have a high preponderance of yentas in the tri-state area who go see it opening weekend because of her publicity. Sometimes they've gone to see *Safe Men* and they've been like, "What the hell is this?" That's why it was good to do *Meet the Parents*. It was one that the yentas could really—

*It brought everyone together.*
JH: Yeah, exactly.

*What were some films that made an impact on you when you were a kid?*
JH: The first movie I became obsessed with was *The Jerk* with Steve Martin. To me *The Jerk* is a movie about a dumb guy written, acted,

and directed by smart guys. I feel like I connected with that. I was into that, and then Eddie Murphy and his *Saturday Night Live* stuff and *Trading Places* and *48 Hours*. *Spinal Tap* must have come out when I was thirteen or fourteen, and I must have watched it a hundred times. I knew every line. And Woody Allen. I just went back and watched *Bananas* and *Take the Money and Run* and those kinds of movies on video. It was silliness, but it was inspired silliness. The stuff that was really deep in my bones was that type of comedy. When I think about the stuff that I've done, a lot of that has seeped through.

*When did filmmaking in any small way enter the picture?*
JH: In the spring of my sophomore year of high school, my parents gave me a video camera. It was a huge half-inch video camera. And that was it. I became obsessed. I remember reading in *Film Comment* about how they did the shots in *Raising Arizona*, and I just became really into it. Then I made a short film called *Ernie*, which was about a meek freshman who became a superhero and sort of beat up the bully, and it was comic and it had some funny camera work in it. We showed it in our school assembly. If it had been a preview screening, it would have tested in the high 90s. I was like, this is great! This is what I want to do! I remember someone coming up to me, this girl who was a year or two older and she was like, "It wasn't just the story, but the way you directed it." So that was pretty much it.

*Was* Ernie *about any kind of wish-fulfillment thing for you?*
JH: Definitely. I was pretty skinny as a kid. I think there're a lot of moviemakers who do movies about a sort of wimpy guy who beats up the big guy. You don't see a lot of jocks being movie directors. The movies I've done have always been about some guy who is a decent guy at heart just trying to make sense of the world around him and trying to overcome some type of adversity. It started with that movie.

*What did you study at Brown?*
JH: I was a history major, but that was because it took the fewest requirements of any major. In my sophomore year I started getting back

into making movies. My senior year I took playwriting classes, and I feel like that's where I learned how to be a writer. I started to write monologues, and that was great because that got me really deeply into characters.

*In looking back, was there a sense that this was going to be a snap? Were you naive at the time?*
JH: It was just what I wanted to do, and I just had a feeling that I would be able to do it. I had two close friends in a class and we each were writing comedy, and the teacher sat us down and said, "You know, guys, you're not all going to be able to be writers for *Saturday Night Live*. Maybe you should venture out from comedy." I remember when she said that. Not for a second did I think she was right. Maybe that delusion was healthy.

*You had a short film at Sundance. Tell me how you got there.*
JH: I made it the first year of NYU grad school. It's called *Tick*. At the time there was this school of high-concept comedies. I wanted to make the anti-version of that, which is just as high concept but then you completely forget about the concept and it's just this small character story. So I wrote this movie about two freelance bomb defusers in a make-believe town where bombs keep going off. It cost, like, two thousand bucks. I screened it for the professors at NYU, and it went over really well. If I look back on it, it was a tightly structured three-act movie. It was eight and a half minutes, but it had a beginning, middle, and an end. And it was a comedy. And at NYU, there weren't a lot of guys doing comedy. There were a lot of movies about homeless people in Washington Square Park.

*Because it was different from the norm at NYU, did your classmates enjoy it, or did they think, "This guy has gone commercial already"?*
JH: I remember getting into arguments with people who were like, "Oh, you just care about the audience." And I was like, "Well, I don't just care about the audience, but movies are *for* an audience." You sit down in a theater and watch them with an audience and you want to

provoke some type of reaction. People say, "Oh, you're just being manipulative. You're manipulating people into laughing." To me, moviemaking is manipulative. Whether you're making *Breaking the Waves* or *Zoolander*, you're manipulating people by the choice of shots, by the actors, by the music. I never felt like I was selling out. I was just writing what came to my mind.

*And what was the biggest thing to come out of Sundance? Was it getting financing for* Safe Men?
JH: Yeah. By the time I got there I had written a feature, *Safe Men*, that I had wanted to make. Endeavor read it and they called me and said, "All right, we're going to sell this script for a million dollars." I was like, "OK." I mean, I wanted to direct it but I literally did not know what was going on. At the same time I had decided to leave NYU. I just felt like I wanted to make features, write features, and direct. So I left NYU. They sent the script out as a spec script to everybody in town and everybody passed. They went from being like, "You're going to be a millionaire," to two days later, "Everybody passed." But I wasn't really depressed, because I wanted to direct it. And two of the producers I had met at Sundance found the money quite quickly for *Safe Men*.

Safe Men *had a million-dollar budget?*
JH: That's right. At that time, those types of movies were a million. You kind of get that million and then figure out how to spend it.

*A million dollars was obviously a lot more than you'd ever worked with before.*
JH: My last movie was three thousand dollars.

*How did you feel walking onto a set with that kind of budget?*
JH: There is a feeling I've had on the two movies I've directed of arriving on the set the first day and there is just a machine that exists. You don't quite know how these trucks got there, how this city was created.

*Like a military campaign has been erected for your cause.*
JH: Exactly. Driving up the first day, there were campers and you just go, "How did this happen?" We had scouted a location but I hadn't visited it the night before, and suddenly it looks the way we talked about it looking. That feeling is hard to beat. Definitely when I stepped on the set and called action, there was a moment where I was like, "Am I playing the role of the movie director?"

*How were you working with actors at first?*
JH: I felt pretty comfortable from the beginning with actors. I think there's something when you've written the piece and people like the script where you feel like they give you a level of respect. Maybe you can't say exactly what you want in precisely the way Lee Strasberg would tell you to say it, but you can still go, "I'm feeling like this is not right."

Safe Men *was released on only twenty screens in August of 1998 by* October Films.
JH: They dumped it. I think October had just been bought by Universal. They were trying to turn them into Miramax, but that wasn't ever going to work. They were the *Secrets & Lies* and *Breaking the Waves* guys. No one did any publicity.

*That must have really hurt at the time.*
JH: In truth I couldn't wait for the movie to be over. They hired a guy named Bud Smith to recut it. He was a sort of Universal edit hatchet guy. He had no idea how to cut a comedy, and he just butchered it. We had to yell and scream to get it back to a version I could be happy with. I did a lot of reflecting. I was like, "The next time I do this, I want to have more control, be more involved," and I also wanted to build up a little more cachet before I directed another movie again. And I felt like the way to do that was through screenwriting.

*How did you meet Ben Stiller?*
JH: *Safe Men* was at the Nantucket Film Festival. We were on a panel together. We met right before the panel for a minute but he was like,

"Maybe we can hang out in New York sometime." And then during the panel Ben was like, "Have you guys seen *Safe Men*? Because it is one of the funniest movies you will ever see."

*Thus a friendship was born.*
JH: Exactly. Anytime somebody tells me they like my work, they're pretty much in. We never intended to make all these movies together. It just happened. We're very different people, but we find similar things funny. We like more low-key things where you're not trying so hard to get a laugh. You're more playing the character and letting the character get the laugh. I think we both have a real appreciation for a lot of similar actors, like supporting actors that are a little off the beaten path. Ben always loves Sam Rockwell. They'll work together someday because he just loves that kind of offbeat thing. Ben champions those kinds of people. Owen Wilson was one of those guys. Ben saw *Bottle Rocket* and put him in *Cable Guy*, and everything happened from there with those two guys.

*What was your main contribution to* Zoolander?
JH: I think overall the thing I'm proudest of in it is the work I did on the Hansel/Derek relationship and trying to make that emotionally involving. There are things that I wrote in that movie that were sort of absurd that I couldn't get away with in *Meet the Parents* or *Safe Men* or anything I'd done—silly things like Derek calling a eulogy a "eugugoly" or picking up the scale model of the reading center and thinking that it's the real one. It was like, "Can we make this guy that stupid but have you also care about him?" I think the reason it's done quite well on DVD and the cult seems to be building up is because there is that emotional core to it. There's a real sweetness to characters like Derek and Hansel.

Zoolander *was one of the first films to be released after 9/11. Did that event inform your work? You're a New Yorker.*
JH: I've thought about it a lot. Literally the best view from my office was of the Twin Towers. I live twenty blocks away from where the

World Trade Center was. I was in the middle of writing what became *Along Came Polly*. I definitely remember going, "Man, what I do is so pointless." I remember also going, "I have to go to my office and write funny stuff" and just not feeling funny at all. *Zoolander* was the first comedy to come out after 9/11. A couple of people told me it was a real relief to go and be able to laugh at something. We can acknowledge that tragedy has happened and the world has changed, but you can still laugh. You're allowed to laugh. The reason I think there will always be movies is there's a need for that communal experience. Now we're in a world where people are creating their own home theaters. In spite of that I still think there's a need, because people love sharing an experience. And with comedies you can *hear* the communal experience. I read a review of *Along Came Polly* where the critic was saying she went on a Friday night and the audience was into this movie and laughing together and she was like, "Maybe that was part of the reason I enjoyed it so much." That made me happy, because that communal experience is a necessary human thing—to laugh together.

*How did you get involved with* Meet the Parents? *The initial screenplay was written by Jim Herzfeld.*
JH: They were feeling that *Meet the Parents* needed some work. It was originally written for Jim Carrey and Bill Murray. It was going to be a different kind of thing. Ben told Jay Roach and Jane Rosenthal, "There's this young guy in New York who made this cool little movie; he did a really good job on the first draft of *Zoolander*—you should meet him." I went to a meeting with them and had some ideas about it and how I thought it could be better. For some reason I felt like I had a connection, because I understand familial relationships and being Jewish and dating a non-Jewish woman.

*Did any of those initial ideas make it into the film?*
JH: One particular throughline: I felt the movie should be more about the private war between De Niro and Stiller. They should have a lot of conflict, and the family shouldn't know quite what's going on. And that throughline I think was a big one in the movie.

*One contribution of yours was "the circle of trust" concept, and the phrase itself.*

JH: Yes. I made it up. I remember sitting with De Niro and he was talking about CIA agents. He knew some agents because he has a CIA movie he's been working on. And I remember listening to De Niro, and I couldn't quite understand what he was talking about. I got the idea of it, but the specifics were a bit cloudy. I remember thinking that this character would use a term that sounds like you understand what it means but if you really look into it, what does it mean? And that became "the circle of trust." When he says it to Ben, I could picture Ben's face nodding but not really understanding what the hell [De Niro] was talking about. It echoed my reaction to De Niro.

*It's an unusually talky film for a successful mainstream comedy. There are some comic set pieces, but there's also a lot of sitting around tables and in living rooms.*

JH: It's that thing I really love about movies—which is that there really are no rules. If it's good, you'll just sit there and watch it. Part of that movie is you have to put the time in, because you put yourself in Ben's shoes. And part of the identification is sitting there for an excruciatingly long time. The scene that probably embodies that most is the dinner-table scene. That scene is eight or nine minutes. In the script it's probably ten pages. You would never do that in a comedy. I think none of us expected that scene to end up being as long as it ended up being in the final movie. In *Safe Men*, Paul Giamatti has a long monologue in the bar, and at the end he finishes and [he and Sam Rockwell] just stare at each other. If I had final cut, it would have gone on for ten more seconds. I think it got funnier. It got weird, and then it got funnier. Those silences are great because that shit happens in life all the time.

*Where did the idea for* Along Came Polly *begin?*

JH: I had finished *Meet the Parents* and was taking my first adult vacation with my girlfriend. There was this beautiful, handsome naked French guy walking on the beach, and I of course felt very clothed and inadequate compared to him. When I got back from vacation, I didn't know what movie I was going to write. I was thinking about that vacation, and I had seen movies where the girl gets dumped. I was also thinking about my life and the lives of my friends—how once you hit thirty, you're at that age where you're planning things out. I thought, "What would be interesting about that type of guy who plans everything out down to a tee and the rug gets pulled out from under him and he has to rethink his plan?"

*Can you point to anything in* Along Came Polly *as evidence of your evolution as a director?*
JH: I'm just trying to tell a story. There's a lot of subtle stuff that I think we're trying to do to make it look effortless and try to make you forget that you're watching a movie and just focus on the characters. I'm proud of that. If you watch it a few times, you'll see how specific the production design is of Reuben's apartment, which looks very different from Polly's apartment. There are technical things I'm proud of. Reuben's big dance routine—that took a lot technically, with extras, tons of camera angles, Steadicams, lighting, slow motion, and I'm happy with the way that turned out in the movie. I'm proud of the racquetball scene, which is just a very involved scene that wasn't working in the beginning and then we decided that they'd be playing but we'd take the ball away. You can't tell, because of the sound. There's one shot where we digitally put a ball in. I'm proud of something like that as a director because you go to the set and you're like, "This isn't working, the clock is ticking," then we all have to think on our feet.

*What filmmakers do you admire?*
JH: When James L. Brooks does a movie, I'll go see it. Some people didn't love *As Good As It Gets*. I loved it. There's a reason that movie did as well as it did—because it connected with people. I sat in the movie theater, and the whole audience was rapt the whole time. I read a review in *Variety* of *As Good As It Gets*, and the review literally was as if the movie was an unmitigated disaster. I remember the review saying "destined to make no money" or something like that. And you watched it with an audience and it was clear something was working.

*Do you see any common denominators among your peers today?*
JH: I honestly think it's too early to define. If you look at the people, they always cite, like, Wes Anderson or Alexander Payne . . . I don't know yet what defines their stuff. There's definitely a winking. Those guys aren't making films like *Shampoo* which are just simple slices of life. They're letting you know who the filmmaker is. There's definitely a postmodern feel to those movies.

*Your films are a little bit different.* Along Came Polly *in many ways is a return to a classic romantic comedy. So where do you fit in there?*
JH: When I started getting into making movies, I was more in the Coen brothers' school of really out-there characters and crazy camera angles. I think that's a more self-conscious school of moviemaking. And then I started to think, "What movies do I really love, that really stay with me?" I started to think I just want to tell stories about characters. The movies I love are movies like *Broadcast News*, where those people live with you, not the tracking shot. So a guy like me you can say, "Oh, he doesn't show himself in his movies," but I think audiences connect with the stuff because they're just seeing something they can relate to.

*So there's something to be said for someone who can pull back and tell a story and have an audience forget he's directing this movie?*
JH: Far and away, the best example of that is Billy Wilder. It took a while for people to realize what a great director he was. He never shows himself, yet he really does. That's what I think the dream is. A movie like *The Apartment* is beautifully directed, but you can't put your finger on why it's such a good movie. It just is, because of the characters and story and all these things that he's subtly doing. That level of filmmaking is something I aspire to.

*On the other end of that spectrum is someone like Tarantino, who is so present in every shot of his films. At the time of* Safe Men's *release, the dialogue in it was sometimes called Tarantino-esque in the reviews.*
JH: It wasn't Quentin Tarantino that I was trying to copy. It was just that my world was a world of pop culture, and that was similar to

Quentin Tarantino's. Like Tarantino, I grew up watching TV and movies and having action figures. So when I was writing *Safe Men*, I was not thinking of Quentin Tarantino, I was thinking of what my friends and I argued about, like *Charlie's Angels* and who was the hottest angel and things like that.

*Perhaps that is one of the common denominators for this generation? Pop culture is such a part of our consciousness that it can't help but come out in the work.*
JH: It's who we are. You look at *Bottle Rocket*, and it's clear that there are references to heist movies. He's deconstructing that kind of thing. I just think we grew up on it, so we incorporate that stuff into our lives. There wasn't syndication before our generation, so we grew up watching every episode of *Happy Days* and that's going to creep into what you think about.

*Not to mention the explosion of VHS in the eighties. Everyone could be a cinephile.*
JH: You could watch these movies over and over again. Quentin is the ultimate embodiment of a guy for whom movies and TV were his reference, and not really literature. It's a combination of him being first and being brilliant.

Safe Men, *while it's become a cult film, got mixed reviews.* Along Came Polly *got mixed reviews.*
JH: I don't read them. They weren't for the most part positive.

*Do you think comedies are generally not given the respect they deserve by critics?*
JH: I do think there is a thing where critics think it's very easy to make an entire audience laugh. In the grander scheme of things, they think *Cold Mountain* is much more difficult to do. Philip Seymour Hoffman and I were doing a press conference together for *Along Came Polly* and the interviewers were like, "Is this just an easy time after *Cold Mountain*?" He's like, "It was harder than *Cold Mountain*." I try

to take a Zen attitude about it. I care about how I feel and what the audience thinks. We had a critics' screening for *Along Came Polly* and the entire audience was laughing the whole time, and there's a row of critics in the back, not smiling and writing into their pads. I just think they watch movies differently sometimes than the audience. If I had listened to the critics, I would have given up after *Safe Men*.

## THE DIRECTOR'S TAKE
## JOHN HAMBURG

*What is the first film you ever saw?*
*Escape from Witch Mountain*

*What is your favorite film of all time?*
*Annie Hall*

*What's your favorite line in a film?*
"Make sure that everyone sees the cake before we cut it."—Hyman Roth in *The Godfather, Part II*

*What movie made you realize that film was an art?*
*Raising Arizona*

*What movie do you consider your guilty pleasure?*
*Runaway Bride*

*Who is your favorite movie character of all time?*
Broadway Danny Rose

*What's your favorite movie snack food?*
Goldenberg's Peanut Chews

*Who is your favorite director of all time?*
Woody Allen, Billy Wilder, Martin Scorsese, Joel Coen

*What quality do the best directors share?*
Confidence and openness

*Who is your favorite actor or actress of today?*
I want to work with too many people, so answering this could come
back to haunt me.

*Who would you cast as yourself in a film about your life?*
Dana Carvey

*If you could remake one movie, what would it be?*
Truffaut's *Day for Night*

*What is your best quality as a director?*
A desire for world-class craft service on the set.

*What is your greatest weakness as a director?*
I have a tendency to wear the same outfit every day of production.

*Finish this sentence: I'll never direct a movie about . . .*
a wayward youth and the eccentric but wise homeless man who
teaches him the meaning of life.

*Finish this sentence: The perfect movie is . . .*
uninteresting. Great movies need to be a little messy.

*What will they be saying about your work fifty years from now?*
"What's the deal with all the awkward hugs?"

*What piece of advice do you have for aspiring filmmakers?*
Do what you want, not what you think you should want.

*What are you as passionate about as moviemaking?*
Family. Friends. Televised golf.

# PATTY JENKINS

"I wish I could make bucketloads of money . . . but more
than anything, I realize the only thing that makes that
kind of work worth it is to be engaged."

*Monster* (2003)–writer/director

The first line of the very first feature film Patty Jenkins ever directed is "I always wanted to be in the movies." And so Jenkins is today, after an aborted attempt to be an artist and no less than six years as a camera operator. Character studies like *Monster* can become dominated by their central performance. And so it was with the story of serial killer Aileen Wuornos when star Charlize Theron received scores of accolades while Jenkins found herself often overlooked. But the powerful filmmaking by the writer/director was not lost on everyone. Roger Ebert, for one, called it the best film of the year. Jenkins says she is something of an emotional filmmaker and, to look at her first big-screen effort, it's not a surprise. Few filmmakers, man or woman, could create such a full-bodied portrait of a human being who was so seemingly beyond the pale of our understanding. It is the fine line between empathy and sympathy that Jenkins navigated so well that makes her future efforts so eagerly anticipated.

---

*Where you were born?*
PJ: It's sort of a misleading answer. I was born on an Air Force base in Victorville, California. But I was only there for like a week.

*Your dad was a pilot?*
PJ: Yeah, my dad was a pilot.

*You traveled around a lot, from what I've read.*
PJ: I lived in a different place every couple months or year up until I was five or six, and I lived in Kansas while my mother went through school. I moved during high school to Washington, D.C. And then to New York.

*Was it in Kansas that you first started getting into the arts?*
PJ: Yeah. It was somewhere around junior high school. I don't remember making any conscious choice about it. It was just kind of automatic that all my extracurricular things were art, photography, and drama. And I was really into music. I remember watching movies all the time, but it never really occurred to me at all to be a filmmaker. It

was kind of like you could be a fine artist or a graphic artist, so then I put my sights on being a fine artist. I couldn't act and I didn't want to play music, so . . .

*And filmmaking wasn't something you could even conceive of as a career?*
PJ: It's funny. I've found notes that I wrote when I was in high school that were like movie ideas. But it was actually something that was pure fun to me at the time. It was like, "This is something absolutely impossible that real people don't do but wouldn't this be a cool movie?"

*Do you remember some of the ideas that you had back then?*
PJ: There was this one idea that sort of stuck around for a long time, about these kids in the hardcore scene—because I was in the punk rock scene in high school and junior high, so it was about this group of people that I knew. A lot of this stuff strangely went on to influence *Monster*. It was me trying to figure out how to explain some of these really damaged lives that I had encountered.

*Can you tell me a bit about your first moviegoing experience?*
PJ: My first few really vivid memories are seeing films that I didn't understand at all. I think it was Jonathan Miller's *Alice in Wonderland*. I have these really strong memories of seeing it when I was incredibly young and being mesmerized by the funny feeling that it gave me and not knowing at all what it was about. I was drawn to strange movies like that, even though I couldn't understand them. I particularly remember Hal Ashby's movies. It's funny—now I look back and I'm sure I couldn't have really understood what they were about. I remember them being such a comfortable place to be as a little kid. I liked watching them. And then I remember coming out of *Reds*. I must have been eight or nine, and I remember sitting in the backseat driving home and feeling something very complex and looking out the window, thinking about what an interesting complex feeling I had. It wasn't joy. It wasn't happiness. It was a kind of ponderance of life. And that has always really stuck with me.

*What were you passionate about as a kid?*
PJ: I was into photography and music probably more than anything. I still think probably music is my real love. I think that it's listening to music that made me want to be a filmmaker. When I was in film school, the second I sat down at a Steenbeck with film that I had shot and put in music to it, that was it. Instantaneously I couldn't get enough of it, and it had nothing to do with career or want or desire. I liked to sit there and do that twenty-four hours a day. (laughs) I was like, "I can't stop doing this. This is it."

*By marrying music to images it seemed like you were getting at something close to how* Reds *made you feel?*
PJ: Absolutely. That was it. I was mesmerized. I'm a very emotional person. And it's interesting that I went into the visual arts, because I don't actually think I'm particularly visually talented or interested in visual stuff.

*You don't consider yourself a visual filmmaker?*
PJ: No, I totally don't. I feel very educated in visuals. I just don't feel interested in them. There are people like David Fincher who just paint magic with visuals. I don't have a zing at it, you know? I come from a totally emotional place.

*I know you have a fascination with filmmaking of the 1970s. What is it about that era for you?*
PJ: That's what our generation grew up watching. The subject matter that they took on was fascinating and they didn't meddle and show their hands so much. They kind of stayed out of the way. And the pacing was incredibly confident and comfortable. It seems like the filmmakers who grew up watching films in the fifties went on to make the films in the seventies. Both of those two periods are probably the most evocative, important periods to me. They're both very emotional, very complex, and very character-driven. And both of them have such great films that kind of delve into the underbellies of life.

*How did you end up at Cooper Union?*
PJ: It was a school that a lot of people in the country may have never heard of, but our art program in Kansas knew about it. And it was free if you got in. And it was incredibly hard to get in. So from a very young age I became sort of obsessed with it. I wanted to get to New York. I wanted to get out of the Midwest, to be sure. It was my singular focus. It was the only place I wanted to go.

*Where was your head at when you were at Cooper Union? It's not a film school. Were you seriously considering film yet?*
PJ: I was thinking that I wanted to be a filmmaker. I didn't know anything about film or how to get into it. And for some reason my instinct was, I didn't want to transfer. I didn't want to go to a film school. I just started making short films. I remember somebody at NYU coming and watching my films and making the joke that it was like I had made a film doing absolutely everything you weren't supposed to do. And that was true. (laughs) How did I learn about jumping the line? I literally reinvented the wheel on every single issue.

*Did it seem like a viable career to you at this point?*
PJ: I wasn't thinking it was viable or not. Painting was something I had trained myself to do to get to go to Cooper, and filmmaking was something I couldn't stop myself from being fascinated with. I decided definitely that I wanted to be a filmmaker, and I also decided at that point that I wanted to be a commercial filmmaker, because it was the emotions I was getting so engaged by. The whole point was bringing those emotions to a large audience. So experimental filmmaking was kind of out the window. I decided I wanted to work in commercials for some reason, just because I knew it was kind of the furthest thing from actually what I wanted to do, but it would teach me technique.

*You spent a few years working as a camera person.*
PJ: Yeah. Six years.

*Were you frustrated or satisfied with your work during that time span?*
PJ: The first few years I was pretty happy. I was really excited I was learning so much. I was seeing that this was actually a real world where people could work, and that was thrilling. And I was finding myself in some really cool, high-end commercials. It was really some fun stuff going on. Shooting a basketball game one day and being on top of a Volvo, driving around, the next day. I'd say two years in or so, I started to feel anxious about where I was going and what I was doing and whether I was doing enough. About five years in, I was saying, "OK, I need to do something I'm not." I progressively started to feel more frustrated with my inability to write a feature in my free time.

*How did the American Film Institute program emerge as something you were going to pursue?*
PJ: AFI, just like the Cooper thing, was just something I heard about. I was feeling more and more anxious all the time. I was not at all becoming more interested in becoming a cinematographer or being a crew person for the rest of my life. I sort of knew that I had gotten into this as an education to become a filmmaker and that felt like it was slipping away unless I did something. Having worked on commercials for six years, I didn't want to go to a film school and learn how to do camera work. I knew I wanted to go to write and direct, and that was it.

*Velocity Rules was one of the films you made there?*
PJ: That was my last film, my thesis film.

*What was it about?*
PJ: When I looked around at short films that won festivals, they reminded me of commercials. I don't feel talented at that at all. I'd sort of decided that I wasn't sure how likely it was that even if you won Sundance in short film it was going to be anything tangible. So I sort of decided to just say "fuck it" and just try to make mini-features—four of them, in very different styles. The last one was a campy, poppy, action short about a housewife who discovers she's a superhero. It was kind of like on that wave of superhero debunking that was going on.

*How was it received?*

PJ: It was OK. I wasn't all that happy with it. (laughs) It was too ambitious for a short film. It's too long and it's too much, but I love and adore absolutely everything that it did to prepare me for turning around and doing *Monster*.

*Tell me about the beginnings of* Monster *way back when you first followed the Aileen Wuornos case.*

PJ: Her story broke when I was in college, and I followed it. I watched it on the news and was left incredibly curious about her because to me she didn't fit. Not only the mold of other serial killers, but she didn't fit the mold of how she was being described to me at all. She would be categorically kind of defined as a crazy, man-hating, person. It was [described as] this big mystery and I was like, "Well, it doesn't really look like that big of a mystery to me." She looks like someone who was beaten down for a really long time and lost it. I found her story really disturbing and unexplained. And then years later when Nick Broomfield's documentary came out, I went and saw it and I thought that was really good, but it didn't answer what had happened before the crime.

*And that was the unanswered question for you?*

PJ: That was the unanswered question. She always looked to me like a quintessential war story—a normal person put in insane circumstances who becomes like a feral animal, a killing machine. I was curious what it takes to make a normal person get there. And I was disturbed. I think it was 1995 that I wrote down a note about a *Raging Bull*–style character film about Aileen Wuornos. Then, that wasn't a genre that was a popular idea at all, and it seemed like a depressing idea. So I never ever was going to pursue that.

*When was the first time it reemerged as a potentially viable idea for you?*

PJ: At the AFI fest. I sat down across from Brad Wyman, my now producing partner, and it was like a two-second conversation. It was the most random thing. He said that he had worked with someone who had just done a movie about Ted Bundy. And I said, "Oh, that's weird; I know about Ted Bundy, and I used to read true crime." And he was like, "They're doing all these serial-killer movies." And I said, "I thought of doing a movie about Aileen Wuornos," and he said, "You should do it. You can get it made in two seconds." I was just kind of like, "Fuck it, let me go see what's going on here." And then it's like the door kept opening and seeming more and more viable, and once I started to look into it, I wrote a letter to Aileen. And suddenly she was writing me back and I was completely sucked in. And then it just ratcheted way up, really quickly. And I suddenly realized, "You better not go forward with this unless you're really positive your partners are making the same movie you are, because I have no desire to make a lesbian exploitation film." I decided I couldn't accept any money unless it was a deal that I felt was structured to at least give me a shot to succeed in making the kind of movie that I wanted to.

*What did you write to Aileen initially?*
PJ: I was very up-front. I told her everything I was thinking. And it wasn't like I won her over, either. She responded like, "Yeah, get in line; you're part of the media. You're gonna rip me off anyway so here's what I want." She had no reason to trust people, and she pretty much never did.

*What was most of the correspondence about?*
PJ: All of our correspondence was about meeting. Her execution was not scheduled at the time. We assumed that would be two years in the future. Then out of nowhere her execution was scheduled and she was executed a month later, and we were already in preproduction at that point. And so the plans that we'd had for Charlize and I to go down and meet her went out the window. I always tried to be very up-front with her and very clear about how I felt and that I was not trying to screw her over, that I was trying to protect her story. I was never sure that she believed me. It seemed like she didn't. But then the

night before she was executed she left us seven thousand of her personal letters. And that's for no money. At the end of the day, for nothing, she left me everything, which seemed so quintessentially her, that even though she was a mistrustful, damaged person, she was endlessly optimistic that one day it would work out.

*You passed on some initial interest in the film until you'd written the script. You wanted to ensure the film that was made would be the kind of story that was in your head?*
PJ: Right. And I said, "I'm going to direct it." I've never ever had more confidence about demanding that I was going be a director just for moral reasons. I was, "Either I'm making this movie because I'm now the person who's making these promises to Aileen, or nobody's making this movie."

*How long did it take to write the script?*
PJ: It took me seven weeks. I just locked myself up and I did nothing but write for seven weeks. I didn't leave my house. I didn't talk to people. I didn't go on e-mail. I didn't do anything. I was like, "I'm sitting in this room until this script is done." And that was the only way that I got it done.

*With the script complete, how did casting get under way?*
PJ: We were looking at name actors, but not A-list actors at all. And it was quite possibly going to go straight to video. I was obsessed with who was going to play it, totally obsessed. Charlize was the person I wanted since the first week of writing it. I remember saying it in the beginning of casting, and everybody was just like, "That's nice, you're on crack." It was close to happening with a lot of actors until we got Charlize to say yes, because the script got pretty popular in town. It was a much more sought-after script than I ever expected it would be, and so the level of powerful talent rose really rapidly. And this whole thing, by the way, happens in a matter of four weeks. Like, from the moment I got done with the script, it was four weeks later we had Charlize, and a month later we're shooting.

*This all must have been quite surreal for you, for it to happen so quickly.*
PJ: Well, here's the other funny thing that I've never talked about in interviews but really the more that I think about it is kind of relevant to that question: I'm a speed skater, and I speed-skate outside here in Griffith Park. A week after I was done with the script, I got hit by a car going fifty-five miles an hour while I was skating. It was a horrific accident that I should completely be dead from. But for some unknown reason I didn't even break any bones. I went through the windshield and was in the hospital and on painkillers on like Vicodin at home when Brad [Wyman] called me and said, "We're going to do this movie." So I was high on Vicodin when this whole thing first started happening. It's so funny. Truly, Brad and I have talked about this many times; it was my life before that accident, and the life after the accident. (laughs)

*Like this has all been a dream since you had the accident.*
PJ: Completely. I've always joked that I actually died in that accident. And that this is all my fantasy of what happened. The whole thing was so surreal. I was so distracted by my accident. It's like I'd ripped all my skin off my face, my arms, my back—everything. Suddenly I was trying to deal with my physical body and what was going on, which is the first time in twelve years that anything had superseded my directing career. It was like, "Oh, my God, am I going to live? Do I have a serious head injury? Am I going to die in my sleep?" They were like, "You're making a movie," and I was like, "Uh-huh. OK, well, just call me later. Tell me where I need to be." I never really got that dramatic, jump-up-and-down moment. My life just went from recovering from the accident to walking around in big hats trying to protect my skin, sitting with twenty famous actresses a day in meetings. Once we got Charlize, that was really it for me. Because that was the day I realized there was a shot I was actually not only going to make the movie, but I was going to make the movie I wanted to make. And I had this powerful actress now not only attached but also producing.

*How were you feeling during the shoot? Were you nervous?*
PJ: Yes, I was definitely nervous—desperately nervous from beginning to

end of the entire movie, because I wanted it to be great. The whole time, all the time, I was like, "I don't know how this is going to happen, but oh well. Here we go!" And that continued until the very end.

*The roller rink scene seems to me to recall that moment early on in your career when you realized what you wanted to do—to marry music to images. It just works.*
PJ: That scene by far is my pride and joy. There are lots of parts in the movie that I really like, but that's definitely my favorite scene. I wrote the script all the way through and in the first act, I just wasn't feeling it. I wasn't actually feeling them fall in love. And the thing was, it gets so dark and violent later. That scene actually came out of a very frustrated night with me arguing with myself and saying, "You know, serial killer, lesbian, whatever; this is bullshit. You know what it's like when people fall in love." And it was just one of those great lucky things that I just was listening to music and I suddenly wanted them to be in a roller-skating rink and then I pulled up the "Don't stop believing" song and I wrote that scene. It was just one of those things that happen sometimes, where you just see it happen in front of you and you just feel it completely. And it just comes out. The scene never changed from that half hour or hour it took me to write it.

*If that scene worked, what didn't in the film?*
PJ: First, everything leading up to the roller-skating rink, which is a lot. (laughs) The whole opening of the film didn't work out the way that I wanted it to. Our first week of shooting was pretty disastrous. We fell way behind schedule, and everybody was kind of getting up to speed and finding themselves. I was the most upset about the opening scene of the two of them [Aileen and Selby] meeting in the bar. That was a scene that on the page I really liked. That scene did not live up to what I hoped for it.

*Charlize's performance got such an amazing amount of press and awards. Did you ever feel that your contribution was being ignored?*
PJ: It's funny. I mean, I don't want to sound like the grand master behind this or something, but the interesting thing about my relation-

ship with her performance was that the design of the success of the movie for me *was* that performance. My resolution before we made this movie was that whoever played this was going to be so good, they'd get nominated for an Oscar. I knew that the only shot such a dark movie like this had was for that performance to be incredible. And I remember being stunned when there started to be award shows, and people would be like, "You're not sitting in the award show; you're not the one that was nominated." And I was like, "I'm not?" There were definitely moments. People would shove me out of the way and tell Charlize how her dialogue was so incredible and I was kind of like, "OK, now you're crossing the line!" (laughs)

*Do you ever feel like you're working in a man's world? Or is it something that doesn't even occur to you?*
PJ: It occurs to me, but I don't feel like that. I'm so uninterested in the subject. It's not out of a lack of appreciation for it. I've just talked way too much about it. And my reaction to that was to go, "Oh, fuck it, I don't even care," and just kind of do whatever I want. It's tricky. I don't want to take away from other women who feel oppressed. But for me I feel that it can be a great benefit as much as it can be a problem. There are things about it that piss me off and can be irritating and exhausting. There are also places that I feel that I can get to and observe, and trust that I can establish that I think is probably easier for me than a man. And so I try to just look at it that way.

*Do you feel a need to strike now while the iron is still hot and get that second film out of the way, or is it more about making sure that second film is worthy of following the first?*
PJ: Well, I think it depends on what you want. I have my little panic attacks in the middle of the night like, "What if I've got to get it done right now?" But the truth is, my priority number one is that I got into filmmaking because I would sit there and see those scenes in front of me. And at the end of the day, making *Monster* was unbelievably hard, as making any movie is. And the only thing that made it worth it is not those awards and all those kind of things that I can barely remember

because I was so overwhelmed. It was really that night in the editing room, that day on set. It was those things. So yes, I wish it could happen right away and I wish I could make bucketloads of money and all of those things. But more than anything, I realize the only thing that makes that kind of work worth it is to be engaged. And so that's my priority. I do care about success and all of those things. But I don't care enough to do movies just for that reason.

## THE DIRECTOR'S TAKE
## PATTY JENKINS

*What is the first film you ever saw?*
*Pippi Longstocking*

*What is your favorite film of all time?*
*Pippi Longstocking*. Just kidding. Probably *A Face in the Crowd* or *The Shining*

*What movie made you realize that film was an art?*
I think it always seemed that way to me. Probably films like *The Red Balloon* made that impression when I was very young.

*What movie do you consider your guilty pleasure?*
*Poltergeist*

*Who is your favorite movie character of all time?*
Chopper

*What's your favorite movie snack food?*
Twizzlers/Red Vines

*Who is your favorite director of all time?*
Elia Kazan

*Who is the most impressive filmmaker working today?*
The Coen brothers

*What quality do the best directors share?*
Attention to detail and humanity

*Who is your favorite actor or actress of all time?*
So cliché, but true: Marlon Brando

*Who is your favorite actor or actress of today?*
Warren Beatty

*Who would you cast as yourself in a film about your life?*
Charlize Theron, though I'd have to ugly her up again

*If you could remake one movie, what would it be?*
The Misfits

*What is your best quality as a director?*
Tenacity

*What is your greatest weakness as a director?*
Delegating certain aspects of the process to other people completely

*Finish this sentence: I'll never direct a movie about . . .*
a jewelry heist. No, truly, if the character's story is good, anything is possible. So I guess "pure action" is the answer.

*Finish this sentence: The perfect movie is . . .*
an experiential journey through a story well told.

*What will they be saying about your work fifty years from now?*
I don't know, but I would like it to be that I succeeded at the above.

*What piece of advice do you have for aspiring filmmakers?*
To embrace how truly hard it is and always will be, to be really honest with yourself about whether that's really what you want to do with your life, and then to put one foot in front of the other relentlessly. Also to try to keep your eye on the ball about what you want out of it, and not get distracted by things you don't care about.

*What are you as passionate about as moviemaking?*
The people that I care about, and speed-skating.

# RICHARD KELLY

"I was aware that I was probably developing that reputation of being really difficult, but I didn't care! I thought, 'If it's a good film, everyone's going to forget what an asshole and pain in the ass I was.'"

## SELECTED CREDITS

*Donnie Darko* (2001)–writer/director
*Domino* (2005)–writer
*Southland Tales* (2006)–writer/director

**D**onnie Darko was barely a blip on the pop culture radar when it opened in 2001. It earned an inconsequential $500,000 in a brief theatrical run. As writer/director Richard Kelly says, it was an "experiment failed!" But something about this odd blend of sci-fi, social satire, and teen angst hit a nerve and spawned a massive cult following. Kelly was just twenty-six at the time of the film's release. In the intervening years his stature has only grown as his screenwriting career blossomed and the appetite grew for what his mind might conjure up for a second directorial effort. Amazingly, Donnie Darko was his first script. Now it seems the creative valve cannot be shut, with a myriad of projects in development. So much for Donnie Darko, the film that bombed. The experiment, in fact, continues.

---

*What did your parents do?*
RK: My dad started out working for NASA, and then he became a mechanical engineer working in industrial robotics. My mom taught English and Spanish, and then she tutored kids who were not doing well in school.

*I would think for a kid growing up, your dad's job seemed pretty glamorous.*
RK: Yeah, he worked on the Viking Lander that went to Mars, and then he worked on the top-secret smokeless cigarette project for Philip Morris.

*Did your dad's work appeal to you early on as a potential career?*
RK: For a while I really wanted to be an architect and then I thought of trying to be a cartoonist. There were a lot of different kind of outlets I was thinking of pursuing, and ultimately filmmaking ended up being the hybrid of all those things.

*You drew a lot as a kid?*
RK: Oh, yeah. I had a pretty big art portfolio. I did a lot of black-and-white illustration. Pencil illustration was my biggest focus, and I did watercolors and oil paintings.

*What sort of movies were you into?*
RK: I definitely went to the movies a lot. I remember *Back to the Future* and *Aliens*, *Terminator*, *E.T.*, Spielberg, Robert Zemeckis, Jim Cameron, and John Hughes. This was in the days long before DVD. No one I knew could afford a Laser Disc player. I remember when you could just start renting movies at video stores. I remember the first movie we rented ever was *Romancing the Stone*. We had this VCR that was top loaded, you know? (laughs)

*Do you remember when you started to appreciate the craft behind film-making?*
RK: Probably when I saw Oliver Stone's *The Doors* in 1990. I was fifteen, and I remember a bunch of us were drinking out in the mall parking lot, and I'm with this girl and we went and saw *The Doors*. The Bob Richardson cinematography in that film blew me away. That's when I was like, "This is really an art form." Maybe it was because that film was all about rock 'n' roll and drugs and sex, and it was me discovering the Doors for the first time.

*Were you open with your parents early on about your intentions of becoming a filmmaker?*
RK: I didn't really vocalize film, because I didn't want to come across as being a dreamer and have people roll their eyes. I was immediately aware of the fact that saying you want to go to Hollywood to be a film director, people might laugh at that. I just kept it very general. I think I said, "I might be able to get an art scholarship with my portfolio," and I did get one to USC.

*Did you have any experience with a camera before school?*
RK: I had no experience with a motion picture camera or even a still camera. I never really held a camera in my life until we started doing super eight film my junior year in college.

*What was the first short you put together?*
RK: The first short was called *The Vomiteer*, and it starred one of my

fraternity brothers. I joined a fraternity right away, and that's where I got all my friends. To the film-school people I was the frat guy who they looked at with suspicion—as they should have, because my first film was about a guy who can't stop vomiting. It was very serious, kind of arty, but it was absurd. I guess it was my response to a lot of the people I met in film school who I just didn't fit in with. The most cringe-worthy films I saw there were the ones about a homeless man, or a girl contemplating suicide because she was raped by her dad. You were covering your face while watching these films, going, "Oh God, not again. Not more dark, depressing suicide and rape and molestation." It was some dark shit. (laughs) There's no law that says an art film cannot be tremendously entertaining or tremendously funny. To me, that is the essence of a great story—comedy and suspense. If you can successfully create those two things, the rest is gravy. Not that *The Vomiteer* was any great work of art. (laughs)

*Toward the end of school were you feeling confident about your prospects as a director? It must have been competitive.*
RK: Very quickly people get beaten down in film school. If their stuff is not well received, it's a rude awakening. It's very painful and it's very personal to a lot of people who come to film school with dreams of being George Lucas or Steven Spielberg. Quickly those dreams are dashed when their film is mocked and laughed at by their peers or not well received at all. So they start dropping like flies in terms of wanting to direct. A lot decide, "I'm going to edit or I'm going to produce, or hell, I'm going to law school." I was one of the ones who was still gung-ho and I wanted to do a big 35-millimeter short film. So I thought, "After graduation I'm going to ask my dad for a little bit of money and I'm going to rent a 35-millimeter camera and I'm going to get some of my friends together and we're going to go do this big elaborate sci-fi film," which was called *Visceral Matter*. It was kind of *Mystery Science Theater 3000*–type camp stuff. It was about a mad scientist and a teleportation chamber. I spent the whole summer building this teleportation chamber in my garage in Hermosa Beach. We shot it in late July over a week around the desert and it was a

pretty grueling process—a lot of visual effects, computer animation. I was just putting myself through a self-financed graduate school, was the way I looked at this short film.

*How much did you spend on the film?*
RK: I ended up spending between forty to fifty thousand dollars. And it's about forty-five minutes long. It's got a lot of digital effects and a pretty elaborate sound design. I really went for it. It gave me great confidence to be on a set and finish something and see it through to the end and understand the process of dealing with a laboratory and dealing with postproduction and working on an Avid. I became very confident in my ability to put together a big elaborate film with a lot of different elements.

*It was effectively made to be your calling card?*
RK: Yeah, well, shorts don't get you anywhere unless you have a feature screenplay. So then that's when I set out to write *Donnie Darko*.

*Was* Donnie Darko *the first feature you'd ever written?*
RK: Yeah.

*Did it start with the title?*
RK: That and the engine. It started off as a big piece of ice. I remember a folk legend from my hometown, and this does actually happen—chunks of ice, either flushed from a toilet in an airplane or falling from a wing, sometimes crash into houses. That happened somewhere near where I grew up. That somehow became an engine that fell off a plane and that was what I built it around. Then it became, "I want this to be a piece of social satire and kind of a comic-book portrait of the suburbs as I remember them." I thought, "Well, I can't set this in the present day. It's not going to feel right. I need to do it as a period piece. Let's do 1988, and let's do it right around the election" because I thought a jet engine could also be a satirical rendering of the death of the Reagan era. I thought putting together a comic-book story of a dysfunctional kid and this science-fiction mys-

tery can also uncover the black comedy in the suburbs as I remember them in 1988.

*Your depiction of the suburbs rang true for many people.*
RK: It's very accurate to how I remember them. I grew up in a very right-wing small town. I didn't know any Democrats growing up. (laughs) Pretty much everyone I knew was very conservative.

*Were you more of a silent rebel than Donnie?*
RK: Oh yeah. The only autobiographical thing that happened in the film was that I got in a fight with my health teacher about this sort of new-age curriculum that they were promoting. But I had never mouthed off to the extent that Donnie did. It was more on my wish list than anything. I was on the honor roll. I played soccer and I ran track-and-field and fit the mold of a normal kid, but on the inside I was just kind of a repressed artist maniac trying to get the hell out of this place.

*What films were you thinking about when it came to the time-travel aspect of the story?*
RK: I was thinking of a lot of time-travel films, certainly *The Terminator* and *Twelve Monkeys*, and clearly *Back to the Future*. I thought there was something very elegant about a well-orchestrated time-travel story that pays off and comes together like a very satisfying puzzle. I wanted to make sure that my puzzle operated on all cylinders.

*At any point in the writing of it were you concerned that it wasn't the most commercial story you were telling?*
RK: No. I think it's all about pleasing yourself. The biggest mistake a lot of writers make when they're first starting out is, "Oh, I have to try to please the studio executives or I have to try to write for the marketplace." That's where you lose your voice, and your voice is diluted by what you anticipate studio executives responding to. And that's when you are handicapping yourself. I never once thought, "I need to do this because I need to sell this screenplay." I thought, "I'm going to

write exactly the movie I want to see." It was all about, "If no one else likes it, fuck 'em." I might be the only person in the world who understands this script and wants to see it made, but that was my attitude and it continues to be my attitude, because I think the purest essence of an artist is ultimately pleasing yourself first. Ultimately, if there's anyone else who likes it, great. If not? Fuck 'em.

*How long did it take you to complete the script?*
RK: Four or five weeks, I think. I remember a feeling of enormous satisfaction when I finished it. Not only was it the first feature-length screenplay I had ever written, but I felt like I really had all the pieces that I needed.

*With the script done, things happened pretty quickly for you. Through your friend Sean McKittrick, you got it in the hands of CAA agent Beth Swofford, who read it and immediately responded to it.*
RK: Beth flipped out for it, and the Tuesday morning after that weekend she read it, I got a call from four agents at CAA. And they all said, "Come in, we want to meet you. We want to be a part of this. We want to help you." And then I got signed by CAA, and that was it. Here I am, twenty-three years old and I've got the most powerful agency in Hollywood saying they want to represent me. It was a huge deal for me!

*Did you ever consider selling the script for someone else to direct?*
RK: I was very vocal and very aggressive saying, "I'm directing this, Sean's producing it, and there's no way we will ever sell it and relinquish control." We both knew this was our ticket, and Sean had seen so many other scripts get destroyed by the development process that we knew we'd regret it for the rest of our lives if we let this script go. There was almost a year when the script floated around and we met everyone in Hollywood. Everyone said, "Yeah, we like the script but we don't think you can direct this." It was, "Love the script, great writing sample, would you be interested in writing this for us?" They were offering me a lot of teen slasher films to rewrite.

*Did you do any of that work?*
RK: I turned it all down, and people thought I was arrogant and probably nuts, but I don't know how to do something unless my heart's in it. The first writing job I took while we were trying to get *Donnie* made was *Holes*. I was the first screenwriter to adapt it. Here was this whimsical children's novel, and I was telling them I want to make it a little more dark and adult. I think they thought maybe I would make it ten percent darker, and I went and made it about eighty percent darker. I changed everything. I turned it into a postapocalyptic wasteland, and the warden was Robert Duvall and all the kids were eighteen-year-old criminals. I was like, "Man, I'm so proud of this," and I turned it in and they freaked out. They said, "You have to go back and start from scratch, or you're fired." I wrote a fifteen-page memo pleading my case to [producer] Mike Medavoy, and it was a complete disaster. I got fired and my agent was just like, "Dude, you can't do this again." (laughs) So then we got Jason Schwartzman attached to *Donnie Darko* and all of a sudden all this heat came back on the script and it got resurrected from the dead. And then we heard that Drew Barrymore and her production partner Nancy Juvonen had read it and they wanted to meet us immediately. So we jetted over to the set of *Charlie's Angels*, and we met with them in their trailer and I offered [Drew] the role of the English teacher. So all of a sudden we had a star. We were able to raise $4.5 million.

*How much tension was there for you on the set, considering this was your first feature? Did you have any anxiety?*
RK: No. I'm very confident on a movie set. I know what I'm doing. I feel like that's what I've been waiting my whole life to do.

*How about working with the actors?*
RK: I had no idea how to talk to actors. I had to figure that out as I went along. Somehow it worked out. In terms of the actors, inside I was scared to death, but I just put on a straight face and talked to them as simply as possible. It's a very delicate process on your first film because they're looking at this first-time director going, "Does

this guy know what he's doing?" You want to make them feel secure, like they're in good hands.

*Jake Gyllenhaal says he was mimicking you in his performance of Donnie. Did you know this during production?*
RK: I didn't realize that until we had wrapped. I was literally losing five pounds per week. I was turning into this walking skeleton. I was sort of becoming Donnie Darko! I started channeling Donnie and Jake, playing Donnie, started channeling me. So it was sort of a subconscious thing going on between director and actor that I can't even explain.

*Once you got into the editing room, how did you feel about what you had?*
RK: The editing process was not pleasant for me at all, because I realized this movie is just going to run so long and the story will not make sense. To cut this thing down to under two hours and have the story still make sense was going to be a huge undertaking. I became very paranoid and anxiety ridden because I felt the film was going to be taken away from me and cut behind my back by the financiers. I don't care how good your footage or your performances are, if you're a first-time director it's almost like you need to expect that. "You're a first-time director, we're going to re-cut you—fuck you." That's sort of the attitude. With each passing week it was, "OK, we're going to bring in this other editor and we're going to show the film to this executive over here at Warner Brothers and get his opinion." The writing was on the wall that the film was on the verge of being taken away from me and that was when I really lost my shit. At some point I got a note to streamline the film and focus more on "Donnie's journey." So I went in with the editors and I cut this butchered version of the film. And I had them go in and we put in a temp title up there in this very obnoxious, curly romance-novel font. And I had them color it hot pink and write DONNIE'S JOURNEY on the main title. That was just like throwing gasoline on the fire. I was just this total smartass, and part of me thinks I shouldn't have done that, but another part of me is proud I did. You cannot be a doormat as a first-time director and let them steamroll over you.

*Weren't you concerned about getting a reputation as a difficult director on your first film?*
RK: I was aware that I was probably developing that reputation of being really difficult, but I didn't care! I knew all I had was this film and if it wasn't well received, then I might not ever work again! I kept thinking, "I have got to be a dick here. I've got to fight viciously and yell at people. I'm going to do it because all I have in the end is the critical reception of this film." I thought, "If it's a good film, everyone's going to forget what an asshole and pain in the ass I was." In retrospect maybe I took things too personally, but this was my life at the time and it's all that I had, and I had to defend it. It was a very unpleasant time, probably the most unpleasant time of my life, editing that film. I'm glad that it's over. Now you're making me relive it!

*We can move on to a cheerier topic, like the film almost going straight to TV. You were taking the film to the festivals, but it wasn't getting sold?*
RK: We came into Sundance and everybody wanted to fuck us. And after Sundance it was like we had an STD and everyone decided they didn't even want to risk fucking us. They wouldn't even give us a blow job. They wouldn't even let me eat them out. (laughs)

*But you did get interest from Newmarket?*
RK: They made an offer for $1 million that said "possibility of a theatrical release, not guaranteed, most likely pay cable, Starz network premiere." I brought the guys at Newmarket over to Flower Films and I got Drew Barrymore to put on that sweet, beautiful smile and say, "Guys, you're going to put this in theaters, aren't you?" And they said, "Of course. We were always going to put it in theaters." And it was just like, ugh! Here I am thinking that this movie that I worked so hard on is going to debut on Starz and my career's going to be over. (laughs)

*The film presented quite a marketing challenge, I would think.*
RK: They planned a Halloween release date, and we all decided the best way to try to market this thing was to tap into more of the thriller element of the story and even gear it toward the image of the rabbit

mask. It was a smart decision to make at the time because it's such a difficult movie to market. It's one of those movies you almost need to market with the filmmaker, but I hadn't done anything yet, so they couldn't market it on my name. Everyone did the best they could. And then all of a sudden, September 11th. At that point you're just, like, the last thing anyone wants to have to think about—a very provocative, challenging, disturbing, difficult film like this. I was like, "Just fucking put it out there. Please just put it in theaters so I can not have to live with the fact that this thing just goes straight to pay cable." So everyone decided we're going to stick with this Halloween release date. Literally, like eight movies opened that weekend. It was an awful weekend to open a movie! So the per screen average was like eighteen hundred dollars or something on fifty-something screens. Newmarket was like, "Well, fuck it. We've just got to cut our losses." So there literally wasn't an ad come Sunday. The movie was over! Experiment failed! Failure on every level. Everyone was just heartbroken. But you know that was the end of Act One.

*So what was the beginning of Act Two?*
RK: It was when the DVD came out, and then all of a sudden in New York it started playing at the Two Boots Pioneer Theater. So people started lining up to see it and the DVD started to really pick up. Each month it outsold the previous month, and these Internet sites started popping up. A year later the film was released in the UK, and it just started to explode. Teenagers connected with it and it just became this thing people wanted to talk about. The audience rescued the film from oblivion.

*Did the fact that there were so many interpretations of the film surprise you?*
RK: I was just so excited that people were getting it, even if they were misinterpreting it and saying it's about mental illness or that Cherita Chen is a spy for the Chinese government or Gretchen is really a reincarnation of Donnie's mother and Donnie wants to fuck his mother— all these theories that were completely wrong. I was just glad people

were talking about it. The real, accurate version of the story was the one I ended up doing in the director's cut, with the philosophy of time travel and the comic book—the sci-fi story that I'd always intended to tell.

*Is there a filmmaker today whose status you'd like to enjoy?*
RK: Yeah. I mean, to be able to have the clout that someone like David Fincher can wield to be able to get *Fight Club* made for $70 million at 20th Century-Fox. What Fincher pulled off with that film is just such a coup d'état. Just to imagine the look on Rupert Murdoch's face when he saw that film raised a fist for counterculture. That is the dream—to have the control or clout that people like Soderbergh or Fincher have. As long as the price is right, they can do everything within the studio corporate umbrella, because they've earned the right to do that.

*Is it important to you that someone watching your films recognizes it as "a Richard Kelly film"?*
RK: It's not about the ego of this is "a Richard Kelly film." But at the same time, I write my own scripts and I feel I've earned enough to have that credit just because I do write my own material. It also helps you. It's called showbiz. You've got to get out there and sell yourself. If my name can somehow become something that the public recognizes as here's another weird crazy movie from the guy who did *Donnie Darko* so we'll go see it. It's the same thing with how they market David Fincher's films or even Soderbergh's films or a lot of Spike Jonze/Charlie Kaufman collaborations.

*What do you think will be common to all your work?*
RK: I think someone else is going to have to define that, because all I know is I don't ever want to make the same film twice. But at the same time I always want people to know it's a film I made, simply because there's something recognizable about me in it. I want them to all be personal. I don't ever want to make an impersonal film. It's like, I wrote a movie for Tony Scott that very much has my kind of stamp on it, but at the same time I wrote it for Tony. I'm just grateful to finally also be

in production on the next film that I direct, because I don't want there to be a four-year lag between each film. I'll just go nuts because I'm sick of writing and I just want to direct a film hopefully every year.

*How did your second film,* Southland Tales, *begin?*
RK: I wrote the very first draft of *Southland Tales* when we were trying to sell *Darko* to a distributor in that hellish five months after Sundance.

*Something interesting would have to come out of that rough period for you.*
RK: Oh, yeah! I was very angry and frustrated and I wanted to write something that would cheer me up. I wanted to write something about L.A., this city that I'd spent the last nine or ten years in. It's evolved significantly, but it's still the basic core story of what I first wrote. I just can't wait to get behind a camera again. I think I'm going to pee in my pants on the first day of shooting, either out of excitement or nervousness. I feel like it's a gift to be able to direct a film and it's been so long and such a struggle to even get *Southland* off the ground. It's even more elaborate and ambitious and daunting an undertaking than *Donnie Darko*. And the fact that I'm getting to do this at my age and have this level of creative control, I'm grateful for it and I'm never going to take it for granted.

*It's been described as a combination of a number of genres. It's part musical, part comedy, et cetera?*
RK: That's basically the best way to describe it. I can't speak in movie marketing terms, and I think sometimes my producers, their eyes roll back in their heads when I say things like that, but that's what it is. It's a hybrid of sci-fi, thriller, comedy, and musical. And what those percentages end up being, I don't know. Maybe it'll end up being ten percent musical, maybe five percent musical. I see them, all four, as being right around twenty-five percent.

*Tonally what films will it emulate?*
RK: Well, I'm going to be screening quite a few films. I'll be screening *Dr. Strangelove, Network, Brazil, Blade Runner, The Big Lebowski, Kiss Me Deadly, Heat,* and *Barry Lyndon.* Also *Pulp Fiction.*

*What are you hoping the audience will come away with from* Southland?
RK: More than anything I want it to be something completely unexpected. I want to take people by surprise. I am trying to create a really exquisite piece of pop art, with pop actors appearing in a very subversive and dark political allegory. I am casting faces that you would never expect to see in this kind of film, and therefore it will be subversive on an immediate, aesthetic level.

*What music is informing the film?*
RK: Moby has already completed the score to the film. His music is the film's aching heartbeat.

*And it's something of a love letter to L.A.?*
RK: It is a love letter to L.A. A really, really, nasty one.

*Are you prepared for the inevitability that many of your fans will be disappointed by whatever you follow up* Darko *with, even if* Southland *turns out great? How much of that is on your mind?*
RK: None of it. I know I'm not a one-trick pony. I know I have a lot more in me than *Darko*. I know that's only the beginning of what I'm capable of doing. There might be people who never like one of my other films more than *Darko*, but there's not a thing I can do about that. I wish that I could have gotten another film out already, but all the stuff I'd written after *Darko* was in anticipation of *Darko* being well received and an immediate success and me thinking, "Oh, OK, I can then get $15 million for my next film." In fact it poured molasses on my feet. The slow reception of this movie made it a lot harder for me to get the next project off the ground, because they're just as messed up and weird and provocative as *Darko* and, unfortunately, they're more expensive. The slow-burn success of *Darko* slowed down my career, but it's just made me a better filmmaker and it'll make the second film that much better. I've had the chance to really direct it in my mind, and I think the time will have been put to good use.

## THE DIRECTOR'S TAKE
# RICHARD KELLY

*What is the first film you ever saw?*
I don't remember.

*What is your favorite film of all time?*
2001: A Space Odyssey

*What movie made you realize that film was an art?*
Brazil

*What movie do you consider your guilty pleasure?*
I don't feel guilty enjoying any film.

*Who is your favorite movie character of all time?*
Probably "The Dude" from *The Big Lebowski*

*What's your favorite movie snack food?*
Popcorn

*Who is your favorite director of all time?*
Stanley Kubrick

*What quality do the best directors share?*
I don't know. Having an obsessive eye for detail?

*Who would you cast as yourself in a film about your life?*
I would never allow the film to be made. And if they made it without my consent, I would show up on set with a shotgun and threaten to kill them all.

*What is your best quality as a director?*
I don't know. And if I answered that question, I would appear smug.

*What is your greatest weakness as a director?*
I have many weaknesses, and I don't care to discuss them right now.

*Finish this sentence: I'll never direct a movie about . . .*
delusional teenagers who see rabbits in 1980s suburbia. Been there.
Done that. I'm game for pretty much anything else.

*Finish this sentence: The perfect movie is . . .*
something that cannot exist. There is no such thing as perfection.

*What will they be saying about your work fifty years from now?*
I don't know. I've only made one movie so far.

*What piece of advice do you have for aspiring filmmakers?*
My advice is don't ask people for advice. Just go and figure it out on
your own.

*What are you as passionate about as moviemaking?*
Nothing

# DYLAN KIDD

"Maybe like life, you don't know how to
make the movie until it's done."

## SELECTED CREDITS

*Roger Dodger* (2002)–writer/director
*P.S.* (2004)–writer/director

The tale of how *Roger Dodger* came to be could serve as an inspiration to any of the legions of would-be filmmakers who tote around their script in a knapsack, wondering how they will ever realize their dreams. Dylan Kidd wrote and directed the acclaimed character study of a despicable lothario, played winningly by Campbell Scott. Kidd is an anomaly in many ways among his directing peers. He is a New Yorker who refuses to trade in his digs for Hollywood, and a man more comfortable knocking himself than anyone else: "My self-esteem is too low to assume that anyone is interested in my style." He is also undeniably an heir to a proud tradition in American filmmaking—the New York writer/director.

---

*What are your earliest memories of going to the movies?*
DK: All of my early memories of movies are of being traumatized by them. I saw *Close Encounters of the Third Kind* when I was seven or eight, and my mother had to take me out of the theater because I was so scared. I remember seeing Philip Kaufman's *Invasion of the Body Snatchers*. I couldn't sleep for six months after seeing that movie. I was literally traumatized by it. I remember my father taking me to see *Amarcord* and just being horrified and titillated. There was this scene with a woman with huge breasts. It was like movies can be either terrifying or erotically forbidden.

*Did you rent a lot of videos when you were a kid?*
DK: Absolutely. Like any self-respecting film geek, I was not a happy adolescent and I think the most important moment in my life was when I bought my own VCR. I had a job, working at a library after school. It was the first time I had ever made money. I got, like, three hundred dollars working over the course of an entire summer, and I decided to buy a VCR. I bought this forty-pound monster. That thing only broke down recently.

*What kinds of films were you attracted to early on?*
DK: I liked Spielberg, and I waited on line to see *E.T.* like everybody else. But I think when you're young, you sort of gravitate toward the

more self-consciously arty stuff. *Rumble Fish* was huge for me. After seven years of therapy, I still don't exactly know what hit me so hard about that movie.

*Was there one film that piqued your interest in filmmaking?*
DK: When I was in film school, I was aware that a lot of people were there because of *Star Wars*. But for me, the movie that when I look back was probably the biggest in terms of that little spark of, "I think I could see myself doing that," was *Stranger Than Paradise*. I was getting *American Film* magazine and I saw a production still of it. I didn't know anything about the movie and I just rented it. Thank God my video store had this movie. This was before *sex, lies, & videotape*, so there was no sense for me that some guy could just get his friends together and make a movie. And to see this film, it was not my style or aesthetic, it was like, "Holy shit," and I think a lightbulb just went off. It wasn't like a Godard film. It was, "Some guy in New York made this movie!"

*In high school did you have much direction?*
DK: I was so miserable. I was just trying to survive. I really was. I was clinically depressed all throughout high school. So for me it was movies and sports. I would have been a professional baseball player, until I became embarrassed that I was not gifted physically at all. I went to college and I was a philosophy major, which just shows how fucked up and aimless I was. I was just very spaced out—and remain to this day a very spaced-out kid that loves movies. I never believed that I would succeed at anything. I felt totally ill-equipped for life. I just liked reading and watching movies. Socially I was hopeless.

*What do you think accounts for your depression?*
DK: I think the biggest thing was that there was a history of depression in my family. A lot of people in my family are on heavy medication. There wasn't any one event. It was just that I didn't feel confident as a kid. I never felt that I could do anything. I always felt very clumsy, and that's why film school was so important for me.

*You first attended George Washington University, though.*
DK: I was such an underachiever in high school that I didn't get into any of the fancy colleges that I was supposed to. And I went to George Washington thinking that I would be at this ivory tower, and I got thrown into the biggest party school outside of, like, Florida State. It was just insane! I knew I had to get the hell out of there. I have some memory of seeing an ad for the Tisch School of the Arts. I'm not sure I knew there was such a thing as a film school, and it was only at that moment I knew I had to transfer. I remember thinking that there was no way I would actually make movies. My plan was to apply to the film school and do that for a semester. I knew that wouldn't work out, so I would just go into the cinema studies department because then I could write about movies. And I just remember getting to film school, and that first time when you look through that viewfinder and the shutter starts, something exploded in my head. I was done. I still didn't ever think I was ever going to be able to do it, but I just fell in love with it. It was just, "Oh my God. This is the best!" There's a block down on the campus and every time I walk by there, I glance at the spot where I was the first time I actually operated a camera.

*It sounds like you had found for the first time a place that felt right for you.*
DK: I loved it. I see kids in film school now and my sense is that it's a little more career oriented. I went off to film school, like, six months after *sex, lies, & videotape* had come out, so it was still in the best sense a film school, in that it's just a bunch of people that were nuts about this stuff. For us there was no thought like, "How are we going to get a job?" It was, "Let's watch this obscure Scandinavian film and talk about it for eight hours." It was just the best. I remember being in love with the way the film smelled. You were drunk on cinema.

*When you graduated, what did you do?*
DK: When I graduated, I thought I wanted to be a cinematographer, but we graduated in the worst film economy. There was no work in

New York. I was working at a pool hall. It was ridiculous. The few jobs I got were little goofy things for MTV, loading cameras on the occasional music video. But still there was absolutely no sense that I could do this. I think my mother was expecting me to go back to law school. For me there was never a plan B. There was no plan A, either. Years went by. I honestly don't know what the breakthrough was, but it took me four years after graduation to finally realize that I needed to make a movie. If you love movies and you want to make movies, there comes a point in your career when you're like, "If I don't make a movie I am going to go insane."

*What did you do to make that possible?*
DK: I did a short film in 1996 and I met my producer, Anne Chaisson, through that movie. When I made that short, it was a manic year. The plan was to make this short film, and then I would immediately write a feature. So I started writing a crazy script that was set in real estate, which was where I was working then.

*You wrote another feature besides the one set in the real-estate world, didn't you?*
DK: I did a horror movie script when I decided that I just wanted to get a movie made. I was thinking I would shoot it on 16 [millimeter]. I was going to go the *Evil Dead* route. It was going to be an incredibly erotic vampire thing. It was actually not bad, but I was still clueless. I don't know, a vampire film? What the hell was I thinking?

*What was the short about?*
DK: The short was an incredibly pretentious, Bergman-esque sort of horror movie about a kid whose mother is sick and he goes to stay for a summer with his uncle and aunt. It's a very painful thing to look at now, but it's very competent. It won some awards. I think doing that reminded me no matter how hard it is, the actual process of being on set with everybody is like a drug. It's so great. Once I made the short, there was still no plan B but at least now I had a plan A, which was to

write an original screenplay. "I'm going try to raise some money and I'm going direct the movie." I wanted to direct. The idea was never to be a writer. It was to write in order to get on set.

*How did* Roger Dodger *begin?*
DK: I decided, "Let me write something that I can shoot." There was no Nick character in the beginning. It was just going to be an hour and a half of Roger going from one bar to another and getting more and more sort of tweaked. The idea was to do something that we could literally go and do guerrilla-style. The style of the movie came from the original idea of doing it without permits and shooting all long lenses, hiding the crew and using radio mikes.

*The script seems like it was written precisely to attract an actor to the lead role.*
DK: That, I think, was calculated. I knew that we weren't going to be able to raise money without getting someone attached first. Once Anne got the script, we were both like, "OK, clearly this is not a commercial product, but man, some actor is going to want to do this role." So that was calculated. It was calculated in that she wanted me to write enough juicy roles that there could be three or four actors that would help us, because we were ready to do that movie for a $150,000 if we had to. It would have been insane, but I was just that desperate to make it. Writing that movie literally felt like a fever dream. It felt at the time like this was my last chance. I quit real estate just in desperation. I was as miserable as I'd ever been, but I got lucky and got one of those long-term dream temp jobs where you're working at some huge database project for six months and you're not supervised at all and you can do two hours' worth of work. I just sat there, writing. So that script was started at a temp job, writing in this cubicle.

*How long did it take to finish a draft?*
DK: The first draft just was insane. The first draft was finished I think, in like, three weeks.

*Did you have an actor in mind when you wrote the part of Roger?*

DK: Not when I was writing it. But when I was first done, I really got a sense that Sam Rockwell was going to be a huge star. And Paul Giamatti, as crazy as it sounds. The character was written to be a little bit younger than Campbell. When you're a self-obsessed person, you're obviously going to write about yourself. I was thirty-one when I was writing it, so he had always been less like the adult uncle and more the young adult. It ended up being so much better and spookier to have Campbell be this middle-aged adult and still be so regressed, because it seems like it's not just a phase. You're witnessing a lifestyle choice, not just a bad year.

*The story of how you got Campbell to play the lead is almost legendary by now. How long were you walking around town with your script on you at all times?*

DK: Two weeks, maybe. I ran into Maya Rudolph from *Saturday Night Live* on the street. It was the first time I had ever approached anybody, and she wasn't able to do it. She was in a hurry. She was very nice, but I remember thinking that it would have helped to have said, "Take this script with you just in case." I think that was where I was like, "I should never get caught without a script."

*And how did you meet Campbell?*

DK: I was meeting my friend Louis, and we stopped at the Grey Dog on Carmine. Campbell walked in and my initial feeling was, "Wow, he's too old." I went out on the sidewalk and called Anne and we talked about it for five minutes. It was just like, "What the fuck, he's here. What's the worst that could happen?" It was like a thirty-second conversation. Campbell really is just an incredible guy. Most people would say, "I can't accept this script," but he said two things. He said, "I'm going to be brutally honest with you, and it's going to take me a couple of weeks." I think I might have lied and said we had some money. I honestly don't remember. I didn't think I'd ever hear from him again. He called me back two weeks later. I talked to him for five minutes before I realized who it was.

*What did he say?*
DK: He said, "Hey, it's Campbell" and I went "Hey!" And then I realized, "Holy shit, it's Campbell Scott!" He was doing a reading somewhere and he invited me, and we went out afterwards and just talked about it.

*What did he want to know from you before signing on?*
DK: He wanted to know if I had a plan. He was like, "These are really long scenes." I told him all about my two-camera plan and my long lenses and that this wasn't just going to be a play on film, this was going to be a very visual movie with cigarette smoke and swirling neon and all this stuff. So I think he bought it. He's a very smart guy. He probably thought, "He obviously doesn't have any money, but it seems like he has a plan." Once we met Campbell, it was just like winning the lottery. It was insane. It was April or May when I met Campbell, and within six months we were shooting. It never happens the way you expect it to be.

*Campbell is a director himself. Were you ever concerned that he was going to take your baby away from you?*
DK: Huge paranoia on my part, which just seems ridiculous now, because Campbell really is the most honorable person I've ever met. I remember the one time that I really made Campbell angry early on was when he suggested that I speak to Andy Keir, who had edited a film that he had just directed. I remember just having a real sense that I have to have my own person in the editing room. This was all my own paranoid fantasy, and I remember having that conversation with Campbell and he was just pissed. He was like, "Look, man, if this is the way we're going to start dealing with each other . . ." And he was totally right, but I was obsessed with protecting my baby.

*When you started to rehearse, was it odd for you to be directing actors with so much experience?*
DK: It was. Isabella was the one. Fuck, it's Isabella Rossellini! She's totally cool, but she's still Isabella. Rehearsals are scary for a lot of di-

rectors. It's definitely scary for me. What do you say? Nobody teaches you how to rehearse. You don't know. You just have to do it.

*Where was your head at during the shoot after struggling to get to this place for so long?*
DK: I had a complete Zen calm throughout that entire movie. We were so prepared. Everybody was so on the same page. We had the best crew. There was a total sense that this is what I was meant to be doing. We invited the entire crew up to the editing room to watch the first week's stuff that had already been cut together. And it was an incredible moment—the entire crew jammed in this room where we watched a twenty-minute chunk of the movie, and it was just so apparent that it was really working.

*Visually what were you trying to accomplish with* Roger Dodger?
DK: The game plan was not to make it feel like a movie. We didn't want you to be aware of coverage. We wanted you to feel like you were literally spying, like literally these four people went into a bar and we photographed them without them knowing. We wanted the sense that the camera was chasing Roger through the movie and this was a guy who didn't want to be seen. So in the end when the camera finally does lock on him and pin him down, it means something. I feel so bad for our cinematographer, Joaquin, because other cinematographers who see the movie realize what an achievement it is but a lot of people were like, "Well, they couldn't afford lights or a tripod."

*What were the key differences in how you approached your second film,* P.S., *as opposed to* Roger?
DK: The difference between the first movie and the second movie was that in the first I was listening to my gut and the second I was not listening to my gut. I need to get better about making sure I put myself in the position to succeed. In the first movie, we went to set so ready to make that movie. And in *P.S.*, in a very self-sabotaging way, I put myself in a bad position which has nothing to do with the cast and crew, who were all wonderful. It was my own preparation about what

kind of movie I was making. The script wasn't tight, and I agreed to make the movie without rehearsing. I'm not good enough to make a movie without a rehearsal. I'm not Orson Welles. I had some feeling that I didn't want to be the guy that waited too long before making a second film. You forget that the first one didn't turn out well because you're a genius: It turned out well because you prepped it for two years and spent eight months of your life thinking about the scenes and how you'll cover them and you rehearsed for a week and you meticulously worked on the script. It's self-sabotage, pure and simple, to walk on set before you're ready. And there's nobody else you can blame except yourself.

*It felt like some tough choices had to be made in terms of deciding how much time to devote to the peripheral characters in the story.*
DK: I didn't realize until maybe editing how hard the movie was in terms of how much you're juggling. And how much is too much to give the audience? It was designed to have three or four things happening at all times, and that's not always a good idea. Even if you have four things going on, you have to pick the one thing that the people latch on to. It's like instruments in a symphony. You need some kind of balance. You need to pick one thing and have there be other colors to put underneath. We got into editing and I just felt like, "Jesus Christ!" It ended up being this huge salad of different tones and genres. It's interesting. In a way you make the movie in order to teach yourself why you wanted to make the movie. And that's the great unfair thing. Maybe like life, you don't know how to make the movie until it's done. You're like, "OK, I'm ready to start making the movie."

*You were able to get your second film out of the way pretty quickly. You didn't sit around and debate what to do as much as some others.*
DK: The last thing in the world I want to be is Quentin Tarantino. If you make a movie every five years, then every movie has to be a home run. If you're the guy who makes a movie every year, then you're sort of bulletproof. I want to be the guy that, before you know it, they've

made five movies. I really admire people like Kevin Smith and Spike Lee. They got their careers moving so quickly. I admire the fact that Kevin Smith made *Clerks* and then didn't fuck around. *Mallrats* came out immediately, and then he did *Chasing Amy* and before you know it, Kevin Smith's a viable director. There's a statute of limitations, you know? It's very easy to wait too long.

*So far you've chosen to stay in New York and make your own films. Does the "Hollywood machine" frighten you?*

DK: My biggest fear is the time suck. I feel like just being this sort of broke-ass guy living in Queens and writing my own script, at least now I'm sort of in control of my time. For me the big fear is writing a script for a studio and them being like, "Great, we love you," and then you realize you still have to go out and do twelve different meetings and pitch it and you still might not get the gig. I'm a bit of a control freak and I would rather live a low-key lifestyle and be maybe a little bit more in control.

*Are there filmmakers out there who you'd like to emulate?*

DK: Two guys I would like to emulate are [Richard] Linklater and [Michael] Winterbottom, because they're prolific and versatile. They're able to play in both worlds—big studio stuff and smaller in- dies. There's something less intimidating about Richard Linklater. I watch a P. T. Anderson movie and I feel like crawling under the cov- ers like, "My God, I would never move the camera like that. That guy's a genius. I should go back and work in real estate." With Linklater and Winterbottom there's something that isn't too precious about their movies that I really like. It never feels labored. It feels like a bunch of really smart, passionate people got together and made a movie.

*What are you proud of when you look back at the first two films? They have to be considered successes just by the very fact of their existence in this tough business.*

DK: As disappointed as we were with *Roger Dodger* not doing more business, the fact is our first movie got bought, some people saw it and the same thing with *P.S.* We go to festivals and a lot of people emotionally connect to the movie. We're living in a culture where you don't get to feel good about hitting a double. You have to hit a home run every time. So a lot of times you have to just think, "I get paid to make a movie." That's amazing. Making a movie is the most joyously collaborative thing you'll ever do. It's totally life-affirming. Whatever you want to say about movies' place in culture and whether it's part of the corporate patriarchy, the actual activity of making a movie I can say without question is totally life-affirming and democratic and wonderful. So it's important to count your blessings. If I have any advantage, it's that I have to do this because I'm not doing it for the money. I simply have to do this. And I don't know if it's for some self-indulgent thing that I need to express myself, but I just have to. The only way I'll win is to not quit and keep doing it.

## THE DIRECTOR'S TAKE
## DYLAN KIDD

*What is the first film you ever saw?*
*Fantasia*

*What is your favorite film of all time?*
*Fanny and Alexander*

*What's your favorite line in a film?*
"These blow up into funny shapes?"
"Well, no. Unless round is funny."—*Raising Arizona*

*What movie made you realize that film was an art?*
*Rumble Fish*

*What movie do you consider your guilty pleasure?*
*Vision Quest*. Just thinking about J. C. Quinn's Pele monologue makes me cry. Wait, here I go . . .

*Who is your favorite movie character of all time?*
Travis Bickle

*What's your favorite movie snack food?*
Goldenberg Peanut Chews

*Who is your favorite director of all time?*
Ingmar Bergman

*Who is the most impressive filmmaker working today?*
Michael Winterbottom, Lukas Moodysson, Abbas Kiarostami, David
Gordon Green

*What quality do the best directors share?*
Determination

*Who is your favorite actor or actress of all time?*
Marcello Mastroianni

*Who is your favorite actor or actress of today?*
Campbell Scott, Laura Linney, and everyone else I've worked with so
far. Also Woody Harrelson, Samantha Morton, Gene Wilder, and
Selma Blair.

*Who would you cast as yourself in a film about your life?*
Steve Coogan

*If you could remake one movie, what would it be?*
The last one

*What is your best quality as a director?*
I prepare like crazy.

*What is your greatest weakness as a director?*
I don't like to hurt people's feelings.

*Finish this sentence: I'll never direct a movie about . . .*
a renegade cop whose desk-jockey superiors won't let him do his job (unless Woody Harrelson is attached).

*Finish this sentence: The perfect movie is . . .*
when you leave the theater feeling more human and less alone.

*What will they be saying about your work fifty years from now?*
"Wow, digital video sure looked grainy back then!"

*What piece of advice do you have for aspiring filmmakers?*
Remember: We're all going to die. Life is too short to make movies that don't come from your heart.

*What are you as passionate about as moviemaking?*
Nothing, and that's becoming a problem.

# KARYN KUSAMA

"I've realized I'm a strong-minded director with a very clear sense of what I want to do, and I just want to be left alone to do it."

## SELECTED CREDITS

*Girlfight* (2000)–writer/director
*Aeon Flux* (2005)–director

It seems more than appropriate that Karyn Kusama began working in film under John Sayles, a filmmaker rare among his peers for balancing the commercial and artistic concerns of a career. Kusama, an introspective woman of mixed heritage ("My dad is Japanese and my mom is a farm girl from Illinois") is wrestling with her own place in American film today. Her first filmmaking effort, *Girlfight*, told the story of a young woman channeling her aggression into boxing. The film opens with the protagonist giving the audience her best Kubrickian stare. Kusama has a similar attitude that seems to say, "This is who I am, take it or leave it." Who she is, is a filmmaker with lofty ambitions, creating films that strive to achieve what she calls a poetic sensibility. I spoke with her as she was finishing her second film, the Charlize Theron action vehicle *Aeon Flux*. Even as she was completing her first studio film, the inner turmoil over the route of her young career clearly consumed her.

*You grew up in St. Louis?*
KK: That's right.

*Can you tell me a little about your family and where you grew up?*
KK: I have a brother and sister and grew up mostly in a suburb of St. Louis. My dad's a child psychiatrist and my mom's an educational psychologist.

*Did they have any particular interest in the arts?*
KK: They both do, but my dad especially. His first love is classical music and opera. We actually were lucky as kids to go to a lot of opera, theatre, and dance.

*Were you a good student?*
KK: I wouldn't call it that so much as wanting to get the good grades and get the fuck out of there. The suburbs are interesting. The one I was living in was so racially uniform and basically kind of segregated. I've always gravitated toward city life where there's more variety in the people you see and meet. I wanted that diversity.

*Can you tell me about some of the first films that made an impression on you?*
KK: The first couple of movies that were really important to me were probably the first and then eventually the second *King Kong*.

*Really? The original is often cited by filmmakers, but the remake?*
KK: Yeah, the Dino De Laurentiis version. It's interesting to see how we still love to see such a primal, weird story being told even under pop circumstances. When the gorilla ripped up Jessica Lange's shirt, I was sitting next to my dad just quaking with excitement wondering if he was going to rip me out of the theater. That was really an important movie for me. Then, of all people, my mom took me to see *Eraserhead* when I was ten, and that was pretty mind-blowing. She didn't realize how strange it was going to be. That was a very powerful experience.

*Were you thinking about film as a career when you were in high school?*
KK: I was more interested in writing, actually—poetry and some short stories. That was my obsession at the time, and perhaps that contributes to my interest in finding the "off" moment in a film—the moment that could feel like a digression but ultimately has the heart of the film in it.

*What led you to NYU?*
KK: I really wanted to be in a big city. I always knew from a young age I was going to live in New York. I found that a lot of the film schools on the East Coast were more film-theory oriented. I was more interested ultimately in having a camera in my hand and shooting, so NYU ended up being a pretty good fit for me.

*How would you characterize the atmosphere of the school? What kind of filmmaking was encouraged?*
KK: When I got to the school, there was a very divided soul. There was a tradition of experimental filmmaking still being taught to film students to very little applause. It's not like I watched the Michael Snow movies and thought to myself, "I really want to make those

kinds of movies." But I did think it was interesting and important to be exposed to it.

*What sort of things were you making in school?*
KK: I found myself initially making sort of personal documentaries. I became very interested in the idea of experimental narrative. Documentary was really helpful to me at the time to understand the mechanics of storytelling. And I still find that a good documentary feels as gripping if not more so than a good narrative feature, because you're still crafting a story.

Sleeping Beauties *was your thesis film?*
KK: Yes. I'm not sure if it succeeds. It sort of is what it is. It's something I had to do then. What's interesting, looking back at that time and even before that, is the unconscious quality you can have when you're working, when you're not sure how much you're saying about yourself or your dreams and demons. I hope I can stay there, despite the fact that the trappings of filmmaking are so focused on the physical business of getting the movie done now than ever before. For me it's important to stay in touch with the unconscious brain at work.

*What were you tapping into from your unconscious mind back then?*
KK: I paid somebody thousands of dollars to talk about that stuff. (laughs) A central conflict in my life is definitely how you see yourself as an individual voice, the degree to which you believe in your individual voice, and then the degree to which you need or want or surrender to a will of the community. I found that a lot of the work then was finding that small kind of ambitious part of myself that just kept moving forward. The stories always revolved around how that existed in conflict to some degree with taking care of other people. I think that's always going to be something that interests me, because it's a relevant theme, especially in the American tradition. We're so obsessed with the lone-wolf hero. I'm trying to understand my own lone wolf, I suppose, and where that fits into a real life—or if it fits into a real life.

*Coming out of NYU, did you have a game plan for the future?*
KK: Actually I don't think I had a game plan. I thought maybe I would work in film, you know, in production. So I did that for a while. And it was frankly not all that I'd hoped it would be, because the fact of the matter is when you're working on somebody else's film that isn't particularly good, or a Taylor Dane music video . . .

*Was that one of the things you worked on?*
KK: Yeah. You don't want to commit too hard emotionally to things like that, because it's frankly not worth it. Music videos are pretty grim territory. What started to happen was I realized unless I had a story to tell, working in film isn't teaching me enough. I need to know the world better. I'd lost a really close friend of mine and suddenly felt like working in commercials and music videos was such a pathetic way to spend my time. I was grappling with much bigger issues about mortality and how we destroy ourselves. So I decided to take a backseat to working in film, and took care of kids and painted houses and all that kind of stuff to live and be in the world. And it probably was the most interesting, informative time of my early adulthood, because I was really searching. That's when I started boxing and meeting people in that world, and I went to artist colonies and all that kind of stuff became the focus for me, like, "How do I continue to experience life and stay engaged in the world and also burrow into my work and writing stories?" I think I found a pretty happy balance. To be honest I had no plan really beyond paying my rent and making it towards burrito night every Tuesday.

*It doesn't sound like you're a fan of music videos as a training ground for directors.*
KK: The problem with music videos is first and foremost you're working in an environment where you're selling a product, ultimately. And I think that gets problematic because, with my brief experience in the studio system, it's so important to insulate yourself from those concerns. And if you know from the beginning you can't insulate yourself, it infects you. Spike Jonze and Michel Gondry have figured out a way

to make what I would call personal, interesting work, but there are too many filmmakers who come out of the commercial and music video traditions and I just don't sense they know how to tell stories. I think the way stylistic choices really resonate is if you have some connection to a literary tradition, a poetic tradition, an operatic tradition, a theatrical tradition. There's so much we need to know about art to make art. I feel like sometimes music videos and commercials become so limited and their worldview is so limited, but maybe that's just me being judgmental. As I'm getting older I think I'm talking out of my ass half the time.

*Your entry back into the film world came with a job working for John Sayles.*
KK: I was babysitting for a family that worked in film, and they knew I was looking for a more full-time job in film. They said, "Maybe you could be an assistant to our friend John," and I met him when he was mixing a movie and we got along and he hired me. I worked there for almost three years. I got to see *Lone Star* from inception to release, and I got to see the beginning of *Men with Guns* and *Limbo*, so it was a really great education for me. It was a great match for me because I think he's successfully straddled the independent world in terms of making his own films and then can work pretty comfortably in the studio system as a writer. I felt like I got to see two ends of the business. Eventually he told me I probably shouldn't be working there for much longer and needed to make my own movies.

*From what I understand* Girlfight *came out of your own experience in the ring. What led you to try boxing?*
KK: Honestly I just wanted to try something new. I wanted to quit smoking and be in better shape, and I knew I needed a complete change of environment. And boxing had a certain pull on me as a kid through sitting and watching it with my dad. It's something that presented itself to me, and I just decided that I would pursue it. It ended up being a good thing.

*The inspiration for* Girlfight *came from a moment in the ring for you?*
KK: Yeah. I was in the ring with a very beautiful young guy who felt

that I was being tentative, and he was being tentative with me and he sort of whispered in my ear, "You can hit me." And I found it kind of weird and thrilling that he would give me permission to some degree. It was a very intimate exchange and it really was interesting to realize that's the nature of the sport. You're alone in the ring in a sense, but the one partner you do have is your opponent.

*There must have been butterflies once you got the opportunity to start shooting after dreaming about it for so long.*
KK: I think I was so desperate just to be on a set and making a movie and working with actors that I don't think that point of it gave me butterflies. Just the fact that it was finally happening made it nerve-racking and a release at the same time.

*I know you had to pare down a lot of your ambitions for the film because of the budget. How do you look back at the film?*
KK: I definitely look at the film as a product of its limitations. I look at it with, I hope, a very clear eye of what we were trying to accomplish in a very short time and with very little money. I'm proud of it for that reason, and I hope if I made it for five or ten times as much money, I'd still be proud of it. But there's an inevitable pang of regret in some areas when I watch the film, just because I know we were seriously limited. The fact that it exists means it's inevitably different than how it started in your brain. And I think that's the sort of key experience I'm finding with filmmaking: You're constantly grappling with a sense of loss, with the pure idea and having to embrace the reality of the footage in front of you or the cast or the set or the music or the crew. You accept that the film you have may be very different than the one you have imagined. That's a very difficult process for most of us, and I think that will be an ongoing experience for me.

*You've said before that you want to make films that have a "poetic sensibility." Can you explain what you mean and give me an example?*
KK: To me the idea of a poetic sensibility is finding the moments that are outside of reason and a black-and-white ideology that can com-

fortably exist and won't conflict with whatever else is on the screen in terms of story. It's something about sequences or images or moments in film where you take the film outside of the linear path or the narrative trajectory to give breathing room to the film. I mean, you could look at movies like *Days of Heaven* and the whole movie is a poetic sensibility with a very loose simple story hung at the edge of it. But then again I just recently saw *The Big Red One,* directed by Samuel Fuller. His storytelling tactics were often very blunt and unsentimental, but then there would be these moments of incredible lyricism. It's a hard balance to strike when so many movies are at this point, as Hitchcock said, just pictures of people talking.

*Do you think you achieved any moments demonstrating that "poetic sensibility" in* Girlfight?
KK: There were definitely moments I strived for. I don't know if I achieved them. That movie was always meant to be blunt and consciously simple and unfancy filmmaking in a way. I think there's a way to take those kind of social-realist dramas and do something lyrical with them. Maybe the poetry of the film exists in a sort of heightened mental space of the ring itself. That in itself is an escape to a different sort of world. There's nothing more real than somebody whacking you in the face, but there's a sort of agreement that happens when you get into the ring and face your opponent that I think creates a sort of heightened reality.

*What was the appeal of* Aeon Flux? *What earns a year and a half of your life?*
KK: I'm still grappling with that. (laughs) The script was so full of feeling and expression, and it was all told in a very spare style. I really loved that sci-fi environment that wasn't this clatter of postapocalyptic detritus of the world. It was quite a bit more idyllic than that, and I thought that was a fresh redirection for the genre. There was a very interesting claustrophobic comfort and beauty in this world that reminded me a lot of where we are right now, where the tradeoff to hav-

ing beauty and comfort in your life was that you stopped having a dialogue with others about the nature of your life.

*You did not get final cut on* Aeon Flux.
KK: I don't think I'm going to ever work on a movie again where I don't have final cut. I've realized I'm a strong-minded director with a very clear sense of what I want to do, and I just want to be left alone to do it and I'm not sure studios are necessarily the most instructive places for filmmakers to be, except to maybe learn about the hard realities of commerce and art intermingling. I definitely feel very strongly that I should be kind of left alone to make movies. (laughs)

*So you're saying if you again work on a studio film, you would need final cut?*
KK: Yeah. The fact is, it's very difficult to get final cut but I'm at a point where—

*It's just not worth it to you? You'd rather work on a smaller scale with more control?*
KK: Oh, absolutely. The problem right now with filmmaking is it's very difficult to make those kind of movies. It's hard enough to scrape together $3 million for a risky movie. That's the conundrum I'm facing right now. The independent film world is not this welcoming safe haven for me or other filmmakers like me. I just want to make movies, and it's important to me to make good movies. I feel like you roll the dice every time you take somebody's money, so it's been an interesting kind of experience to be longing to make a smaller movie but not necessarily knowing what my venue would be to do that.

*So if you had to hazard a guess, the next few Karyn Kusama movies will be films smaller than* Aeon Flux?
KK: Well, I say that, but *Aeon Flux* was overwhelming in a lot of ways, and the fact is the money was just a component of what made people say they had to always be interfering in the creative process. The

money is definitely a component, but I feel like it's just the nature of the business. People who finance your movies generally get really nervous. So there's a part of me that feels like after *Aeon Flux* if somebody said to me, "Listen, we have a $100 million action movie that happens to be really dark and challenging and interesting," I'd have to consider it, just because I know I could do it. I frankly find it a lot more creatively freeing to have a very limited budget. That's an exciting challenge to me. You start to really kind of hone what's crucial because you only have so many resources to go around. The only issue I have in terms of these big-budget films is it's just that much more money for a studio to be freaking out about. The irony is they torture you on everything. They'll torture you on a $20 million movie. If they have reason to torture you, they'll torture you. If only they knew how critical I was of myself.

*I know it bothered you when* Girlfight *came out that you were inundated with questions about being a female director. What was bothering you?*
KK: I think what I was resenting was being pigeonholed as some kind of miracle because I was a woman. I know that I have a lot to learn, but I know that I have an instinct for filmmaking. I know that I'm at least marginally good at what I do. (laughs) And it just bothers me that there's an assumption that there's something sort of special in being female. Maybe what's special is how long it took me to get here, and that's worth discussing perhaps, but I just don't really want to get into what it means. I think what frustrated me is oftentimes I felt there was a subtle or not so subtle condescension in the question. I think everyone expected me to be so desperately grateful and just sort of be googly-eyed. And the fact is that's not who I am. I've worked very hard to get to where I am, and I continue to do so. And I could make the argument that I have to work a lot harder than a lot of male directors because, frankly, I have to prove myself every day as opposed to every other day, and that's just the way it is right now. That's what pisses me off. I don't want to be considered like the miracle baby.

*Do you believe that it's a given that it is a tougher road for women today to be filmmakers?*

KK: I think it's a little disingenuous to say it's not a different set of challenges, because people are simply more comfortable with men behind the camera and running the show, literally and figuratively. It's not something I hold against people anymore, because it's almost like a deficiency within the culture that I have to sort of figure out. I don't get too wrapped up in agonizing about it, but I do think it's just a reality of this business. But at the same time I feel like I am very lucky, because I don't think anyone thought I was going to be directing a movie like *Aeon Flux*—least of all me! It's interesting because I complain about the fact I know things would be different if I were male, but the fact is it's very difficult to be a filmmaker, male or female, who tells ambiguous stories or stories that kind of wander or don't commit to a theme. In a way that's the tragedy. It goes beyond gender lines. The field of complexity is very narrow within pop filmmaking today.

*What are the things you've learned to avoid or not avoid the next time from your experience on* Aeon Flux?

KK: Well, my biggest problem is I'm a pretty decent person and I don't believe in being a screamer and I don't believe in big pompous declarations of my identity as an artist and the big bad studio system. I know there's an unholy alliance between commerce and art, and that is something I've been facing for a long time. I feel like what happens to me is I'm for the most part unfailingly polite, and politeness is not rewarded in this business the way brutality is, unfortunately. I'm trying to figure out how to get what I need without always having to raise my voice. That's always been a hard thing for me. I just don't believe I should have to raise my voice, but the fact is nobody pays attention until I do, so it's weird.

*I've heard you say that it's important to you that an audience recognizes your films as your work.*

KK: It's not necessarily that I want people to say, "Oh, that's Karyn Kusama," because I can't really expect that yet. But I want people to feel like they are not seeing a movie that's been made out of a mold. I ultimately want to make movies that people don't examine as much as experience. And that's a way I'd like to believe I had some kind of distinctive filmmaking voice. I think it's important to have a sureness of hand when you're taking an audience through your story, and that sureness ends up expressing itself whether your form is to stand back and let the story unfold, or if it's to be quite crafted and manipulative with every moment. The one steward of that experience for the audience over time is always going to end up being the director. I want an audience to watch *Aeon Flux* or *Girlfight* and say, "I felt like that director was taking me somewhere and shaping the material for me." Because the fact is, I think movies should be experiences. They should be like walking into a dream, and dreams have to have shape even if they feel shapeless. They have to be manufactured and there needs to be an architect to all of that, so I guess that's what I mean.

*What's your take on the state of American filmmaking today? Are you optimistic about the future?*
KK: That's an interesting question. The thing is, it's always been a struggle to make movies but it's harder when the people who are overseeing all that money literally don't even watch movies or care. It's a big change I think from the previous studio incarnation, and it's already affected American filmmaking tremendously. I hope that because we're in a very dicey political situation it helps to incite filmmakers toward a more formally daring or inventive or politicized kind of filmmaking, because the fact is we don't even know how much longer we have on this earth to be lucky enough to work on this art form. At this point, why not get a little faster and looser with it and take chances and fight for your chances. Everyone's so fucking busy trying to keep their jobs, and I think it'd make a lot more sense if people started arguing a point and fighting for something meaningful as opposed to letting every meaningful choice go down the drain again. It's just not worth it to put oneself in jeopardy when we proba-

bly don't even have much longer on this planet. It seems worth it to make good movies now. And I sense that could happen, and I'm optimistic in that way.

## THE DIRECTOR'S TAKE
## KARYN KUSAMA

*What is the first film you ever saw?*
Fantasia

*What is your favorite film of all time?*
The Hustler, Rosemary's Baby, Safe, High and Low, Ikiru, The Elephant Man

*What's your favorite line in a film?*
"Everybody, everybody wants a piece of me! Aren't you gonna have one?"—*The Hustler*

*What movie made you realize that film was an art?*
King Kong (1933)

*What movie do you consider your guilty pleasure?*
Valley Girl, fer sure. I know every line.

*Who is your favorite movie character of all time?*
Ellen Ripley, Fast Eddie Felson, Carol White

*What's your favorite movie snack food?*
Popcorn

*Who is your favorite director of all time?*
Michael Powell, Roman Polanski, Akira Kurosawa, Michael Ritchie, Stanley Kubrick

*Who is the most impressive filmmaker working today?*
Todd Haynes, Edward Yang, Wong Kar-Wai, Claire Denis

*What quality do the best directors share?*
An obsessive love for, and humbling by, the art form

*Who is your favorite actor or actress of all time?*
Barbara Stanwyck, Paul Newman, Toshiro Mifume

*Who would you cast as yourself in a film about your life?*
You're kidding, right?

*If you could remake one movie, what would it be?*
Alice in Wonderland

*What is your best quality as a director?*
High tolerance for absurdity

*What is your greatest weakness as a director?*
High tolerance for absurdity

*Finish this sentence: I'll never direct a movie about . . .*
an alcoholic cop with a chip on his shoulder.

*Finish this sentence: The perfect movie is . . .*
going to keep me up at night.

*What will they be saying about your work fifty years from now?*
I'm just hoping we make it that far—so it's hard to say!

*What piece of advice do you have for aspiring filmmakers?*
Engage in the world.

*What are you as passionate about as moviemaking?*
Cooking

# NEIL LABUTE

"I'll probably never make a *Gladiator*, and I'll probably never make a *Miss Saigon*. I'm not as drawn to the spectacle as I am the people."

Few filmmakers have so quickly established a unique voice in their work as Neil LaBute did in his first two films, *In the Company of Men* and *Your Friends & Neighbors*. He is, as every generation of moviemakers needs, a polarizing figure. To this day he is hailed for his unflinching examinations of the darkness inside all of us and by equal measure decried as a misanthrope. Both may be true. *In the Company of Men* after all began in his mind with one phrase: "Let's hurt somebody." LaBute never had designs on a film career. He was and remains a playwright. Meanwhile, the breadth of his film work has expanded greatly since his initial efforts, taking viewers on a road trip full of violence and black comedy (*Nurse Betty*) and an epic period love story (*Possession*).

---

*Where were you born?*
NL: I was born in Detroit.

*But you didn't grow up there?*
NL: We moved to Washington State when I was about five.

*What did your parents do for a living?*
NL: Both are retired now. My dad was a long-haul truck driver and my mom worked as a receptionist in a hospital.

*Were either of your parents particularly interested in the arts? Did they push you in that direction?*
NL: There was no prompting from either of them towards the arts. My mother was interested in film from a filmgoer's point of view, reading movie magazines and watching films—strictly a fan's sort of interest, not in making them or anything like that.

*What do you thing the first signs were of your interest in pursuing writing and the arts?*
NL: I always had a pretty healthy interest in storytelling, whether it was imagining myself to be somebody else or whatever. It was pretty

early that I found an interest in the church play, the school play, going to the movies, and television. As limited as TV was at that time, I scoured it for movies. There was a program on PBS that my mother probably got me interested in watching. It was the equivalent of what an International Film 101 class would be. Once a week it was either *Nights of Cabiria* or *Wild Strawberries* or *Seven Samurai*. I got pretty hooked on that program even if I couldn't follow the stories. Like they would play *Aleksandr Nevskiy*. I remember that vividly. Following the text or not, I thought, "This is something more than what I'm used to watching. This is something that is really challenging." Still today if I'm working, I'll pop on *La Dolce Vita* or a good art film just to listen to the sound of it, in the way you'd put on a CD. I like the sound of it in the house.

*What moviegoing experiences do you recall?*
NL: I remember going to a revival of *Gone With the Wind* with my mother when I was young, and that certainly made an impression on me. I felt like we were there for part of my childhood, it was so long. I would sleep and wake up and it would be like the war is still going on. I vividly remember waking up at one point and seeing Rhett gathering Scarlett in his arms and carrying her up this amazing set of stairs toward the boudoir. It was a very powerful collection of all the things that can work in cinema—the soundtrack and the overpowering image. I remember being like, "Wow, what is this?" And then as we were older, the drive-in became very popular. You were thrown in the car and you'd go see a couple of movies. It was the drug of choice for me. My parents never had to worry if I was off at a party, because I was always going to the movies.

*Has writing always come easily to you?*
NL: Certainly when I started writing I wasn't the best. You'd read something and go, "Oh, that's something Pinter wrote once or that's an Athol Fugard play, sort of, but bad." But that didn't make me stop and say, "I have got to do something else." I don't think it was, "I'm only going to do this if I'm good." The difficult thing with writing is,

once you're done with something, you're unemployed. And you have to get people to buy this stuff. How do I sustain my life with this stuff? But the positive side said, to me: You can write wherever you are. I don't have to go to California and audition for things or move to New York. I can be working at McDonald's. I can be working as a doctor.

*How did you end up attending Brigham Young for college?*
NL: I ended up at Brigham Young through a high school guidance counselor who suggested it. It was just, "Here's a school that has a very great arts program and there's a fair amount of money you could get for it." Ultimately it really came down to they made the best offer.

*You were not raised as a Mormon, but you were entering a school where nearly everyone is. You must have had a fair amount of trepidation.*
NL: Trepidation, yes. Because you're going off essentially for the first time by yourself. But it wasn't like I'm going off on a tramp steamer with a bunch of seasoned sailors. It was like, "Here's a bunch of people who are quite religious." And I knew several members while I was growing up and always liked those folks, so I was going in with basically positive feelings rather than, "Oh, I don't know what this is. Is this some sort of cult?" There was none of that kind of worry, just the simple worries of how am I going to pay for my groceries and that sort of thing.

*At some point while there you converted to Mormonism.*
NL: Everyone around me was Mormon. And I'm taking classes in the religion. You had to take twelve credits of religion, and several of those had to be Book of Mormon. There's a narrowness of vision anytime you get people of so many like minds together, because you're constantly supporting each other and saying, "Yes, you're right!" (laughs) There was just me saying, "Hey everybody, let's just think about this a minute."

*But obviously you didn't convert from sheer weariness of disagreeing.*
NL: And it certainly wasn't that. Nor was it me playing the angles going, "Oh, I see actually the Mormons get a break on their tuition."

(laughs) I just gradually but steadily became sure that it was something that I wanted to do.

*Were you studying film and theatre extensively there?*
NL: The thing about Brigham Young is they had these steadfast moral principles, where they didn't want people having sex before marriage and drinking and all that, so they provided all this entertainment to keep people busy. (laughs) Anything to keep them off of discovering they could actually go over to someone's house and have sex. So there was a film society that ran a lot of the old classic American films and then there was a great program called International Cinema. I just soaked that stuff up.

*Was a film career something you had seriously considered by that point?*
NL: I loved film, but I really didn't have any designs on it as a practitioner, because theatre was there, and I could practice it and it was relatively simple to do. Get some friends together, put the show on the lawn or in a classroom or whatever. And I was very good about doing that kind of thing.

*When did you consider turning one of your plays into a screenplay? I know you attended the Sundance playwrights lab.*
NL: It snowballed from the Sundance lab. One of the pieces that I did at the lab was read or seen by someone who wanted to have me turn it into a screenplay. And that got me hooked up with [the production company] Good Machine. So I went through that process of, "How do I open this up as cinema?" I was introduced to the long process of film financing in the independent world and how long it can take to put a movie together. But also by that point I had started to hear these stories of guys who had put a little money together in all sorts of nefarious ways: selling their blood, laying money down in Atlantic City and using their credit cards, and all of these crazy ideas for making small films. That attracted me because that actually had more of a theatrical spirit, more like what I was used to. This is really like putting on a show in your parents' barn. Now, this I understand. So I went about thinking,

"Maybe I could do one of these." Happily I was ignorant, because I had heard all these stories about, "Yeah, he made this movie for twenty-five grand" and all of that. While that's what we shot *In the Company of Men* for, it certainly wasn't what it took to get it up on the screen. It took more money, which had to be raised very quickly once we realized that we were going to get into Sundance. But happily I didn't know that at the time, or I'm sure I would have just gone the other direction. I thought $25,000 was going to do it, and off we went and made this movie. And I used everything that I knew as a theatrical director and writer and just sort of applied it to film. Because also by that time I had watched a lot of movies and there were people that I really admired, like Ozu and Rohmer, who had this very still aesthetic as opposed to a camera that was constantly moving. I thought, "I don't need it to move." For me I'm happy just to lock it down and look at these things. I'm not caught up in the dynamics of the camera. I'm much more interested in what happens within the frame than constantly shifting the frame.

*Supposedly* In the Company of Men *began for you with one line: "Let's hurt somebody."*
NL: It really did. It was the first line, in fact, of the screenplay. I just wrote it down and started writing from there. I had a couple of guys sitting in an airport and they say that to each other, and I wrote the first scene off of that, but ultimately I ended up flipping that and making it the last scene of the first segment of the movie. I thought that was a provocative way to start a movie, although I ultimately didn't end up starting it that way.

*Was it written specifically as a screenplay rather than a play?*
NL: It was written as I often write, which is sort of this nebulous world of dialogue and scenes. A play will start just because I start writing and I get excited about it and I want to finish it and it hasn't been promised to DreamWorks or anybody. I've joked before that if they stay in a room, looks like it's going to be a play, and if they go out to the car, then it starts to look like a movie. (laughs)

*Is it true that you initially wanted to do* In the Company of Men *in black-and-white?*
NL: I did. In fact, we shot it in color because it was the cheapest stock that we could find. It had a due-by date that was passed, and we got it cheap. The rough cut that we sent into Sundance was in black-and-white. When we got in, we found that to actually get a sort of pristine version of it ready for the festival, it was a much easier and less expensive road to get the color processed and ready and timed than it was the black-and-white. And so we ended up taking a color version up there, and that was it.

*Why did you want to do it in black-and-white?*
NL: It fit that story to me. I was going off a love of things like *The Apartment*, which always felt so strong in black-and-white. I've grown up probably seeing more black-and-white films than color. And I love the way those films look. It seemed to work for me—the starkness of it, the contrast really seemed to apply well to this piece. But I would have happily done that with *Your Friends & Neighbors* or lots of things. You keep hoping that there'll be one that people will let you do in black-and-white.

*It would have to be the right material that you could make a compelling argument for.*
NL: Or you pay for it yourself, ultimately. You just sort of go, "Well fuck it. I'm just going to go do this on my own, then. And I'll show them how it's done."

*Did you have a concrete plan for what you were going to do with the finished film?*
NL: I was working in a real vacuum. I shot it in Indiana and cut it there, and I wasn't around a bunch of other filmmakers. I just followed the only course that I knew, which was, "Let's send this in and see if Sundance is interested." All the things that came from that, getting it released and going to Cannes, were surprises.

·

*The pressures of being on a film set where time is so sacred and costly must be quite different from your theater experiences.*
NL: You always feel like you don't have enough time or money. We had an eleven-day shoot for *In the Company of Men*, and I could feel that pressure of having to get it all in. Then to have a sixty-day shoot for *Nurse Betty*, it still feels like there's not quite enough time. You're aware that the time is just clicking away. It's represented very nicely by the sound of the film running through the machine. You can just hear it. (laughs) To wipe all of that away and make an environment in which the actor feels completely safe and like they have all the time in the world is tricky. But that is, I think, the game for me because of how important the actors are to me.

*What tricks have you learned to keep actors happy and in a good creative space on your sets?*
NL: You can't always do it one way. I can remember on *Your Friends & Neighbors* I would often put headphones on in between shots and be playing something ungodly like Nirvana, because that chaotic music sort of calmed me down. But Catherine Keener wanted to feel like I was right there and available, so I knew I should take those headphones off and be where she needed me to be. So it's constantly adapting to what you see.

*Did you feel like you were a sought-after commodity as a director coming out of Sundance with* In the Company of Men?
NL: Coming out of Sundance, the film made a lot of what you'd consider "noise." People were very interested in it. It won an award, and it was in a very good place from being shot in the middle of nowhere. But walking away from that festival, it hadn't been tested in the ultimate arena for movie executives, which is, "How much money has it made?" And in fact it failed in one particularly important area, which is it didn't get picked up by anybody for domestic distribution. Later that year I went to the New Directors festival in New York, and Sony Classics picked it up and then it got into Cannes and then it was released in August. It did a humble amount of business—a couple million dollars of

business. It turned a great profit. So that, then, made people go, "Oh, we're interested." Because they always do that crazy math where they go, "Well, if he can make that much profit with *that*, then if we give him *this*, he'll make *this* much profit," which is not necessarily true. That is the way they think, and so then they became more interested. However, by that time I was already involved in making *Your Friends & Neighbors*.

*So there weren't tempting offers of other things to direct after the first film?*
NL: I can remember at one point during the editing of *Your Friends & Neighbors* that the script for *American Beauty* came through. I don't think I actually read it. My agents said, "It's a really good script and you kind of have just done that kind of thing." And I'm like, Yeah, that's probably true." And then when it came out I was like, "OK, I should probably read those kind of things now." (laughs)

*Was jumping into another film so quickly part of a sense for you of wanting to establish immediately that you were not just a flash in the pan?*
NL: Yeah, I think there was a sense of not wanting to agonize over the decision, that you could talk yourself in circles and into not doing anything. So I thought, "I've got something else here," and here's interest from someone I admire, Jason Patric, who had read the script for *Your Friends & Neighbors* and said, "Yeah, I'd like to produce this." So I very quickly jumped on that, and off we went. In retrospect I think it was the best thing I could have done, rather than just having fumbled along and worried about what I was going to do and what did this say about me and should it be a bigger picture? The one-two punch of those films did as much to create the voice of me as anything did, and the plays have continued to do that.

Nurse Betty *was your first film that didn't come from an original story by you. It would seem that it presented a lot of new challenges for you as a filmmaker.*
NL: Well, yeah, there were a number of things that I knew I had to do. I needed to be able to step up and tell, as wacky as it was, a more conventional story in a more conventional way with the tools that

people would expect. It's a road picture. I can't make it static. So now I'm planning a shoot-out and a scalping, and that's going to require makeup and CGI. . . . I had to just suddenly learn how to use these other tools without any real formal training. And again it's very gradual. It was never like, "I don't know how I'm going to learn this by tomorrow." It was stuff that you kind of have to sit down and go, "OK, now, how am I going to make this work?" And I also knew that once I had signed on to something like that, I wanted to be honest and true to the material rather than I'm going to try and make this movie more like my other pictures. It needed to be taken care of in the way it was designed. I liked the challenge of doing it. Yes, there are headaches of logistics of "Now we're going to go shoot in the desert or go to Rome, and how are we going to make all this work?" But I found that to be fun.

*Possession* didn't do well at the box office. Do you agonize over the commercial prospects for your work? Do you feel pressure to make a hit?
NL: I'm aware of it because it is a business that I'm working in. And as much as you'd like to keep it in this pristine realm of artistry, what you are doing at the end of the day is a commercial venture, and you are hoping that people go see it. So that's tricky to try and slay both of those dragons. There was a kind of dumping of *Possession* due to a changing of the guard at Focus. The people who said, "We're going to make this movie," were not the same people who were releasing the movie a year or so later. And it's a shame. You want it to get out there and have its life. But it doesn't take away how I feel about the movie. The only thing I walk away from *Possession* saying is, "I wish it was a little bit longer." We had a cut probably fifteen minutes longer that I liked even better. But we were always trying to cut it down for time, I guess for some imaginary audience of young girls. I always just felt we should make the picture we're interested in. But that's always hindsight. In the more general sense, yeah, I think I'm always aware that to continue to be able to do this, I need to, on a very basic level, be able to return on what I spend.

*Whether it's a $1 million film or a $20 million one.*
NL: Exactly. I never felt more beholden than to the guys who gave me

the money to do *In the Company of Men*. Those were real people with real money taken out of their bank account, as opposed to millions of dollars from Universal. I mean, you can't really comprehend $20 million as opposed to these guys who had $25,000. So yes, I'm aware of it without being completely shackled by, "Oh God, I must make something that people like." They say the worst thing that can happen to you is to make a movie that makes $100 million, because then people are expecting you to do that again.

*Is there any less of a sense of ownership over films like* Nurse Betty *and* Possession *that come from other people's work?*
NL: Well, I never felt like the hired help, because they were projects I'd pursued. But the fact that those were from some other source, yes, you can't help but feel that they probably required a certain kind of filmmaking that was less like what I had established as my own aesthetic. I think you can see my hand in them easily, but I think that they're probably less like signature pieces than the others are naturally.

*And because of that, are they any less satisfying?*
NL: Not for me. I feel like they're all kind of my babies in the end. It's just some of them I've seen from conception and the others I've adopted. (laughs)

*Whose films today do you make a point of watching?*
NL: I'm a big film viewer, so I am constantly watching movies. If there's a new one by Woody Allen, I always go see it. I haven't been as satisfied lately in his material but I always go take a look. I'm always curious about what Eric Rohmer is doing, and Mike Leigh and Jane Campion. I'm always curious about what the Coen brothers are going to do. I like Paul Thomas Anderson and Wes Anderson.

*You mention Woody Allen, and he strikes me as someone who, like yourself, has a very distinctive voice in film. He's been criticized in recent years for continuing to mine the same territory. Is that a concern for your work?*
NL: I can see *Annie Hall* and *Manhattan* and *Hannah and Her Sisters*

and yet I don't feel like he's repeating himself. This is an area in which he wants to work. He feels like he has something to say, and I'm happy to see that. Hopefully that's what people see from my work. In that regard, someone who'd be a sort of hero to me would be Eric Rohmer, who's made a number of films about the foibles of men. He goes back to the same ingredients of, "This guy wants to be with this woman but she actually likes his friends." He's dipped into that well a number of times. They're aesthetically not particularly different, but they're each their own kind of creature. That's probably more the way in which I'm headed rather than I need to do one science-fiction movie and one western. I'll probably never make a *Gladiator*, and I'll probably never make a *Miss Saigon*. I'm not as drawn to the spectacle as I am the people.

*You've mentioned before that your relationship with your father was less than ideal. Do you see a connection between that and the unsympathetic men that recur in your work?*
NL: Sure. My men are often harsh and untrustworthy, and that probably comes out of early experience. The male figures in my life early on were probably more like that—more aggressive and more quarrelsome. And a lot of that has seeped into my work. If you look at the gallery of rogues I've created, most of them are pretty tricky characters and I think that comes from somewhere. But it's not something I give a lot of credence to. It's also because I know that to create drama, you've got to have somebody that creates drama. So why not make it the guys? They can take it. (laughs)

*Have you ever considered returning to some of the indelible characters you've created, such as Chad from* In the Company of Men?
NL: Actually right before *Before Sunset* came out, I talked to Aaron Eckhart. It'd be fun to drop in on Chad every ten years, sort of like *7 Up*—that sort of thing. We could see where he is, if he's now married, what he's doing. Those kinds of things do interest me.

## THE DIRECTOR'S TAKE
## NEIL LABUTE

*What is the first film you ever saw?*
Gone With the Wind

*What is your favorite film of all time?*
La Dolce Vita

*What's your favorite line in a film?*
I love the last line in *Manhattan*: "You've gotta have a little faith in people."

*What movie made you realize that film was an art?*
Probably *Deliverance* or *The Godfather*

*What movie do you consider your guilty pleasure?*
A Don Knotts film called *The Ghost and Mr. Chicken* used to make me laugh out loud when I was a kid, mostly because Don Knotts is some kind of comedic genius. I bought it immediately when it came out on DVD. It still works.

*Who is your favorite movie character of all time?*
Marcello from *La Dolce Vita*, Rooster Cogburn from *True Grit*

*What's your favorite movie snack food?*
Popcorn. No question. Butter, salt, napkins.

*Who is your favorite director of all time?*
The guy who moves me the most as a filmmaker is Eric Rohmer.

*Who is the most impressive filmmaker working today?*
Scorsese and Spielberg are such brilliant technical directors and still work extremely well with actors, and yet, someone who works in such

a relatively simple way as Kiarostami makes me incredibly happy as a viewer.

*What quality do the best directors share?*
A desire to understand the human spirit is essential.

*Who is your favorite actor or actress of all time?*
Hard not to pick Brando because of his sheer ability, but I love guys like Gary Cooper as well.

*Who is your favorite actor or actress of today?*
I never tire of watching Meryl Streep.

*Who would you cast as yourself in a film about your life?*
I'd shoot for Tyrone Power, but should probably go for Albert Brooks. The best would be down the middle—a young Elliott Gould.

*If you could remake one movie, what would it be?*
The Wicker Man

*What is your best quality as a director?*
An understanding of text, an ability to work with actors, an undying fear of being able to say, "I don't know."

*What is your greatest weakness as a director?*
A certain reticence to be more forceful. I could stand to be a bit more assertive as both a director and as a person.

*Finish this sentence: I'll never direct a movie with . . .*
singing and dancing as a strong, central part of the whole.

*Finish this sentence: The perfect movie is . . .*
one that takes me to a place that I haven't yet been, whether it's down the street or across the earth.

*What will they be saying about your work fifty years from now?*
"Talky. Static. Bruising. Unsettling."

*What piece of advice do you have for aspiring filmmakers?*
Never take no for an answer. Believe it when someone says it to you, but immediately move on to the next person until somebody says yes.

*What are you as passionate about as moviemaking?*
The theatre

# DOUG LIMAN

"I'm not that guy who's making the cookie-cutter movies.
I don't mind a little reputation."

**D**oug Liman makes the conventional unconventional. That could describe the unique take he's brought to films like *Swingers, Go,* and *The Bourne Identity.* It could also describe his approach to moviemaking itself. Liman's films have been besieged by reports of delays, re-shoots, and problems with their respective endings. Even his collaborators have questioned his methods at times. *Mr. & Mrs. Smith* producer Akiva Goldsman calls him a "madman." *Swingers* star Jon Favreau says, "There's a whole air of chaos around the way he does things." Both also swear by his talent. There is a method to Liman's madness and the proof is in the work, films that have been lauded for their energy, originality, and ingenuity.

---

*Your father, Arthur Liman, was one of the most noted attorneys of his day. Was the law something you ever considered as a career?*
DL: No, because my older brother really was following in my father's footsteps. My mother is a painter and an artist so it wasn't like I came from a family of just lawyers. Ironically it was because of my father that I got into film. He had a client called Bell & Howell who made super eight movie cameras and he won a case for them. As a present they gave him a super eight camera and a projector. He had no interest in this camera, but I did. So as a six-year-old I started running around with it making movies.

*What sort of movies did you make? What were they about?*
DL: They were about our family dog, Licorice. That was the only actor a six-year-old could get their hands on and control.

*What do you think it was about film that drew you in at that age?*
DL: I love film. I like [watching] almost any movie that's 35-millimeter projected. Just the experience of seeing images on screen excites me to this day. I love having a roll of 35-millimeter film in my hand. So that's part of it and I'm a storyteller. My father was a storyteller. That's what trial lawyers do. There was a theatrical component to his courtroom appearances. I think at the end of the day that's ultimately why

I love filmmaking, telling stories. And that's how I know there's a movie I want to make. If I find myself, after reading a script, wanting to tell people what happens in the story and tell people this great moment, that's indicator number one that I'm likely to make that movie. The other criterion is that I have something really unique to say. If you look at the films I've chosen to do, they're films with a lot of room for the director to put his or her story into it. *Swingers* is a script Jon Favreau wrote about getting over an ex-girlfriend. Meanwhile the film that I made was about male friendship. In no way is that more obvious than that his script ended with his character getting a call from his ex-girlfriend and his hanging up on her. The film that I made couldn't end like that because the love story I was telling was between Jon and Vince [Vaughn]. The story that was in my head was not the movie that Jon had written.

*Even though you knew you wanted to go into film, you didn't go straight to a USC or NYU.*
DL: I went to Brown. I decided that I needed to get a real education first so I would have stories to tell. So I would go to Brown and get away from film, which didn't exactly happen because I ended up starting the TV station at Brown. Then I applied to USC film school and got in.

*What did you think of USC?*
DL: I pretty much immediately hated it.

*Why such a strong reaction?*
DL: Brown had an attitude of, you pay a lot of money to come here, you're an adult, and if you don't want to come to class it's your loss. At USC they're treating you more like you're in medical school. I was like, this is ridiculous. I'm at an arts school. Why should there be any requirements? Why should attendance be mandatory?

*Did you graduate?*
DL: I did not follow the rules while I was there. I got through it in about a year and a half or two years. I didn't get a degree, but I

ended up with a thesis film. I broke huge rules. The deal I ultimately made with the dean of the school was for me to swear never to talk about it.

*How much confidence did you have in yourself coming out of USC?*
DL: The crazy thing was, for my entire life I had been preparing to do this one thing [making movies]. Now I actually have to do it. And suddenly all of the insecurities I was able to dodge in high school and college came back with a vengeance. Everybody else in high school was like, "What am I going to do with my life?" and I was so mellow and I'm not a mellow person at all. Now out of film school it suddenly occurred to me, what if I'm not good at this? I had literally prepared to do nothing but this. I had lived a very charmed life. And suddenly with my first outing, *Getting In*, I wasn't the overnight success everyone was expecting me to be. It also became clear that my father ultimately expected me to get a real job in film, meaning do something where one day you'll ultimately be running a studio. He was a very practical person and he was like, "How are you ever going to get a mortgage on a house?" He really started to worry that I was becoming a dilettante. We would have huge screaming fights. Our relationship really hit a low point.

*What were the lessons learned on that first directing effort,* Getting In? *It was a film that no one really took note of.*
DL: *Getting In* was made for a million dollars and was [released] direct to home video. I very quickly realized why a million dollars at that time was the worst number to make a movie for. I sort of knew that going in and had some ideas about how an independent film should be made, but I didn't really have enough confidence to fight for those ideas. But I did go shoot the title sequence using those ideas. Unfortunately I did it at the end. But it really paid off and the title sequence is the best thing in that movie. It involved a cat and a rat. I spent five hundred dollars on it and it was better than anything else in the movie. That gave me the confidence when I read *Swingers* to say, "That's how I want to do this whole movie."

*How did you and Jon Favreau come to work on* Swingers *together?*
DL: Jon Favreau and I had become friendly. We both had scripts under our arms that we wanted to get made. But neither of us had read each other's scripts. I had no idea that my destiny was under his arm because everybody in L.A. has a script and usually the best thing is to see how long you can get away with not being asked to read it. Finally Jon asked me to take a look at it, and I fell in love with it. And I realized I could apply my theories about independent film to *Swingers*. Jon had been working with my housemate Nicole [LaLoggia] on the script for a while and they had the budget set at about a million and a half. I told Jon, "I don't want to step on anyone's toes, but that's the wrong way to make the movie. We should make it dirt cheap." I showed him the title sequence to *Getting In*. I said, "I did this with animals. Now I want to try it with humans." He ultimately went for it. The problem was I didn't have any money. It was a good pitch but ultimately you have to back that thing up. So the next step was to try to find money. I turned to my dad and I was like, "I'm trying to raise some money for this film, and he was like, 'maybe I can help you.'" This is after all those screaming fights. He got one of his clients to give us $200,000 and my dad did all of the paperwork. Obviously he had grave reservations. Suddenly he had a client's money on the line. So my dad became my studio and called me every day. He really instilled in me a sense of, someone's given you money to make a movie and that's a sacred trust and that's something that's stuck with me to this day. I'm often criticized by friends for flaking because I put a movie first, because those are my father's words resonating in my brain. I needed to do everything in my power to protect that investment of $200,000. It was not a license to go party with it.

*It was also a big decision for Jon to make, to allow you to direct this pet project of his.*
DL: It was huge, especially because everyone was telling him he couldn't make that movie for less than a million and a half. So here I am with basically no track record saying I'm going to go make it for $200,000. I don't have a great film under my belt. I have a thing I did

with a rat and a cat for five hundred dollars and I'm saying, do the math and imagine this with you and Vince. Of all the things that have happened in my career the single best thing to happen to me was for God knows what reason Jon Favreau chose to trust me.

*Favreau told me codirecting the film with him was a scenario that was discussed.*
DL: That was never an idea I was open to but I also was very sensitive to the fact that this was his baby. When I approached him and said, "I want to direct your movie," I was approaching someone who had spent two years thinking he was going to direct it and just hadn't gotten anywhere. If you talk about making a movie with a real budget anyone can direct it. Making a movie for $200,000 requires a specific set of skills from the director. They better know how to DP. They better know how to do every single job on that set. And when the money runs out, as it did on *Swingers*, the director is going to have to do every single one of those jobs that's left because there won't be any crew left. In *Swingers* every postproduction sound was recorded by me with a DAT machine I bought from The Good Guys, used for twenty-nine days, and then returned with their money-back guarantee. I was insane. But I had to do what I had to. I had taken somebody's money. I had to finish the movie.

*You were also the DP of* Swingers. *How often were you behind the camera?*
DL: Who else would be behind the camera? I don't think you understand how small our crew was. There was almost no crew. The gaffer was this guy known around L.A. as "Rod with a truck." You hire him because he comes with a truck with some lights in it. The majority of the lighting in that movie was done with lightbulbs I bought from Home Depot.

*Favreau says he felt like you ran the set a little chaotically at times.*
DL: Of course it was chaotic! I can't fucking believe it worked. The one thing I try to communicate to aspiring filmmakers about *Swingers* is that the film gives the impression that it was easier to make than it was. The film is probably the most storyboarded of anything I've ever done because that was the only way we could get away with shooting in bars that were open to the public. For the actors the experience was

pretty insane. There were situations like where Jon walks across the bar to talk to Heather [Graham]. Days in advance I had blocked this out in my mind and I preset some lights in the ceiling, including a spotlight on Heather. Heather Graham is shockingly beautiful and here she is with a gorgeous backlight on her so she's slightly brighter than anybody else at the bar. There was no camera anywhere near her because I was shooting her from across the bar. And there's a shot where I walk all around the bar with Jon and by the time we'd get to her some guy would be talking to her and I'd have to call cut and shoo them away. We never got a clean shot. In the finished movie, there's some dude talking to her like, this is a hot chick. So there's stuff from an actor's point of view that doesn't surprise me that Jon's like, this was insane because that would never happen on any other set ever.

*But you have said in the past that you actually like an environment of chaos on a set.*
DL: Yeah. I usually find that my ideas in advance aren't as good as the ideas I come up with in the moment. So I like to have an environment that's thought provoking, that gives me enough variables that are changing so I don't have to generate every single idea. I really don't like wooden filmmaking, and obviously with *Swingers* I developed a technique to just hand-hold the camera and suddenly it's not wooden. Wooden filmmaking is the thing I'm most terrified of.

*So it's all about avoiding wooden filmmaking even if that means scrapping a plan for a scene on the day of filming? That's something that you're said to do from time to time.*
DL: If I come up with a better idea I can no longer shoot the less good idea no matter how much work has gone into the less good idea.

*Did the success of* Swingers *feel like you anticipated it would?*
DL: There's a superficial component to that that I missed out on a little bit because my father was very sick at the time we finished the movie. I had been in L.A. for about five years and wanted to experience being the guy who shows up at the party who everyone's looking

at because he just sold a script or a movie. By the time I became that guy I just wanted to be back in New York with my dad.

*Was he ever able to enjoy* Swingers?
DL: Probably the best compliment I ever got on a movie was when I showed him and my family the movie after we sold it. My father had been battling cancer, and every test was more bad news. He never got a break. When the film ended my dad turned to my mom and said, "Maybe our luck is changing." He got to come to L.A. and come to the premiere. Six months later I got a call that MTV had selected me as their best new filmmaker. This was just a couple weeks before my father died. He was in the hospital and they didn't have MTV in the hospital so my mom got a hotel room across the street and snuck him out of the hospital in a wheelchair in the pouring rain and they went and watched it.

*So he didn't have that worry about you being able to pay the mortgage by the time he passed away.*
DL: We had a dispute about how to sell the movie. Miramax originally offered us $750,000 and he thought we should just take it. I meanwhile had been talking to this producer, Cary Woods, and he told me he wanted to come on board as executive producer and my dad's like, "You're just being taken advantage of. Why do you need another producer on the movie?" And I disobeyed him and made the deal with Cary Woods and turned down the $750,000. Three days later I got to send a fax to my dad with just one line, "Miramax. 5 mill." So he also got to see that I did have some good business sense.

*Tell me about the decision to make* Go *your follow-up to* Swingers.
DL: *Go* was not the wise decision after *Swingers*. The wisdom that was being forced onto me by my agents was to do a studio film while you can.

*Was there anything your agents were pushing on you in particular?*
DL: There was an Alicia Silverstone romantic comedy that was the perfect step up. It ended up being *Heartbreakers*. It was going to be Anjelica

Huston and Alicia Silverstone. It was the perfect kind of thing to do, but I happened to fall in love with a little script called *Go* that was another little indie movie [like *Swingers*]. The thing that I had in my back pocket going into *Go* is that I had a pretty wild childhood, the usual outrageous stuff. What was unique was that nobody got hurt. The thing that I was wrestling with when I was going to do *Go* was, how was it that all these bad things had happened to me led to me being in such a good place? Like the jobs I didn't get that ultimately led to me doing *Swingers*. Just two years ago I was ice-skating in Central Park at night on the boat pond and I was arrested for unlawful ice activity. It was worth it. *Go* was a celebration of stuff like that. My experience has been, while you're young you have a get-out-of-jail-free card and you should use it.

*With* Go, *you had some difficulty finding an appropriate ending and that's been a problem in virtually all of your films.*
DL: I try to not do it the way it's been done before. With *Go*, there is no other movie like *Go* so there's just nobody to turn to. It was very obvious how to end *The Bourne Identity* right off the bat. It's called the WIJ. It stands for "woman in jeopardy." It's such a common thing for action movies they had a nickname for it at USC. One of my first pitches to Matt Damon when we were talking about the film was, "I am not going to have a WIJ. There's got to be a way to end a spy movie without taking the woman hostage." There's a reason why all these spy movies have WIJs. They work. The problem is it's clichéd now. I was so frustrated with trying to come up with a non-WIJ thing that I actually came to a point where I said to Matt, "Fuck it. Maybe Chris Cooper should just grab her. That literally solves all our problems." And Matt's like, "You can't give up now." He gave me a pep talk. And we did find another way.

*In the case of* Mr. & Mrs. Smith, *you filmed a more conventional ending with villains that you decided not to use.*
DL: What happened with *Mr. & Mrs. Smith* is that I didn't like anything about the villains. I kept pushing the villain stuff off saying we'll

worry about it later. Let's get the love story working because none of the villain stuff written was really working. And then we got into the situation where we had a stop date with Brad Pitt. He was going to have to leave to do *Ocean's Twelve*. So we had to shoot the ending. It was the only fight I ever really had with the studio because I was like, this ending doesn't work. And they were like, you don't have script approval. You have to shoot this. So we did it in two days and it didn't work. I tried to make it work. It wasn't like I tanked it.

*Were you satisfied with the ending that you ended up using?*
DL: Honestly *Mr. & Mrs. Smith* I consider my most flawed of movies. But given the constraints and the politics of making a movie like that I could not be more proud of it. It's a movie where I'm still working on the director's cut. Basically that was a cut of the movie I did that's in the theaters. I like George Lucas's approach to filmmaking, that a movie is never really done. It's a work in progress.

*Unlike* Mr. & Mrs. Smith, The Bourne Identity *was a project that you developed over a number of years.*
DL: *Bourne Identity* was my movie. I developed that from scratch. Nobody got between me and the script. I predated every single person who worked on that movie. The script came from my head. The writer had never even read the book. It was very clear that it was my baby. *Mr. & Mrs. Smith* wasn't my baby. It was developed by a producer [Akiva Goldsman] long before I was involved. No producer could exert themselves creatively on *Bourne Identity* because it was my vision. *Mr. & Mrs. Smith* was Akiva Goldsman's baby before it was mine. And you can't compare working with Matt Damon to working with Brad Pitt and Angelina Jolie. When I was working with Matt there wasn't a single paparazzi during the many months of filming. Early on in the process he was like, "My last two films have tanked. If you screw this up I'm really in trouble. I'm really counting on you now." The unique position that *Bourne Identity* put me in was making action movies with actors that don't make action movies. I actually put myself in an

awkward position because I told Matt we were making an art movie and I told the studio we were making a spy movie. And my goal was to make a good dramatic film that could be sold as a dumb summer movie. I made that bed. Then with *Mr. & Mrs. Smith* you're working with two of the biggest stars in the world who have much more on the line than I do. If Brad Pitt chooses the wrong movie and becomes Vin Diesel, that's hundreds of millions of dollars of potential revenue gone. He had more at stake than anyone I'd ever worked with. I understand the terror that someone like Brad Pitt feels when he considers doing a film like *Mr. & Mrs. Smith*, which originally had John Woo on as the director. The wrong version of that movie and suddenly Brad Pitt is not cool anymore.

*It's also dangerous for you, isn't it? If* Mr. & Mrs. Smith *had bombed, you probably wouldn't be trusted with another $100 million film so soon.*
DL: But the thing that makes me so infuriating to the studios is I don't care. I made more money off *Swingers* than off any of these movies. I can go make a movie for a couple hundred thousand dollars again. Michael Bay needs the studios. I don't know if he knows how to make a movie for $200,000. But I haven't forgotten. I'm not in it for a career. I don't know how many more movies I'm going to make. I just don't want to repeat myself.

*You don't think you're going to be making movies when you're eighty?*
DL: I don't think so. I'm honestly not in it for the career. I like telling the stories. It's like, I just read a script that I like that's a big-budget film. It needs a lot of work. It's a situation where it's already a good script and there are filmmakers who would just go make it. If I'm going to go make this thing, it's suddenly going to take on a whole other life. It's going to be something you haven't seen before. And it will be something I've never tried before; therefore, I won't necessarily know how to end it. There are a lot of stories I want to tell. I'm like, I need to try to use film to say something about politics in America. But then I'm like, film might not be the best medium for that. That's why you

hear me having thoughts about leaving film just because I worry about the world right now and I'm not sure how much good I'm doing.

*You haven't overtly tackled a message movie yet.*
DL: Mostly because those movies are usually too preachy for me so I try to be a little bit more subversive. *Bourne Identity*, that's Iran Contra. Chris Cooper is playing Oliver North. *Mr. & Mrs. Smith* is ultimately meant to be a celebration of marriage. I'm certainly developing a lot of material that's more serious. It just usually comes out a little too preachy for me. I'm also not sure what it accomplishes. I might help the world more by doing popcorn movies and take the money that I make and spending it on things the way Angie [Jolie] does, directly helping people.

*There's been a lot written about your clashes on* The Bourne Identity *with producer Frank Marshall. In an* L.A. Times *article he said, "I'm not saying I directed the movie. But as the producer, it was my job to get the movie finished."*
DL: Clearly that article started with Frank disparaging me to this reporter. I hadn't even thought about Frank Marshall in two years. Success has many parents. If people want to take credit for work that I so clearly did, that's a huge compliment and I'll take it. I think when my father was warning me about Cary Woods and *Swingers* and being careful of the producers in Hollywood the person he was really warning me about was Frank Marshall. He just didn't know it.

*Does it bother you that you have a reputation for being "difficult"?*
DL: I take it the way Akiva Goldsman put it to me: "How can anyone have any issue with your methods when you're four for four? Who's to say there's a quote-unquote right way to make a movie?" Frank stole my franchise that I lovingly created myself. Whatever he has to do to sleep at night. I'm not that guy who's making the cookie-cutter movies. I don't mind a little reputation. I'd rather fail trying to push myself. I learned that early on with *Getting In*. Bowing down to the

producers and playing it safe I ended up with a movie I wasn't proud of. I'd rather have a movie I'm proud of and burn some bridges than have everyone love me and me not love the movie.

*You haven't really failed since your first film. Are you prepared to fail again?*
DL: You have to be. That's the thing I worry about the most. It's like when you're playing poker and you've won a lot, now suddenly you have this stash you're trying to protect and that's the surest way to fail because you stop being bold. The moment you play it safe you're dead.

## THE DIRECTOR'S TAKE
## DOUG LIMAN

*What is the first film you ever saw?*
*The Poseidon Adventure*—I remember running out of the theater in the middle, I was so terrified.

*What is your favorite film of all time?*
Too many to name. My first favorite film was *The Four Feathers*.

*What's your favorite line in a film?*
The exchange in *What's Eating Gilbert Grape* when Juliette Lewis catches Johnny Depp having an affair with the townswoman and she asks him if he cared about the woman and Depp says, "Yes," and she responds, "Good."

*What movie made you realize that film was an art?*
*Diva*

*What movie do you consider your guilty pleasure?*
Anything with Chevy Chase.

*Who is your favorite movie character of all time?*
Anything Katharine Hepburn played, especially Susan in *Bringing Up Baby* and Tracy Samantha Lord in *The Philadelphia Story*.

*What's your favorite movie snack food?*
Nachos with cheese.

*Who is your favorite director of all time?*
Like my favorite movies, too many to mention. I would include Spielberg and Scorsese and Coppola and Lasse Hallström.

*Who is the most impressive filmmaker working today?*
Tom Tykwer

*What quality do the best directors share?*
Original voices

*Who is your favorite actor or actress of all time?*
Katharine Hepburn

*Who is your favorite actor or actress of today?*
I have loved all of the actors I have worked with.

*Who would you cast as yourself in a film about your life?*
I did cast Adam Brody in *The O.C.*

*If you could remake one movie, what would it be?*
*Star Wars: Episode I*

*What is your best quality as a director?*
I love telling stories.

*What is your greatest weakness as a director?*
I'm a lousy writer.

*Finish this sentence: I'll never direct a movie . . .*
that is preachy.

*Finish this sentence: The perfect movie is . . .*
entertaining and substantive.

*What will they be saying about your work fifty years from now?*
"He never repeated himself."

*What piece of advice do you have for aspiring filmmakers?*
Succeeding is much harder than a book like this could ever communicate, but the thick skin you develop now will serve you later because ironically it never really gets easier.

# MCG

"I think people create rooms where they have fake feedback sessions with their own staff and no one is truly empowered to say, 'This is shit.'"

## SELECTED CREDITS

*Charlie's Angels* (2000)–director
*Charlie's Angels: Full Throttle* (2003)–director

The man born Joseph Nichol knows what is said about him. He is fully aware of his reputation. And that's precisely why McG, the director of pop entertainment like the *Charlie's Angels* films, is dying to show off what else he can do. Of course, Hollywood isn't about to make him apologize for directing two blockbusters right off the bat of his career. In fact, with his debut film especially, he confounded the conventional wisdom that a film as "troubled" as *Charlie's Angels* was said to be could stand apart from the cookie-cutter blockbuster crowd. In an impressive body of music-video work and two features, McG has proven he can create images that pop off the screen and connect with an audience. Whether the other facets of this Midwest-born man who says "There's a great deal of darkness in my spirit" emerges in future work, only time will tell.

---

*You were born Joseph Nichol, but I understand you've pretty much always gone by McG? Why?*
McG: Yeah. My uncle was Joe, and my grandpa was Joe so they called me McG, short for McGinty, which is my mother's maiden name.

*And that started early on?*
McG: Day one. My name has never ever been anything but McG, and it serves as sort of an unfortunate name at this point because everyone thinks it's sort of a Hollywood nickname and thinks, "What an asshole." But it'd be fraudulent for me to call myself Joe or Joseph. No one has ever addressed me as such in the history of my life.

*You were born in Kalamazoo, Michigan. How long did you stay there?*
McG: Just until I was about two. My dad worked in pharmaceuticals and he took us all out west to Newport Beach, California. There were five of us in a Volkswagen Bug, with my Big Wheels strapped on the top.

*You're so identified with California today. Is there any of the Midwest left in McG?*
McG: Oh, yeah. There's no doubt the family ethic in the household

was very much a function of the Midwest, or even more so of the East, because my family's largely from Pennsylvania.

*When you say "the family ethic," are you talking about a work ethic?*
McG: Yeah, a work ethic and sort of the patriarchal vibes of the screaming father. I sort of always respected my dad's no-excuses, get-up-and-work ethic. He was always a really hard worker, even at the expense of his own health sometimes. And hopefully I can have the wisdom to balance that out a little bit, but I always looked up to him for that and respected that he was an entrepreneurial guy that never took no for an answer and just got up and got it done.

*Was music a big part of your family's life always?*
McG: My house was always filled with music. That's sort of my earliest memory—my dad listening to jazz, my mom listening to Motown, my sister listening to disco, and my brother blasting Led Zeppelin.

*Did you gravitate in one musical direction?*
McG: I really enjoyed them all. I became a big fan of melody, independent of the genre that it existed in. I'd be my sister's dance partner to the *Thank God It's Friday* soundtrack. My brother and I would go see *The Song Remains the Same* with all the stoners at the local art-house theater. It was interesting.

*I understand theatre was also a big part of your life as a kid?*
McG: Yeah. I was an actor as a kid, and I did Ronco commercials like the Mr. Microphone commercial.

*You're kidding!*
McG: No. And I was part of a theatre group down in Orange County. I really enjoyed acting. There's sort of a famous line in my family, when my parents were informing my grandparents like, "Oh yeah, McG's taking acting lessons," and without a beat my grandpa said, "What for?" So you know there wasn't a great deal of sympathy for the arts in my household. But my dad went to Japan and he came back

with an SLR—my first camera—just a cheap Japanese camera with three different lenses. And then I started taking pictures of things I found interesting. I would go rent darkroom space at this place in Costa Mesa and develop my own pictures. I started shooting in different film stocks and experimenting and figuring out how to manipulate the print time in the bath for color saturation and control of the graininess and blacks and whites and getting rid of the grays. I started to really develop a visual imprint in those earliest days.

*This is when you were about thirteen?*
McG: Yeah, twelve or thirteen. Basically I'd do two things: I'd ride the bus to go to the darkroom, and I'd ride the bus to go to a place called Music Market that was ninety minutes away by bus. I'd have five or six dollars and records were $5.49. I'd buy one record that I'd be excited about and wouldn't be able to go to the fast-food spot to get a cheeseburger and have to ride home starving. (laughs) But I had to make that sacrifice because I knew I could eat something when I got home, but the record would last forever.

*Why do you think pop culture, whether it be music or film, so resonated with you early on?*
McG: I always remember responding very emotionally to film. I had a lot of lonely time on my hands because I wasn't really the best-looking kid in town and I sort of pined after girls. I had to sort of immerse myself in the arts because girls weren't particularly interested in me.

*What were the first films that made an impact on you?*
McG: I'm going to have to go with *The Sound of Music*. And watching *The Graduate*, when I'm probably nine or ten years old, had a very profound impact on me. There's no doubt that there're certain songs and arrangements of music and certain pieces of film that release a chemical reaction in my brain. This sounds a little goofy, but I really believe that. It's such a euphoric experience that I sort of want to chase that experience as often as possible. And it's also that set of chemical cir-

cumstances in my brain that makes me fucked up. So, you know, you take the good with the bad.

*When you say that you're "fucked up," what are you talking about?*
McG: I'm pretty convinced that there's a chemical reality to who I am, regarding my brain, that makes me kind of a strange guy. And there's the behavioral component of growing up in a house where my dad would lose his temper a lot and my mother has a little bit of a hypochondriac streak. It doesn't take a genius to see the writing on the wall. I'm fundamentally a pretty neurotic guy, but I've come to terms with that. In high school I read Freud and I got really into that. I was convinced I wanted to go to school and become a psychiatrist and go on to become a psychoanalyst. [Later] I came to terms with the fact that my interest in psychiatry and psychology was basically because I was so fucked up. And once I sort of came to terms with that, I was free to immerse myself back in the arts, which is really my passion and my love.

*Who was the first filmmaker you studied?*
McG: It's clearly Alfred Hitchcock. I sort of did the same thing with Hitchcock that I did with Freud, and went out and diligently studied every picture he ever made. All this stuff I was picking up from what he was doing was making me very excited, but I was also very excited about things that I thought were visually stunning, like *Sound of Music* and *Wizard of Oz* and *Gone With the Wind* and all the Busby Berkeley stuff. I liked films that were larger than life and spoke to my Walter Mitty escapist lifestyle. That's why my earliest work was a reaction to what was going in Seattle at the time. I loved the Seattle movement like the next guy, and immersed myself in Nirvana and Soundgarden, but I never bought into the stare-at-your-shoes-and-be-bummed-out thing. I mean, I was legitimately bummed out in my life. But I just liked big performers and big explosive movies that were exciting, like *Raiders of the Lost Ark* and *Star Wars*. Even though I would identify quietly with *The Graduate* and *The Conversation*, my whole thing was a reaction to Seattle. I'm going to bring out this Busby

Berkeley component of color and excitement. To me that was sort of the start of the McG video.

*Clearly one of the most important personal and professional relationships of your life has been with Sugar Ray's Mark McGrath.*
McG: We've been best friends since we were about eight years old. We went to elementary school together, and junior high and high school. And we're best friends today. We were into breakdancing together. We were very excitable young kids that thought everything was cool, except for what we were about.

*You sang back then, didn't you?*
McG: Yeah. We had a band called the Q-Tips in high school, and Mark was sort of my sidekick. He was too shy to sing, so I would, but all the girls would swoon and stare at him. I'd just sort of do everything I could to command attention. I wasn't all that successful. At the time I was very interested with what Rick Rubin was able to put together from his NYU dorm room. Here's this dude who realized hip-hop is real, there's a culture out there, and he taps into it and breaks LL Cool J, gets behind the Beastie Boys, Run-DMC . . . And that was my inspiration to take Mark and say, "You're a very charismatic, good-looking guy. You're a great performer; let's shoot a video." I didn't really know what it even meant to be a director, but I knew what I wanted the end result to look and feel like.

*And you were essentially managing what became the group, Sugar Ray, with Mark.*
McG: I produced their first record, and I was going to produce their second record, but they sort of marched in and said, "We don't want you." It was a very emotional, sad sort of parting of ways. But I kept doing all the videos for Cypress Hill and then Korn, and before I knew it I was pushing film through a camera every single week, which is a great way to cut your teeth and get your style. You can go to film school, but there's really no substitute for putting film through a cam-

era and working with people. You just go out there and get it done and have your successes and have your failures. It's just trial by fire.

*How did you even know how to approach directing that first music video?*
McG: Well, I didn't. We shot the first video for three thousand bucks on 35-millimeter, which is unheard of. I didn't know that to shoot on a location; you need permits and insurance. We didn't know anything. We just stole the locations and ran from the cops. I would put the film into the lab knowing I didn't have any money to get the film out of the lab. It was as do-it-yourself as you could possibly imagine!

*Are you sensitive to criticism of music-video turned film directors like yourself?*
McG: I have a very strong opinion about that. I always quote Mark Romanek. He's a music video superstar who I really admire, who's truly this auteur and artist. He got some vanguard lifetime achievement award and said, "Let's face it: Most music videos are shit! But the three percent that are interesting is some of the most compelling filmmaking that's out there." And that's true! Because you look at what Michel Gondry was doing, you look at what Spike Jonze was doing, you look at what [David] Fincher was doing, and that's truly filmmaking. It's beautiful and it's unapologetic and it's storytelling and it's affecting kids' lives and adults' lives, and there's no shame in that. Under no circumstances do I think it should be a liability to say that you came from music videos, because you learn how to be responsible and get your work done in a day and get all the shots to tell your story. You learn to deal with difficult personalities and communicate with talent. It's arming you in an excellent way to step into *Charlie's Angels* and deal with Bill Murray and deal with a $100 million budget and a studio that's not interested in fucking around.

*Do you feel that directors who come out of music videos are treated as second-class citizens?*
McG: Less than it used to be, but yes, there's still some of that. I really look forward to that being brought to a rapid end. But that's the

privilege of a fan. Listen, if you look online, it's not cool to say, "I like McG." When I was doing *Superman*, people would fucking kill me day and night. That's their privilege. I'd only made two popcorn easygoing *Charlie's Angels* movies. But under no circumstances am I going to apologize for taking a movie that everybody thought was going be a disaster and making a pretty entertaining film and, most importantly, films that are tonally their own. You can't look at the *Charlie's Angels* pictures and go, "Oh, that's just like this or that's just like that." It's a little like Bond. It's a little like *Austin Powers*, but in the end it's its own thing, which I think is an interesting achievement. But obviously as a filmmaker I want to grow in my ability to tell stories and become more subtle and have more depth and grow into my nineteenth-century-literature/Merchant-Ivory phase.

*I get the sense from you that you're just itching to show the public that you have more in you than* Charlie's Angels.
McG: That's what matters to me most, and it's real difficult! It's so easy to put people in a box. And like I say, that's the privilege of the public to just take what they see and draw conclusions. I'm not trying to deny anybody that, but I definitely want to get into a different filmmaking phase. But under no circumstances do I want to apologize for films that reacted with the public. I loved *E.T.* I like *Star Wars*. There was a time when the event movies were the best movies. Sometimes the Beatles are the biggest band in the world because they're arguably the best band in the world.

*How do you go from music videos to a huge summer action film as your first feature? How did you land* Charlie's Angels?
McG: I was doing the music video route, which was fun. You get a call on Monday. Everclear needs a video quickly. You come up with an idea. Four days later you're shooting, and five days after that it's airing. That kind of turnaround was tremendously satisfying. And to this day I sort of miss that. I had the best experience with a Gap commercial with Dwight Yoakam. We went in the studio and redid the song "Crazy

Little Thing Called Love" because I like Freddy Mercury and Queen. And he did this little country version, and people really reacted to that campaign. It helped turn Gap around. Then I heard that there was a *Charlie's Angels* movie out there. I was frustrated with what I felt like were bad movies that came from old television shows. I thought, "Why can't somebody just get this right and make an entertaining movie that comes from an old TV show?" So I said, "Look, I'd just like to talk to Drew Barrymore," because I knew she was behind it and she was kind of a rock 'n' roller and I figured we would have a similar aesthetic. But she cancelled on me like seven times. Finally she acquiesced and agreed to meet me. I remember meeting her at this Vietnamese restaurant in L.A. I said, "I want the movie to be funny and self-aware. I want it to have all the action that the boys' films have and an elegant subversiveness that only the most discriminate viewer will even be aware of." She started getting more and more excited until by the end of the meeting, we were both bouncing around the couch and just jumping out of our skin with enthusiasm. And she committed completely to us doing the picture together, which was insane for her because I'd never made a movie and Sony's counting on this being a big franchise. They want the movie in capable hands, not some shithead like myself. I one-hundred-percent owe it to Drew Barrymore, digging her heels in and giving me a shot.

*Was the script close to being locked as you began the shoot?*
McG: Oh, my God. No! We never had a script, period! We had no script.

*How could that not have scared you to death?*
McG: Well, that created a great deal of stress, but I really knew where I was going and that it was going to all come together. So I stayed the course. Sometimes those desperate times create the best stuff. Look, I'd prefer to have a locked document and really get into the nuances and subtleties of what you're trying to achieve. I look forward to the day I can make that kind of picture.

*It does boggle the mind though to think that a studio can allow a film of that size to go into production without a locked script.*
McG: It's miserable. I wouldn't advocate it for anybody. It's no way to do your thing, but when Cameron [Diaz] has this window and Drew has that window and Sony says, "This bus has left the station, we need that movie for November of 2000," that cart drives the horse, so you just keep going.

*You opened the film in a way that really sets the tone, with a long, seemingly unbroken shot on the plane. Is that a nod to Scorsese or De Palma or anything in particular?*
McG: Of course. Scorsese and De Palma all the way! And *I Am Cuba*.

*What statement, if any, were you trying to make with that opening?*
McG: I was excited about the prospect of an impossible shot and taking advantage of computer-generated components. I wanted to clearly establish the tone of the thing. *T.J. Hooker* comes on and you say, "Ugh, another movie from an old TV show. What are you going to do, just walk out?" And then they jump out the window. I'm trying to say to the audience, "I get it! I know! You think this sucks. Give me a chance."

*You're probably tired of talking about all the reported on-set conflicts that occurred on* Charlie's Angels.
McG: There were a lot of heated conversations, though.

*So when, as was reported, people like Bill Murray and Lucy Liu are getting into it on the set, where does that leave you, the director?*
McG: It was strange for me, because I had the highest title on the set but in reality there were probably seven or eight people who had more juice than I did. So there's the title of director, and there's the reality of who's running the show. Fortunately there was a lot of trust between the actors and myself, and that went for Murray as well. I had a really good thing with Murray. He's really passionate about being the best he can be every time he steps out in front of the camera, and that's going to lead to some heated conversations, artists having dif-

ferent ideas about how different character arcs should play out. And I always encouraged that. And that's not to say people didn't have words with each other. Of course they did. To me that's representative of passion. That's fine so long as everyone fights fair and comes to a reasonable conclusion and you get out there and you shoot some film and you make your day. The bigger nightmare is people just sleepwalking through it and never challenging you and each other and not giving a fuck.

*So from your perspective at least this passion is coming out of wanting to improve the film.*
McG: I'm telling you straight up that's the truth. It was all coming out of passion.

*Were there test screenings for* Charlie's Angels?
McG: Yeah, we test-screened it once in Peoria, Arizona, and it went average. I remember a look that Drew and I gave each other across the hallway of the multiplex afterwards that was just a mix of so much desire for people wanting to respond to our film and seeing that the response was average. We put our nose to the grindstone, made a few changes, cut a few things, added a few things, and then three or four weeks later we tested the film again and it tested through the roof.

*What did you adjust?*
McG: Story clarity, and we changed the cut-down a bit. People were able to lock down more and enjoy the scenes and emote with the characters. The difference was huge.

*Do you think you'll always test your films?*
McG: Well, it's a double-edged sword. My fundamental inclination is to test, because you get caught up in your own little bubble of a universe and you want to believe what you want to believe. You have to have a lot of faith in the virginal eyes of the viewer who has no agenda. When you make films that are your own personal art offerings, I wouldn't test it, because it's your own and you don't care. But if you make films with north of $100 million of someone else's money and

the object is for it to be received well by a great many people, you're doing yourself a favor by testing a picture. But you have to understand how to read the results. You can't just whore yourself out to every little whim and comment. If you think something is funny and you test it and three times in a row no one laughs, you need to swallow your medicine and realize that's not funny. To deny that is just being ridiculous. I think that's how a lot of errors in filmmaking are made—when directors insulate themselves in environments where they aren't subject to feedback.

*That's the exact criticism often made about the last generation of directors—that they often lose touch with the real world and what made their work relevant in the first place.*
McG: I'd like you and I to do a book on this subject. I think people create rooms where they have fake feedback sessions with their own staff and no one is truly empowered to say, "This is shit." You look at how many directors out there who [once] made great films, and you just scratch your head wondering why can they not make a film? What is going on? The last five films have been crap! First of all, an ability as an artist to be relevant is fleeting. Look at your favorite songwriters. Far more often than not they had a period of greatness and then fell the fuck off. And it's the same with filmmakers. They have a period where you love everything they're doing, and then they fall off. If you go to 7-Eleven for your coffee and you go to the multiplex to watch your movies, you have certain sensibilities that make you in touch with the reality of the human condition. If you start living behind gates and only seeing special screenings at your house and have your coffee custom made by your own barista, you're not as relevant as you want to believe you are.

*Do you worry about that for yourself?*
McG: No, because I haven't made it yet. Hopefully I'll be subject to making shitty films, and hopefully you and I will have enough of a relationship where you'll call me and say, "What the hell are you doing?" And maybe I'll get with it. I really believe that.

*After* Charlie's Angels, *did a lot of filmmakers you respect come to you who enjoyed the film?*

McG: I was put on the creative rights council of the DGA [Directors Guild of America], and all my heroes are on that, like Peter Weir. Steven Soderbergh chairs it. I'm able to have very intimate one-on-ones with these people. They all seemed relatively amused and pleased with *Charlie's Angels*, but they were very serious about what my choices in the future were going to be and what my plans were to show growth. And I wanted to honor that challenge and become a more accomplished storyteller.

*Is it important to you to earn the respect of people you respect?*

McG: It's the single most important thing. I'm still insecure enough that I really want to be respected by David Fincher. I want a nod of appreciation by Steven Soderbergh, and those nods aren't given away. So it's my goal to earn them. To some degree I'm proud of what I've put together, but at the same time I feel a very distinct chip on my shoulder when people think I'm a lightweight, untalented, "Oh let's blow up the building and shoot it with twenty cameras" guy. From the bottom of my heart that's truthfully not who I am. I try to identify what's right for any given picture, and I tried to make the right moves for *Charlie's Angels*. And I think we definitely got it right in the first one and more or less got it right on the second one.

*Do you have any regrets about making the sequel your second film? It's delayed, by a few years at least, an opportunity for you to show off what other kind of filmmaking you can do.*

McG: That's such a tough question. I think if you have the good fortune of creating a franchise, you have to see it through. Not to mention, these people are my friends. These are people I'm emotionally invested in. None of us were planning on making a sequel, but we all sort of agreed it was all or nothing, Cameron, Lucy, Drew, and me. We were all going to do it, or we all weren't going do it. And when it became clear that the public wanted another one and my friends at Sony wanted to do it, it was the natural choice. I don't regret it. There were some other films that I was circling that could have allowed me to flex different filmmaking moves and maybe not put me in that position where it's so fun to talk shit about me on the Internet.

*So what did you learn not to do?*
McG: Never be redundant. Always show growth and keep your toes tapping. I wanted to do more with that picture than I was ultimately able to do.

*You have a reputation for being extremely high-energy and positive on the set. How much of that is the genuine you and how much of it is a front for motivating the crew?*
McG: The *Charlie's Angels* projects were particularly difficult because we never had the benefit of a locked script, so I needed to be that cheerleader and can-do guy. But ironically there's a great deal of darkness in my spirit. I would like to not just be that cheerleader. I would like to focus on artistry and spend a little more time behind the monitor and not in front of the camera cheerleading everybody on in the interest of making our day and getting our work done.

*What films have resonated with you in recent years?*
McG: I appreciate what Charlie Kaufman has been up to with Spike [Jonze] and Michel Gondry. It makes me hungry and want to get out there and show the world what I've got. I really believe given the right piece of material, I can draw those performances out of the actors. I want that chance. I want that great piece of material where you know going in the script is phenomenal. This is going to be our *Million Dollar Baby*. This is going to be *Shakespeare in Love*, our *American Beauty*. There's nothing about who I am to the layman to suggest I'm worthy or capable of doing any of those things, but that puts a perverse little smile on my face. I look forward to the challenge. I don't want to be doing karate and explosions the rest of my life.

## THE DIRECTOR'S TAKE
## McG

*What is the first film you ever saw?*
Chitty Chitty Bang Bang

*What is your favorite film of all time?*
The Graduate

*What's your favorite line in a film?*
"She's totally serious, asswipe."—Sixteen Candles

*What movie made you realize that film was an art?*
Strangers on a Train

*What movie do you consider your guilty pleasure?*
Waiting for Guffman

*Who is your favorite movie character of all time?*
Boo Radley

*What's your favorite movie snack food?*
Hot Tamales

*Who is your favorite director of all time?*
Alfred Hitchcock and Spike Jonze

*Who is the most impressive filmmaker working today?*
Michel Gondry

*What quality do the best directors share?*
Originality

*Who is your favorite actor or actress of all time?*
Cary Grant

*Who is your favorite actor or actress of today?*
Sam Rockwell, Charlotte Rampling

*Who would you cast as yourself in a film about your life?*
Philip Seymour Hoffman

*If you could remake one movie, what would it be?*
Midnight Cowboy

*What is your best quality as a director?*
Endurance

*What is your greatest weakness as a director?*
Tunnel vision

*Finish this sentence: I'll never direct a movie about . . .*
the Vichy government of France in World War II.

*Finish this sentence: The perfect movie is . . .*
Risky Business.

*What will they be saying about your work fifty years from now?*
"He was hungry."

*What piece of advice do you have for aspiring filmmakers?*
Never give up.

*What are you as passionate about as moviemaking?*
Aviation

# TREY PARKER & MATT STONE

"The honest truth is we just fucking hate actors."
—Trey Parker

## SELECTED CREDITS

*Cannibal! The Musical* (1996)–Parker, writer/director
*Orgazmo* (1997)–Parker, writer/director
*South Park: Bigger, Longer & Uncut* (1999)–
Parker: cowriter/director, Stone: writer
*Team America: World Police* (2004)–
Parker: cowriter/director, Stone: cowriter

Trey Parker and Matt Stone hate watching movies. In fact, I'm not entirely sure they even like movies that much to begin with. That's as good a place as any to start when listing what sets them apart from virtually all other filmmakers working today. They began as two Colorado film students who shared a love for Monty Python and making each other laugh. Their collaborations thus far share the latter criterion: a musical about a cannibal, the story of a Mormon acting in pornography, a cartoon featuring Saddam Hussein and Satan in a homosexual affair, and a satire of Jerry Bruckheimer spectacles made with puppets. Meanwhile, they continue to produce one of the most popular comedy series of all time, *South Park*, and operate in film with near autonomy, insisting always on getting final cut for their projects. Those who embrace the status quo are just bracing for what could possibly come next.

---

*Trey, can you tell me a little about Conifer, Colorado, where you grew up?*
TP: It was a typical small town. I definitely had feelings sometimes like I was in the middle of nowhere and wanted some excitement in my life, like probably every kid in the world does. But it was a great place to grow up. There was a lot there that bred creativity, in that there wasn't much to do but try to entertain yourself and your friends. And I think that really helped, because when I got to be about twelve years old, I started making movies all the time. Every weekend, we'd get together and make some dumb little ninja movie or something. We were all in Tae Kwan Do, and we all thought we were badasses, so we loved making martial-arts movies. I would be Karate Man Dave, and Karate Man Dave just thinks he's fucking awesome and he actually kind of sucks. It's really weird because looking back on it now, I'm twelve years old and I would, like, paint a total handlebar mustache on.

*Matt, you grew up in Littleton. Were you also making movies when you were a kid?*
MS: No, not at all. I think it's weird that I ended up here, because I didn't do any of that stuff. I was into music. I played drums. But I was

much more like a math kid. That's what I was good at—math and science—and that's what I did. I hadn't even thought about film until I took this summer class. It was just to get credit, because it sounded easy. I liked it, so I did the 16-millimeter class and that's where I met Trey. I never really even thought about films or filmmaking until I was in college.

*What were the first films you were into as kids?*
TP: For me it was all comedy. It was Zucker brothers' stuff like *Airplane* and *Naked Gun*, and then anything that Monty Python did, of course. That really was the huge obsession.
MS: I'd say for me Monty Python were the movies I remembered.
TP: It's just sort of who we are as people, too. We just deal with everything with comedy, basically.
MS: I remember one of the first movies that made me think about making movies, though, was *Raising Arizona*. It was kind of transparent that they were guys kind of fucking around behind the camera. That was the first time I thought that maybe I could do that. Before that I don't even think I thought that people made movies. They just somehow got to my TV or movie theater.

*Trey, how serious were you about film when you were making these movies as a kid?*
TP: It was serious. Even when I was eight, I knew I wanted to be Steven Spielberg. My mom just dug up this thing from the sixth grade, and I guess you were supposed to draw what you wanted to be, and it's me sitting in a director's chair. If I had only known how hard and shitty it was, I would have changed my mind.

*Were you as focused on a career, Matt? Was it all about math?*
MS: I was like a little prodigy at math. I drank that prodigy element away some time ago. Other than math, I wanted to be Stewart Copeland of The Police. I didn't really have big ambitions. In high school I remember thinking, "Fuck society, I'm going to go ride around Latin America on a motorcycle," and of course I didn't, because I'm too wimpy, and I just went to college.

*How did you two start to collaborate in college?*
TP: We met in a 16-millimeter class. We just got paired up because everyone else in our class wanted to make black-and-white sexual-exploration movies and shit like that, and we wanted to make fucking *Monty Python and the Holy Grail*.

*What was the film program like at the school?*
MS: It wasn't much of a program. It was just like thirty people in the production part. And then there was a film-theory part. There was a definite epic struggle between the film-theory side and the film-production side. The film-theory people were the ones sitting around talking about . . . you know, I don't know what the hell they talk about. And the production side was people like us who really didn't care about deconstructing film as much as just making it. It was a nothing department compared to USC or NYU. But on the other hand, there was very little structure and everyone had to chip in, so Trey would be the boom guy on my film and then I would be the costume guy on his. Everyone kind of did everything and, in doing that, you got to do a little of everything. It was really just "Let's make movies and then we'll fucking figure it out when we get there."
TP: It was nice, too, being in Colorado. The first big thing that we did that really jump-started the whole career was *Cannibal! The Musical*, and because it was in Colorado we were able to go around to people and go, "Hey, we're making a movie, you wanna help?" And they were like, "Sure! Have my house! Have my restaurant! You're making a movie?" People were so excited that a movie was actually shooting in Colorado that you could get whatever you wanted.

*Do you think you would have floundered at a more competitive film school like NYU or USC?*
TP: Sure. Because when there's too much competition, we just get pissed off and leave.
MS: Yeah. I would have gotten out.
TP: We're the first guys to bail on anything difficult.

Cannibal! *was originally made under the name of its subject, Alfred Packer, who was hanged for cannibalism in the 1800s. His story was a well-known one where you were.*

TP: It's a pretty great story. We even talked about the idea to remake it now that we're all, like, thirty-five—the age those guys were supposed to be when all that shit happened. We could just go and spend $25 million and remake that. We love stupid ideas and we thought this would be a really stupid one.

*Was it fun to be shooting this bizarre musical while still in school?*
MS: No.
TP: No. It's like making anything. You hate it. And anyone I've ever talked to that's worth their salt actually kind of hates the process. Like, I think Michael Bay probably goes out and has a really great time making movies, but that's because he doesn't give a fucking crap. It's so funny, because as stupid as our shit is, we think about it way too hard and we just agonize over, "Is it the right joke? Is it the right point?" And that was sort of the beginning of that. Looking back it's like, "Yeah, that was a pretty great time wasn't it?" But then when we really think about specific days, it's like, "Man, we were fucking miserable making that movie out in the snow and you've got, like, a broken camera and six hours to shoot."

*Looking back it was a pretty risky move to make a film like that for more than $100,000. Was it confidence or simply not knowing any better what a gamble you were taking?*
TP: Yeah, it's the thing that's made us all the money because it's the same ignorance that said, "Hey, let's go do an animated show." We don't know how to fucking do an animated show, and we didn't go to anyone and say, "Hey, how do you do an animated show?" If people knew how we do *South Park*, their fucking heads would explode. We come up with the idea on Thursday and it's on the air Wednesday. There's not one thing of animation in before that. And if we had gone and said, "How do you make animation?" we probably would never have

been able to do it. But just not knowing, we approached it in a totally different way and sort of invented a new way of doing animation. It was the same thing with *Packer*. It was just stupidity and naiveté, but it's the thing that has really helped us through our careers.

*Was there a plan for what you were going to do with* Packer?
MS: Our plan was to come out to L.A., sell it for a million dollars, pocket some of the money, come back to Colorado, and make another movie.
TP: We immediately learned how stupid we were to think, "Well, you just make a movie, and you make money." We came out here and of course it was just the kind of thing that turned into, "Oh, well there's this company that's interested; let's hang out in L.A. another week and see what happens." And so it turned into a month and years.
MS: I still want to go back to Colorado.
TP: Our bags are still packed.

*Trey, before* South Park, *you'd done a little bit of that kind of animation in school.*
TP: Yeah, it was an animation history class, but instead of having to write an essay I said, "Can I make an animated film?" and they said, "Yeah." Not knowing anything about animation, I decided to try to do a sort of Terry Gilliam kind of thing and make everything out of construction paper because the way I drew was super-crappy and child-like. It was absolute shit and total crap, and it got me a Student Academy Award. They flew me out to L.A., put me up in a hotel, and there's the other four finalists and their stuff is, like, beautiful pencil and watercolor animation. And my thing comes up and everyone's like, "What the fuck?" I learned there that crappy shit is totally funny. And I've made a whole career out of it.

South Park *fans know that the show essentially happened because of the short you made for producer Brian Graden. How did you guys hook up with him?*
TP: We had finished *Packer*, and we came out and had a little screening and Brian came to that and afterwards he came up to us and was

like, "Whatever you guys want to do, let's do it." Of course, at the time we were like, "Holy shit, that's awesome!" We didn't know that it was like, "Whatever you guys want to do, we'll do it and then you'll get five hundred bucks to make it."

*And that became* The Spirit of Christmas *video you created for him as a holiday greeting card for his friends?*
TP: Yeah. He had seen the one we had done in college and said, "Make me another one of those, and I'll pay for the film plus you guys can each have, like, four hundred bucks" and I was like, "Wow!" So we went and worked our asses off.

*When did you realize that* The Spirit of Christmas *was becoming this mini-phenomenon—that everyone in Hollywood was talking about it?*
TP: When people were coming up to us in bars two months afterwards, saying, "You've got to see this thing. I got this off the Internet" or "I got this thing from my friend and you guys would love it." And then going and showing our own stuff to us. It would happen again and again and we were like, "This thing is fucking everywhere."
MS: Brian only sent out about forty copies of it. He was going to send out a lot more, but when he saw it, he thought it was too offensive. So he only sent it to his select group of people who he thought would get it. It was a very fortunate time for us because the Internet had just kind of started and because the animation is just so shitty, it was one of the first things that you could watch over the Internet. You could download it and it was super-shitty, but it still was what it was.

*How did* Orgazmo *happen?*
TP: *Orgazmo* was actually the movie we came up with while we were shooting *Cannibal!* We were like, "After we go sell *Cannibal!* for $10 million, we'll come back to Colorado and make this new movie, which was a musical called *Orgazmo*. The only regret I have is that we got talked out of making it a musical. Paramount saw *Cannibal!* and said, "What do you guys want to do next?" and we were like, "OK, so there's this Mormon and he wants to be in porno" and they were

like, "OK, no thanks, see you around." We found [producer] Kaz Kuzui, and her little company found a Japanese guy who was like, "Here, take a million dollars." It really was the perfect next step from *Cannibal!*

*Was it any more of an enjoyable experience than* Cannibal! *was?*
TP: Once again, it was miserable. It's always miserable. I have never had a good time on a set. I've never had a good time making an episode of *South Park*, either. I always hate it, and I always say, "I'll never do it again."

*When* South Park *came on the air, it quickly became huge. You guys were everywhere. What was the point where the frenzy hit its peak to you?*
MS: Actually it was the same week that the Denver Broncos won their first Super Bowl which was, for us, the greatest part of that week. We were at that game, and I think it was the first Broncos game I ever got to go to. That was the week we were on the cover of *Rolling Stone, Newsweek*, and *Spin*. It was crazy.
TP: I think for us it was like, "This is the machine that churns you up and spits you out, and so before it spits us out, let's do as much shit as we can. Let's do *Baseketball*. Let's do a *South Park* album. We just said yes to everything because we were like, 'fuck it!'"
MS: Because it's all going to be over in a year.
TP: It's all going to be over in a year! You might as well just cash in. And everything sounded fun, like "Yeah, we'll do an album. Sure, that sounds fun!" It was a pretty confusing time. It also seems like about that time was when no one in the world would tell Matt and Trey that something wasn't funny or that something sucked. All of a sudden everything you say is funny.

*You've said that one of the valuable lessons you learned from working with David Zucker on* Baseketball *was choosing which battles to fight?*
TP: Yeah. Just with studios and how they were like, "Well, that joke worked. Do that again!" And we're like, "Well, that won't work again.

That's why it was sweet—because it was one time." And they're like, "No, it's testing well. Do it again."

MS: On the *South Park* movie, when we were signing agreements we said, "No preview screenings, none of those cards, and Trey has final cut." That's the first day of negotiation. Unless you give us all this, we won't talk.

TP: And they were like, "Guys, this is your first studio movie. Nobody gets final cut."

MS: And we were like, "OK, see ya."

TP: And one of the big fights was that they wanted the *South Park* movie to be PG-13. And we wanted it in there that it had to be R. And that actually served us really well. And it was the same on *Team America*: "OK, we're doing this weird-ass movie and we have final cut and there's no preview screenings." They really hate it but in a way I think they kind of like the fact that, OK, all the responsibility is on you.

*Many filmmakers swear by test screenings—particularly for comedies. Why don't you believe in them?*

TP: The reason we don't do test screenings is because *South Park* came so very close to not existing because of test screenings.

MS: Yeah, the pilot tested horribly.

TP: And it's like we knew from personal experience that the comedy that we love, Monty Python, tons of people totally didn't get. So when we were doing shit that even only a small group of people really responded to, we thought we were doing something good.

MS: Those preview screenings are especially insidious because it's not even like thumbs up or thumbs down on a show, but thumbs up or down on this joke in the beginning of the third act. I'm a math guy. I like math. But it doesn't apply to movies. We make comedy for ourselves.

TP: That's the thing that's really served us well. When I'm sitting down to write, I just think about my friends at home and I think about them watching it and I try to make them laugh. I can't try to make everyone laugh.

*Why did you do the* South Park *movie?*
TP: Part of it was because we could, and another part was here was a chance to do an R-rated version and not bleep everything. But more than that was we had a sweet idea for it. To this day they are still at our heels for a *South Park* movie sequel. But the *South Park* TV show is such a hungry baby, every good idea we have goes into that. And until we have another sort of epiphany, like, "Here's a sweet movie to do," we're not going to do it.

*The* South Park *film landed you an Oscar nomination for one of the songs, and you attended in drag as Jennifer Lopez and Gwyneth Paltrow. Did you ever consider performing the song yourselves for the show?*
TP: Hell no. We honestly were debating even going. We were the guys that were totally against that shit. That's what *South Park* is all about. It's anti-celebrity. It's anti all that crap. And it's like, can we really walk down the red carpet in a tux going, "Here I am, I'm one of you now"? But on the other hand it was like, "Dude, it's the fucking Academy Awards. We should go for once in our lives." And that's when we came up with the idea to go in dresses. We could go but still say "fuck you" to everybody.

*It must have been a tough moment to step out of that limo dressed as you were.*
TP: It was super-tough. It was really hard.
MS: It was fucking really hard, yeah.
TP: But not as hard as fucking sitting through that goddamn thing. I mean, we got up and left halfway through, and it was still fucking brutal.

*If you look at your work from* South Park *to* Team America, *it seems like you've always gravitated toward seemingly crude techniques for telling stories.*
TP: We're not the guys who would be happy making fucking *Deuce Bigalow,* you know what I mean? We always want to do something that's just really fucking weird, because at least if it's not funny, it's

really fucking weird. The honest truth is, we just fucking hate actors. Having to work with any people and trying to get them to do your comedy, it pisses us off so much.

*Why do you hate working with actors so much?*
TP: I think it goes back to the way I made movies as a kid. The way I was brought up, making movies was to turn the camera on and I go get in front of it and I think of the lines I'm going to say, and I do it. And I tell my friends around me what to say. So it's really hard for me to stand back. When we were doing *That's My Bush* with real actors, I told them beforehand, "Look, I know the way you actors are, but the way I'm going to direct you is I'm going to act out your shit for you." Because it's the only way I know how to do it. I'm a horrible communicator. I have no patience, and I don't like people. I just have absolutely no respect for actors. I really don't. I honestly believe that eighty percent of people in the world can be pretty good actors. I just have no respect for their art at all.

*Matt, are your views as extreme as Trey's?*
MS: No, I think actors are sweet. (laughs) We have to play good cop/bad cop if we make a movie with actors so we don't have a reputation. I'm not as good of an actor as Trey, so maybe I have a little bit more respect for them. But when you're someone who is behind the scenes—a writer, producer, or director—you do see the inordinate amount of acclaim that actors get sometimes and you're like, "Man, that's not even the fucking hard part."

*You talked about how much you work to the last minute on* South Park *episodes. The same thing happened on* Team America, *didn't it?*
MS: Oh, yeah.
TP: You can ask Scott Rudin. He said he's never seen anything like this. He's like, "I've never seen people write so much in postproduction." Because he saw it so much in the *South Park* movie, too. He's like, "You guys wrote half that movie in postproduction." It's just how we work.

MS: There were whole scenes in *Team America* that were shot with the puppets saying one thing, and then we'd sit in the editing room and turn the sound off, and basically we'd *Mystery Science Theater 3000* it and completely change the entire scene. There were at least two or three scenes that we did that with.

*How close to the release were you still fiddling with it?*
MS: Oh, two or three weeks. Paramount was going crazy. We did the whole post-schedule in six weeks, beginning to end. Yeah, it was pretty hellish.

*You've said that* Team America *was a difficult filmmaking experience. Was it the technical complexity that frustrated you?*
TP: Yeah. Because we had to rewrite the entire script every single day. We'd get to the new scene, and the puppets couldn't even begin to do what was written, because we wrote the script without even knowing how to do this. About two months into shooting that movie, we became really good at making puppet movies, but we were already two months in and we had about a month to go.

*Was ever there a point during the film where you thought you would not be able to complete the movie?*
TP: Every single day. That's why it was so miserable too—because we're working our asses off with no sleep. And in the backs of our minds we're going, "We're never going to make it. We are going to completely fail." So yeah, it was brutal.

*You've had many run-ins with the MPAA over the ratings for your films. How do you feel about the organization?*
MS: We have a lot of problems with the ratings board itself. When we originally submitted *Orgazmo*, we got an NC-17. And we wanted to make an R movie because that was really important for our career. We were like, "OK, what do we have to cut? What's the most offensive shit?" And they just wouldn't tell us. They were like, "Well, that would

make us a censorship organization. It's just the overwhelming sexual content. So maybe try another crack at it." But the thing is, we were doing an independent film and to get an Avid was like three or four thousand dollars a week, and we couldn't afford it. And then when we did the *South Park* movie we got an NC-17. We were like, "Well, we've gotten an NC-17 before," thinking we knew how to deal with it. And Scott Rudin was like, "Here are the notes they gave us: At a minute thirty-eight, cut this word; at a minute forty-one, cut . . ." It was in excruciating detail. And people won't say it, but as one of the signatories to the MPAA you get preferential treatment. And with independent films they just give you an NC-17 and say "fuck you." For *South Park*, one of the last jokes we were arguing about, Rudin called and says, "We've got to cut this," and I just went crazy. I called him back and said, "Fuck that! This is bullshit!" I just freaked out on him. And so he called somebody and somebody called somebody and the next day we had an R. We didn't change a frame. We had an NC-17, the studio bitched, and then we had an R.

*Matt, Trey has directed all of the films himself, even as you two continue to write together. Have you ever wanted to codirect one of the projects?*
MS: No. I think that this is where my lack of ambition has really helped our partnership. Trey is the director and always has been. On *Team America* I got a little experience being second-unit director, but it's just not one of my strengths. And I'm just not as interested in it. I'm better at other things that Trey isn't good at.

*Are there any significant differences in your comic sensibilities?*
TP: No. It's pretty damn similar.

*What about in terms of the direction of the career? You're always on the same page?*
TP: We're totally the same person in the sense that neither one of us thinks more than about three months into the future. We don't plan at all, and I think that's helped us too, because by not planning we

don't pigeonhole ourselves into anything. We're always sort of mentally available when something good comes along.

MS: I think that's why we kind of freak people out a little bit in town, because we don't have a publicist and we don't have a managed career. We just kind of do what we feel like doing.

*You say you don't have a managed career and that also seems to extend to the way you speak. You both are notoriously candid. Has it ever cost you anything in terms of your career?*

TP: Never. There have been times when we felt like, "OK, this is over. Everyone's sick of us. It's time to leave town." But we've always been able to say "OK, we can leave this town with our heads pretty fucking high" because the nature of what we do is so anti-selling out. Of course we've sold out in more ways than either of us ever thought we would, but we've always had that in the backs of our minds—that we better always do shit because we think it's cool. Especially now it's like we really better just do shit because we think it's cool and to fuck with people and to not make another million bucks.

*Do you go to the movies a lot?*

MS: I don't really watch movies.

TP: It's weird, because that's sort of the last thing that either of us wants to do. The last thing I want to do is think about story and structure and character and all that shit. I fucking hate that now.

MS: I don't even have a TV at my house. I gave it up about a year and a half ago.

*What's wrong with movies today, in your opinion?*

TP: There's so rarely that film now where you get knocked over the head, like, "What the fuck was that?" Now you go and you know what you're going to get. You sit there going, "Well, here they are, giving it to me. I know what scene is coming next." I hate to sound totally jaded and bitter and cynical, but it's like really there are so many movies where you just see the studio in it and you see the Ivy

Leaguers sitting around a table saying, "Here's how you do this scene."

*Do you feel like your work is given short shrift because it's full of fart jokes and profanity?*
TP: I know that we work way harder then the Michael Bays of the world, and I know that we put a lot more thought into our stuff than most people think. I remember when the *South Park* movie came out, a lot of critics were like, "Well, they obviously didn't have a lot of ideas so they just filled time with music." And it's like, "Do you know how fucking hard it is to make a musical work?" But on the other hand you've got to stop and look around and say, "Dude, we've made a lot of money off of this, and that's pretty great."
MS: Yeah, somebody must like it out there. And a good fart joke is—
TP: We still laugh our asses off at fart jokes.
MS: I just laughed at Trey this morning. He farted on our friend Jennifer, and it made me laugh.

## THE DIRECTORS' TAKE
## TREY PARKER & MATT STONE

*What is the first film you ever saw?*
Trey: *Fantastic Voyage*
Matt: *Around the World in Eighty Days*

*What is your favorite film of all time?*
Trey: *A Christmas Story*
Matt: *Babe*

*What's your favorite line in a film?*
Trey: "Don't talk to me, I'm thinking."—Ralphie, in *A Christmas Story*
Matt: "A man for a husband."—*Raising Arizona*

*What movie made you realize that film was an art?*
Trey: *Timecop*
Matt: *The Road Warrior*

*What movie do you consider your guilty pleasure?*
Trey: *The Devil's Advocate*
Matt: *Raw*

*Who is your favorite movie character of all time?*
Trey: The Outlaw Josey Wales
Matt: Mad Max

*What's your favorite movie snack food?*
Trey: wine
Matt: Milk Duds

*Who is your favorite director of all time?*
Trey: Don't have one
Matt: Trey Parker

*Who is the most impressive filmmaker working today?*
Trey: Definitely not me
Matt: Besides Trey, Pedro Almodóvar

*What quality do the best directors share?*
Trey: They're not completely stupid.
Matt: Insanity

*Who is your favorite actor or actress of all time?*
Trey: I hate them all.
Matt: Eddie Murphy

*Who would you cast as yourself in a film about your life?*
Trey: Tom Wopat
Matt: Eddie Murphy

*If you could remake one movie, what would it be?*
Trey: *Orgazmo*
Matt: *Megaforce*

*What is your best quality as a director?*
Trey: I'm really nice.

*What is your greatest weakness as a director?*
Trey: I hate actors.

*Finish this sentence: I'll never direct a movie with . . .*
Trey: any chance of making money.

*Finish this sentence: The perfect movie is . . .*
Trey: funny, sad, and not longer than one hundred minutes.
Matt: less than ninety minutes.

*What will they be saying about your work fifty years from now?*
Trey: "Why did anyone ever give him money?"

*What piece of advice do you have for aspiring filmmakers?*
Trey: Don't listen to any advice from me. Or Michael Bay.
Matt: Have a backup plan.

*What are you as passionate about as moviemaking?*
Trey: Lovemaking
Matt: Drinking margaritas

# TODD PHILLIPS

"For me it's much more recognition having fifteen-year-olds quoting your movie than having Roger Ebert commenting on whether it's funny or not. *Old School* wasn't made for fat guys struggling with their weight."

ELLIOT MARKS © 2004

## SELECTED CREDITS

*Hated* (1994)–director
*Frat House* (1998)–codirector
*Road Trip* (2000)–cowriter/director
*Bittersweet Motel* (2000)–director
*Old School* (2003)–cowriter/director
*Starsky & Hutch* (2004)–cowriter/director

Todd Phillips grew up with the antiestablishment comedies of the 1970s. They obviously made an impact. With the 2003 hit *Old School* he contributed his own classic comic tale of rebelling against authority. Phillips obviously is proud; "Letterman said it was the funniest film he had seen in ten years." But for those who think this filmmaker is easy to peg, Phillips is full of surprises. For instance, the cursory fan of *Road Trip* or *Starsky & Hutch* probably has no idea that the director has devoted a sizeable portion of his career to making documentaries. Of course, even those films carry the unmistakable Phillips stamp of irreverence and unpredictability. In many ways, Phillips's abuse at the hands of overeager frat boys in *Frat House* is as hysterical as anything Vince Vaughn put his recruits through years later.

---

*You were born in Brooklyn?*
TP: Yeah, in Brooklyn. I grew up mostly on Long Island.

*Your parents split up when you were just five years old. Did you divide your time between your mom and dad?*
TP: Oh, no. I probably haven't talked to my dad in twenty years. We just grew up with my mom. I have two older sisters.

*Did you find yourself ever wishing you had a brother or some other male presence in your life?*
TP: Yeah, which is actually why I think it sort of found its way into my movies. All my movies are about relationships between guys. I don't think I had a lot of male bonding. (laughs) It's something I've thought about a lot. Every movie I've done is generally about guys and how guys relate to one another.

*What were you like as a kid?*
TP: I was a bad kid. I had sort of a delinquent group of friends, honestly. We always had to go to family court. I was fifteen and I remember I had two JV cards, which were Juvenile Delinquent cards. If you get three, you have to go to reform school.

*What did you get them for?*
TP: One was for shoplifting and one was for trespassing.

*When did you start getting into movies?*
TP: I got into movies at a young age. I got into [the kind of] movies you normally get into as a kid. I didn't discover Preston Sturges at twelve. It was *Stripes* and *Meatballs* and that kind of stuff. I didn't understand what a director did, but I loved movies and comedies in particular.

*Do you remember the first films you became obsessed with?*
TP: The first thing I became obsessed with was probably *Stripes* and probably *Revenge of the Nerds*.

*Highbrow from the start.*
TP: (laughs) Yeah, all the way. It's the stuff I love. To me, what was great about those late-seventies and early-eighties comedies was that they were antiestablishment. It's the tone of that I always responded to. All the good comedies are antiestablishment movies. *Animal House* is the classic antiestablishment film, and *Stripes* is the same.

*Did you enjoy NYU?*
TP: NYU was a good experience. I didn't officially graduate from NYU. I went through three years and then I kind of just stopped. You get what you can out of film school and then you realize, "OK, I'm done." That was my approach because it's not like you need a degree. It's just like, "What can I get out of this, and what can I do with this?"

*Why do you think you gravitated first toward making documentaries at NYU?*
TP: Everyone's eighteen years old when they go to NYU and they expect you to sort of sit down and write a screenplay. Unless you're a to-

tally gifted writer, what do you really have to write about when you're eighteen years old? Ninety-nine percent of people write from experience. They're not necessarily gifted writers. So you have a lot of people writing about where they grew up, and maybe if they were lucky, their parents were divorced and they had some conflict in their lives, but it was ultimately nonsense. I always felt the better route was to do documentaries and, in essence, live life on fast forward by absorbing experiences that you're not necessarily otherwise going to have.

*Were you thinking that documentaries would be a means to get into fiction films?*
TP: I never saw them as a separate thing. Documentaries and movies are all storytelling. A good documentary has a beginning, middle, and end. There are a lot of people who call movies "documentaries," but they are basically journalistic pieces. The way to direct a documentary, you have to have a point of view. Michael Moore, whether you like him or hate him, has a point of view behind his movies. He doesn't claim to be a journalist. He's making movies with a beginning, middle, and end the same as *Road Trip* has a beginning, middle, and end. So to me, I never saw them as separate things. I think documentaries as a means of breaking into film are a really interesting way to go, because documentaries are seventy percent the subject matter you choose, so it's a little bit of an easier road. Ultimately all you are as a director is a storyteller, and if I can tell a story about GG Allin, why can't I tell a story about Will Ferrell going back to college? I was probably naive in thinking that, but it worked and it probably works easier now. Back then it was treated as the ugly stepsister of filmmaking. The word "documentary" made people yawn. I think I was ahead of the curve—mentally, at least.

Hated *was your first serious stab at a documentary?*
TP: I was a junior at NYU when I did *Hated*. I had only done photography because I didn't have a video camera when I was younger, so *Hated* was the first movie I had done.

*Can you tell me a little bit about the subject of the film, GG Allin, and how you hooked up with him?*

TP: I was really into punk rock from when I was probably fifteen, and GG was always the most extreme character in punk rock. At the time he was sort of legendary, so I knew he would be an interesting subject. Just by going to shows I ended up becoming friends with his brother, Merle. I told him I wanted to do a documentary with GG. He was like, "You should write him a letter." He was in jail at the time. I wrote him a letter in Michigan and he wrote me back. He was getting out of jail in three months and he was going to be on probation for a year. He couldn't leave Michigan. I was like, "Fuck, I want to do it now." He was like, "Well, if you send me a bus ticket I guess I could do it." (laughs) So we send him a bus ticket and he comes to New York. The whole time we're filming the movie he's broken parole, and then he gets caught at the end of the movie. He served another year in jail while we were editing. Then when he got out of jail, he came to the premiere of the movie at NYU and then he died a month later. I was actually with him, shooting some stills of him for the press kit when he OD'd on heroin. We didn't even know he was dead. We just thought he was passed out.

*His routines onstage were pretty out-there, including hurling excrement at times.*

TP: Yeah, there was that, but it was more about just violence. He was incredibly extreme. (laughs) I mean, this is not Marilyn Manson. This is the real thing. It wasn't like you were into GG's music when you went to see his show. It was just the excitement of the stage show and the adrenaline of the room, and that was what we tried to capture in the movie. It's sort of the danger of it, and to me it's the thing that I've always been attracted to. I even think it carries itself over into *Old School*. As punk rock as fuckin' GG is, I think that comedy can be as punk rock as that, because there are no rules with it.

*I understand you got the money for the film in an unusual way.*

TP: The movie cost $14,000, which I didn't have. GG was friends with John Wayne Gacy who was, at the time, on death row. This guy was a painter in prison. He painted clowns. I wrote him a letter and I said, "Hey, I'm doing this movie on GG and you know what would be great is if you could paint the movie poster and then I could sell it and then I would have money to make this movie." Gacy calls me at home from the Menard Correctional Facility in Illinois, and he said that he would do it for fifty dollars and art supplies and a photo of myself. And he sent me this bio that I had to fill out, which was sort of sexual and weird.

*Oh my God.*
TP: So I did all that, sent him the fifty bucks. Two months later he sends me the painting. He numbers and signs the posters. I put ads out in these punk-rock magazines. I sold them for fifteen dollars apiece in three months—every one of them—made $15,000. (laughs) I actually spoke to [Gacy] three days before he died. He really took to me in a weird way.

*Your next documentary took you inside a fraternity's hazing rituals. Wasn't* Frat House *supposed to be a project for HBO?*
TP: [HBO vice president ] Sheila Nevins loved *Hated*, but she couldn't air it, because at the time they didn't air documentaries that are made outside of HBO. She was like, "I can't air this movie, but I fucking love it. What do you want to do next?" I hooked up with my friend from NYU Andrew Gurland, and we pitched a few ideas. We made a three-movie deal with HBO. We were going to make three documentaries based on eighties comedies that we grew up on. So we were going to do *Animal House*, which was *Frat House*. We were going to do *Stripes*. Andrew and I were going to join the army and go through boot camp. And then we were going to do *Bachelor Party* because Andrew was getting married. (laughs) It was a way to make documentaries entertaining which, by the way, now is happening all over the place, and it's great.

*Did you go into* Frat House *with any kind of preconceived feeling about fraternities?*
TP: Look, I went to NYU. I'm not a fraternity guy, even though I've now made two movies that have them in them. To me, the thing I was

always fascinated by was the male bonding. I just want to understand why guys put themselves through that kind of thing.

*You become part of the pledge process in the film. What was the worst part for you to endure?*
TP: I think the worst thing was when I was in that dog cage, because I'm a bit of a germ freak. They're, like, pouring tobacco spit on my head and urine and whatever. I couldn't believe I was in a dog cage.

*Thinking, "How did I get to this place in my life?" You suffered through it all and you don't even get to be a part of the fraternity.*
TP: (laughs) Yeah, exactly. I didn't even get to fuck any of the girls.

*Frat House never made it to HBO despite doing very well at Sundance. What happened?*
TP: The movie got a little press, and a lot of the kids started to come out and say it was a setup and we told them what to do and we paid them. Well, first they came out and said they were drunk and stoned when they signed the release, which was absolutely true. (laughs) We found the best time to hand them paperwork was when they were drunk and stoned, which to me was logical. Otherwise, they're like, "Maybe I have to fax this to my dad." So they got us on that, but that didn't really matter, because the process of releases isn't really that legally binding. You don't necessarily need a release, because it's not like we're filming with hidden cameras. It became a big legal headache with parents threatening to sue and saying it was going to ruin their kid's life. So it went away after that. Andrew and I were fighting it for a little bit because we really wanted the movie to be seen, but we now look back on it and kind of like that it's this underground sort of thing.

*It was at Sundance that you met Ivan Reitman, who would be important to your career. How did you two meet?*
TP: I met Ivan because his son was there with a short film. His son, at our Q&A, raised his hand and asked, "What was your inspiration for

this movie?" And I told him the story I told you about how we wanted to make three movies based on eighties comedies and two of those three movies were his dad's movies. Two days later that same kid comes up to me and goes, "Hey, Dad, this is the guy I was telling you about."

*He's produced two of your films. Would you consider him a mentor?*
TP: Yeah, for sure. I didn't know anyone in the film business, ever. It wasn't like I had an uncle in the business, so I always think of Ivan as that guy.

*After* Frat House *you made some money directing some commercials for a while?*
TP: I directed over a hundred commercials probably.

*Did you feel your commercial work honed your skills behind the camera?*
TP: You know what it is? You finally to get to really play with all the toys that you'll have available to you on your first feature. So it wasn't really just for the money; it was great experience and the best way to learn how it works on a real movie set, because I had never been on a real movie set before.

*How were you working with your cast on* Road Trip? *It wasn't a terribly experienced cast.*
TP: I feel bad for these first-time directors that somehow luck out and get Tom Cruise in their movies. These guys were great for me because they really hadn't done a ton of stuff and we were all sort of in it to-gether. It took a lot of the pressure off. Vince Vaughn is the greatest in the world, but I don't think I could have directed Vince in my first movie. He's just intimidating.

Road Trip *was called a "gross-out" comedy by some, much in the same way that* There's Something About Mary *and* American Pie *were at that time. Do you find that term belittling?*
TP: I think it's belittling to all the movies in a way, but it didn't bother me, because at the time it was a marketing tool. I just find it dismis-

sive of all those movies, because there're plenty of gross-out movies that don't do well because the story doesn't work. It's easy to be gross. It's hard to be funny. So it has to work on more levels than being just a gross-out thing.

*You've said casting is one of the most important parts of your job. Did you have the guys in mind when you were writing* Old School?
TP: We wrote the movie for Vince Vaughn. That was the only part we had in mind because I think Vince is the funniest guy ever, and I don't think he'd ever done a comedy like that. And we had to fight for Vince.

*Vince is one of your favorite actors to work with. Why?*
TP: Out of anybody I've ever worked with he's the funniest guy in real life. And whether it comes across in his movies or not, I know having him on the set it's going to be great because when you're in those weird situations, he's going help you out. Vince is somebody who thinks more like a producer than an actor, and that's not a negative thing. He actually thinks about the movie as a whole as opposed to his role. So he's tracking story, which is what you should be doing as the director. It's always nice to have somebody else involved that's doing that.

Fight Club *was obviously on your mind when you made* Old School. *There are a number of references to it.*
TP: Yeah, I always saw the movie as the comedy version of *Fight Club. Fight Club* is my favorite movie of the nineties, other than *Boogie Nights.*

*You've said that you see* Old School *as a pull between responsibility and irresponsibility.*
TP: It is. It's about that moment in life where you have to decide, "Am I going to go this way or that way?" I personally put off going "that way" for a long time. I'm definitely still "this way." I think it's why *Old School* connected. It's not so much, "Oh, it's funny when Will gets shot with a dart in his neck." Comedies that last have to work on more than that one level of just being funny. *There's Something About Mary*

is great because it's funny, but it's also great because you're so invested in Ben Stiller's desire to get back with this girl, to get a second chance. It's something you can so relate to.

*You're in* Old School. *What's your one line?*
TP: "I'm here for the gang bang." I know it because I live here in L.A. and across the street they rented a house to eight college kids. Without fail on a Friday or Saturday night they have a party, and without fail at three in the morning they buzz my buzzer and say, "I'm here for the gang bang." And they all run away laughing. And then I see them when they're not drunk in the daytime and they're taking out the garbage and I'm like, "Guys, enough with that." And they're like, "Sorry, man, it was my buddy. It's not going to happen again." And then the next Saturday it happens again.

*That character and your character in* Road Trip *seem to have a lot in common.*
TP: It's the same guy. It's an alter ego, and actually I had a part written for him in *Starsky*, but we didn't have time to shoot it. I very givingly gave up my part. (laughs) That's Mr. Creepy, and he's very sexual. He finds sex in everything. He's so straight that sometimes he's even gay, if that makes sense.

*What was the genesis of* Starsky & Hutch?
TP: I met with Ben Stiller and he liked the stuff I'd done, and we started talking about doing a movie but we didn't know what. Suddenly a week or two later he called me and said, "Hey, I found a movie we should do. It's more of an idea: me and Owen Wilson as Starsky and Hutch." And I said, "All right, I'm in." Because I knew we could have fun with that, and I was just dying to work with Ben and Owen.

*Tonally the film must have been a challenge. It has comedy and action and it's not exactly a spoof, but—*
TP: That's what was difficult about the movie. I always saw it as kind of a love letter to the show as opposed to an homage or a spoof of the

show. Our goal was, "Let's write a prequel to the TV show; do the same thing tonally, but put different actors in it and thus hopefully make it funny."

*With* Starsky, *you were again working on a film about the relationship between men. Do you think this recurring theme might go back to the absence of your father?*
TP: It could, quite possibly. I don't know if it goes back to my dad. It more goes back to the fact that I was raised by three women—two older sisters and my mom. I've sort of been protected in that way, and I always was surrounded by women. I didn't have a brother. You can't help but explore something that's foreign to you in a way.

*Interestingly, the relationship between Ben and Owen in* Starsky *almost mirrors a traditional romantic comedy.*
TP: I always said to Ben, "This is going to be a romantic comedy between two straight guys." It follows the beats of a regular romantic comedy because they're thrown together, there's tension, and they're thrown apart and then they come back together stronger than ever. A typical romantic comedy to me is like R&B music. It's just not my thing, but to take two guys and virtually make a romantic comedy with all those beats just seems interesting to me. I find romantic comedies are rarely romantic and rarely funny, which is why what P. T. Anderson did with *Punch Drunk* [*Love*] is like the greatest romantic comedy of all time—because it's actually funny *and* romantic.

*What sort of mood do you like to establish on set?*
TP: Extremely relaxed and light, almost too much so. Ben told me when we were shooting *Starsky,* "I feel like we're making a student film." And Owen used to say, "The inmates are running the asylum." Maybe it is too light. I don't know. Look, I'm not delusional. Plenty of people don't like my movies. I've sat down with reviewers who don't like the movies but they'll always say, "Boy, it looks like you had a great time making it." And I think that is true and that the energy finds its way into the movie. So if you're not into the story, I think the enthusi-

asm and the energy of the fun sucks you in. Or that's what I'd like to believe.

*Speaking of critics, does it bother you when a film as successful as* Old School *still gets panned by prominent critics?*
TP: No. For me it's much more recognition having fifteen-year-olds quoting your movie than having Roger Ebert commenting on whether it's funny or not. *Old School* wasn't made for fat guys struggling with their weight. I mean, it's tough to make that guy laugh. Just look at the poor guy. I'm not picking on critics. While some people hated that movie, it's also been loved by critics. I don't have any reviews framed, be they good or bad. Ebert loved *Starsky*, but that didn't make me suddenly feel better.

*Do you test-screen your films?*
TP: Every film I've done. I think testing a comedy is absolutely one-hundred-percent crucial, and I think testing a movie in general is crucial. I always find it amazing when directors—outside of Steven Spielberg—just say, "Here's the movie; take it or leave it." I find it astounding because, ultimately, you really don't know what you have until you put it up there. Certainly comedy, when you watch it with an audience, then you know, "OK, that works; that doesn't work." You're making a movie for the audience. *Road Trip* was not the story I needed to tell. It wasn't going to be the pinnacle of my career. It was a movie I was making to be funny and I think ninety-nine percent of directors who make comedies will tell you the same thing. It's totally different for Paul Thomas Anderson and people making films that are personal stories that are like, "This is exactly the way I wanted to tell it. If it doesn't work for you, it doesn't work for you; so be it." When you're making a film [where the] sole purpose is to make people laugh, to not test it is kind of shocking because how do you know? It's not funny to you anymore. Are you going to just assume that [other people are] going to love it? And then you're shocked on that opening Friday night when you go to the theater and nobody is laughing?

*At a certain point, wouldn't you want to trust your own instincts?*
TP: No. I would never not test-screen a movie. Ultimately it's a fine line, because you are a director and everyone wants to consider themselves an auteur. Certainly as a writer-director it's important that it maintain that original vision you had for it. It's not like you can change your movie a hundred-eighty degrees by testing it. It's still the movie you shot. If a joke fell flat and I'm taking it out of my movie, am I changing my vision? Did I compromise what I set out to do? No. The joke didn't work, and I'm adult enough to know it didn't work. Big deal.

## THE DIRECTOR'S TAKE
## TODD PHILLIPS

*What is the first film you ever saw?*
*Deep Throat.* I was five.

*What is your favorite film of all time?*
*Gimme Shelter*

*What's your favorite line in a film?*
"Better to be king for a day than schmuck for a lifetime."—*The King of Comedy*

*What movie made you realize that film was an art?*
*Under the Rainbow*

*What movie do you consider your guilty pleasure?*
*One Night in Paris*

*Who is your favorite movie character of all time?*
Rupert Pupkin

*Who is your favorite director of all time?*
Hal Ashby

*Who is the most impressive filmmaker working today?*
Paul Thomas Anderson

*What quality do the best directors share?*
Persistence of vision

*Who is your favorite actor or actress of all time?*
Al Pacino

*Who is your favorite actor or actress of today?*
Sean Penn

*Who would you cast as yourself in a film about your life?*
Hilary Swank

*If you could remake one movie, what would it be?*
*Sullivan's Travels*. Not that it needs to be remade; it is just a film that really connects with me.

*What is your best quality as a director?*
Are other people really answering these questions?

*What is your greatest weakness as a director?*
Low tolerance

*What will they be saying about your work fifty years from now?*
The same thing they say now, "Me and my friends got really high and watched (fill in title) . . . it was sooooo awesome."

*What piece of advice do you have for aspiring filmmakers?*
Don't agree to answer lame questionnaires. It's like doing someone else's homework.

*What are you as passionate about as moviemaking?*
Gambling and drugs and my dog

# BRETT RATNER

"Why do I need final cut? Final cut is for artistes
quote unquote—directors whose movies don't
make a lot of money."

*Money Talks* (1997)–director
*Rush Hour* (1998)–director
*Family Man* (2000)–director
*Rush Hour 2* (2001)–director
*Red Dragon* (2002)–director
*After the Sunset* (2004)–director
*X-Men 3* (2006)–director

From the time he saw *Raging Bull* as a kid, Brett Ratner knew he wanted to follow the path of Martin Scorsese. Today he may not be Scorsese, but no one else can claim to be anything like Brett Ratner. Start talking with him, and that is immediately clear. You soon realize he could probably talk his way in or out of any situation he wanted. It's no wonder he is up for so many high-profile projects. And it's not as if he has gotten by on enthusiasm alone. He is a student of film, throwing out film references with obvious love and affection. Ratner makes movies for the masses and would not think of apologizing for it. It is hard to argue with the results. The *Rush Hour* series is one of the most lucrative franchises going today. And his Hannibal Lecter film, *Red Dragon*, attracted one of the finest ensembles of the last decade.

---

*Can you tell me a little bit about your family and where you grew up?*
BR: I lived in one house with my mom, my grandparents, my great grandmother, and my mom's brother. It was a little house in Miami Beach. We were upper middle class. My grandfather was the patriarch. My whole life, since I can remember, I have dreamed of being a filmmaker. I don't know why. The thing my grandfather and I would do every weekend would be to go to the movies. He's Cuban, so we'd mostly pick action movies. He loved action movies because with them, you don't really have to understand the dialogue.

*When did you start to make movies of your own?*
BR: My mom knew this guy named Nile Rodgers who became a record producer. Every Christmas he'd come to town, and one year he came and brought me a film camera.

*And you were off to the races?*
BR: Yeah. And so I started using that to make my little films. Around that time they were shooting the pilot for *Miami Vice* on the street, and I would ask my mom to let me skip school. She was a very liberal mom and she let me. She'd drop me off on the set, and I would watch them film. When you're a kid, it's all fantastic. I was there, seeing it live, and

then I would see it on the TV. So I started to connect the dots. I was like, "Oh, I understand what that camera movement was." I used to stalk movie sets, and the other set that I stalked was *Scarface*. I stalked it so much that Brian De Palma said, "Hey, kid, get into the shot." I must have been twelve or thirteen. I'm in the background of that scene in the pool. I'm on a raft. Al Pacino was so cool, but I remember that is the day I decided I don't want to be him. I said, "I want to be the guy telling him what to do," and that guy was Brian De Palma.

*What do you think you were being drawn to?*
BR: I think it was the control. I saw him collaborating with everybody, and I saw Pacino just sitting there. I was happy because I could focus at a very young age on what I wanted to do. *Raging Bull* was my favorite movie, so I said, "OK, how did Martin Scorsese become a filmmaker?" He went to NYU film school. I go, "Well, that's where I'm going to go." So I did whatever I could. All I did every day was skip school or get home from school early, and me and my friends would get together and make these little short films. They were like mock *Miami Vice* episodes. It's actually my best work.

*It obviously paid off. You got into NYU.*
BR: I went and the interviewer said, "How dare you apply to this school? You have the worst grades and the worst SAT scores." She said I should go to community college and after I got straight A's, maybe they'd consider letting me in. And I was like, "No, you don't understand." I brought my little projector with me and they were like, "No, we don't look at this." I left devastated. I literally walked down the street with my little suit and my projector and my films and I was like, "My life is over! How can I let this woman decide my future?" So I go to the dean's office, saying I need to see the dean. They let me in. I said, "Dean, my whole life I've dreamed of being a director. I need you to let me in here, or I'm going to be living on my mom's couch for the rest of my life." A few weeks go by and I go to my mailbox and [a letter] says "You've been accepted to NYU." That was a defining mo-

ment, and the fact that I got accepted made me realize that "no" wasn't a response that I was ever going to accept.

*That seems like a lot of tenacity for someone so young. Where do you think it comes from?*
BR: The tenacity is from my grandmother. And my mom is a very outspoken, outgoing person. But the thing that I got [from them] that I think made me successful was the fact that I got a lot of love. I was never afraid to fail. If I didn't get into NYU, I would be OK. I'd still be making films, but they'd be in my backyard with my friends instead of with NYU students in Washington Square Park. My state of mind was, "If I can't be a director, my mom's still going to love me, so no big deal. I'm going to do the best I can."

*You've always been a film buff, but was it in film school that you started to study the history of the medium?*
BR: In film school I started going back. In film school you're taking a lot of film history classes and a lot of film theory classes, which were all bullshit to me, but—

*Why were they bullshit to you?*
BR: It's kind of like that joke with Woody Allen in *Annie Hall* when he's in line and the film professor is talking about some writer, and Woody Allen pulls the guy out of the line and the guy says, "You have no idea what you're talking about." That's what I felt like for some of the professors. They were analyzing these films and saying, like, Daffy Duck was racist. I don't think Walt Disney was thinking about race. These professors act like this is the Bible, even though it was their theory. I didn't always agree.

*What do you think your fellow film students made of you?*
BR: They didn't like me very much, because I was the mainstream guy there. My sensibility was to do comedies, and they were doing films about someone dying—really artsy kind of films. But my biggest inspiration was this professor who was a cinematographer of documen-

taries. He was the least commercial guy ever. Some kid did a film and it was so genius, it literally made me want to quit. I said, "There's no way I will ever make a film as good as this." The execution, the composition, the movement in the frame, it was literally genius! The film was about getting high. Only a few guys in the class had gotten high, so ten kids out of forty laughed. The professor said, "This film doesn't work." They started screaming, "You're a fucking communist! You're a fucking asshole!" I mean, NYU is very vocal. He was like, "Wait a second. What's the greatest story ever told?" Someone's says the Bible. He says, "Yes. The Bible is the best story ever told, because a small child can understand it and an adult can understand it. That's what your approach to your films has to be. If you're going to make films for just you and your friends, you're never going to succeed. If you want to get paid to make films, you have to make films for all audiences." That stayed with me.

*You did a short film at NYU called* Whatever Happened to Mason Reece? *What did you take away from that experience?*
BR: NYU teaches you how to make films. They don't teach you how to get a job. My professors told me, "Brett, you have to make a film. That's your résumé." So I shot this film. One night before I was supposed to shoot, the professor calls me. I'm shooting at seven in the morning. He says, "I read the script. It's not funny." He spoke with broken English. I said, "What do you mean it's not funny? You don't know if it's funny. You're from Poland! You don't speak English. How do you know what's funny?" He said, "No, you rewrite it, right now!" I sat there until one in the morning, rewriting the script. Ten years later, on *Money Talks*, Chris Tucker and Charlie Sheen come in my trailer and they say we can't shoot this scene. They go, "It's not funny." I said, "What?" I had to rewrite it right there in front of them! And then I realized *that's* what the fuck my professor was doing. He was preparing me for when I'm on the set of a $25 million movie, where the stars come to me and say we can't shoot and I only have six hours left in the day to shoot it.

*Didn't you go through some unusual channels to pay for* Mason Reece?
BR: Yeah. Before I finished the film, I came across a *Forbes* magazine where I saw the forty most powerful people in Hollywood, and I sent a letter to all of them with a clip from the movie, asking for money. I didn't need the money, but I wanted the relationships. I got thirty-nine rejection letters, and I could not have been happier—letters from Peter Guber, from Steve Ross, from all the heads of all the studios. I thought, "One day I'm going to go out to Hollywood and I'm going to say, 'Hey, you wrote me a letter!' Even though it was a rejection letter, you wrote me a letter." The dean calls me in. I'm thinking I'm getting kicked out. I was the worst film student ever. I would keep equipment [overnight] when I wasn't supposed to. I was using the editing room when it was closed in the middle of the night. I was just crazy. He goes, "Steven Spielberg's office called. They're looking for you. Here's the number." I go back to my dorm room and call the number. They answer the phone, "Steven Spielberg's office." I'm like, "Is Mr. Spielberg in?" They say, "Who's calling?" I say, "Brett Ratner." "Hold on one second, he's expecting your call." My heart was pounding out of my chest. I'm like eighteen, nineteen years old. They finally go, "Mr. Spielberg's going to call you back." I remember falling asleep on the phone. I woke up with slobber all over my phone. When I woke up, the phone rang and it was Kathleen Kennedy. She said, "Steven saw your clip and we're very impressed, but we don't give money for short films and thank you for sending it to us." And I was like, "You don't understand. I'm going to be a big director like Steven Spielberg. You've got to trust me. This is an important film." I kept her on the phone for, like, ten minutes. A month goes by and I get a check from Amblin Entertainment. I was like, "Oh my God!" I blew it up the size of my wall in the dorm. I would show it to girls in the hallway to try to impress them to try to get laid. I don't think I ever cashed the check. I just carried it around in my wallet for three years. When I became a music video director, Quincy Jones called me and said, "I want to meet you." He said, "Come to this party with me." So I think there's going to be like a hundred people there. There are three people there. He goes, "Brett, this

is Penny Marshall, Robert De Niro, and Steven Spielberg." I was like, "Oh my God!" Spielberg sat down next to me and he goes, "So did you go to film school?" I said, "It's funny you should ask, because you gave me money." I picked his brain for four hours. I said, "Where did you get that shot from in *Schindler's List?*" He goes, "Oh, that was Michael Powell's *Peeping Tom.*" Every shot I asked him about was from another movie. And I realized, "Shit, I do the exact same thing!" So anyway, it was great. He gave me his phone number. He tried to fix me up with his daughter. I didn't want to go there, because I thought if I hurt his daughter, I'll never make it in Hollywood.

*One of the most important relationships that you made at NYU was with Russell Simmons. How did you two meet?*
BR: When I was at NYU the first guy I met was Russell Simmons. I lived in the dorm where they started Def Jam. Russell and I became best friends. I did all the early Def Jam videos. I knew I had to do a hundred music videos to practice my craft. Music videos were like another film school to me. I was getting paid to learn. Because in film school, you don't really have all the tools. So I said, "OK, I didn't pay attention in film school to all this type of stuff, so I'm going to learn about every single piece of equipment." And that's what I did.

*How did your first feature film,* Money Talks, *come about?*
BR: Russell had just started the Def Comedy Jam, and I was at the auditions. Out of the hundreds of comedians one of them was Chris Tucker. I said, "This kid is a genius!" And I asked him to be in a music video I did with Heavy D. It was a big video on MTV, and it was the first thing he'd ever done. He went on to *Friday*, and he was about to do *Money Talks*. Chris was like a cult underground comedian, so Mike De Luca gave him a development deal to do *Money Talks*. Mike hired a big commercial director, and a week before production he went to Mike and said, "I can't work with Chris Tucker. He wants to improvise. He wants to change the lines." That's the genius in Chris Tucker! At the end of the meeting, Mike said to the guy, "You're fired." So Chris said, "I remember this cool white boy named Brett Ratner."

And Mike remembered my name because he's very hip to all the hot music directors. He called me in and hired me.

*Were you nervous going into the shoot? You had almost no prep time.*
BR: I had no clue as to what to expect. I had nothing to lose. I was like, "This is my dream." I didn't know what the fuck I was doing. But my instincts turned out to always be right.

*There was never a worry of, "What if I'm making a bomb here?"*
BR: I didn't know what a bomb was! I'd never done a movie. I became more scared as I went. Each time I did a film, it became scarier and scarier. On the set of *Money Talks*, I'm like, "Fuck, this is the greatest time of my life." I always had that fearless attitude.

*How did* Rush Hour *come about?*
BR: Mike De Luca said, "What do you want to do next?" I said, "I want to do a movie with Jackie Chan and Chris Tucker." So I read four or five different scripts that were all buddy cop things. I wanted to do a contemporary version of *Beverly Hills Cop* with *Midnight Run*. Out of all the scripts I found, *Rush Hour* was the best. It was written for Stallone, originally. The idea was to do a movie that was serious in tone but put a comedian in the middle of it. And we crossed the hip-hop and the Asian culture.

*I've heard that you like to watch movies every night while you're shooting a film?*
BR: Yeah. I always do that. It keeps it fresh for me. I tend not to watch movies in the same genre. I watch movies in different genres and there might be a similar scene. I have so many references. That's why Scorsese and Spielberg are so quick on their feet and do such great work—because they have all the references. They've seen what works. I think that's what helps me too. Look, I'm not like De Palma or even Paul Thomas Anderson. I can watch Paul Thomas Anderson's films and tell you in every scene what movie he's taking from. I know those references, but that's kind of blatant stuff that he does because

he wants to show you how he loves those movies. My stuff is sublim-inal. You would never even pick it up, really. It's very subtle stuff.

*In the wake of* Rush Hour, *what conversations with other filmmakers meant a lot to you?*
BR: Warren Beatty called me and said, "It's my favorite film of the year. I have got to meet you." And we became very close friends after that.

*You were going to remake Cassavetes's* Killing of a Chinese Bookie *with Warren, weren't you?*
BR: Yeah. I got cursed out by a lot of friends of mine who were just like, "That's a classic!" It's Paul Thomas Anderson's favorite movie, so to Paul I was the antichrist. Mike De Luca was going to greenlight it, and then I got *The Family Man.* I literally had to beg for that job. They didn't want to hire me. They said I was too young. I wasn't a family man myself. I said, "But I *am* a family man. I'm just not the father in the family. I'm the son in the family." And the way I convinced Nic Cage, I said, "Watch this scene of *Kramer vs. Kramer* where he's making French toast with his son. That's the relationship I want you to have with your little daughter." I gave him references so that he would understand.

*The argument could be made that* Family Man *was your most important work to date. After your first two comedy/action films, this one showed some range.*
BR: It's because of that film that I ended up getting a film like *Red Dragon* or why I was even being offered *Superman.* Fifty years ago a di-rector would go from comedy to drama to romance to westerns to mu-sicals. It didn't matter what genre it was; that was your job. Look at Billy Wilder. But nowadays it's like, "OK, this is who we go to for com-edy. This is who we go to for the action stuff." They put you in a box.

Rush Hour 2 *had a very large budget. Many filmmakers believe that per-haps a smaller budget encourages greater ingenuity. What do you think?*
BR: I agree with that. But you can't make *Rush Hour* on a small bud-get. But yeah, creatively my best work was my work when I was ten years old. (laughs) Because it's about the creative ideas. Films today

are always based on the formula. They don't make movies like *The Long Goodbye* anymore, or *Harold and Maude* or *Being There*, which are full of heart and humanity. People don't die in the end of movies anymore. Warren Beatty died in the end of every one of his movies. Tom Cruise dying at the end of a movie? No way!

*You've worked with a lot of exceptional actors, in particular on* Red Dragon. *How do you work with actors? Do you give line readings?*
BR: Oh, yeah. I got yelled at three times a week on that movie. I always give line readings. I mean, that's a mistake. I'm not an actor. What I do know is what I like and what I don't like. It's my job to rein the actors in and express to them the tone of each scene based on where we've come from and where we're going. And that's what I'm very good at, I think. Because Philip Seymour Hoffman can say the line upside down and it's going to be good, but how does it fit into the puzzle?

*You also have to be able to work with actors who come from different backgrounds and levels of study.*
BR: Yeah. I got yelled at because I would talk to Anthony Hopkins sometimes like I was talking to Jackie Chan. And it's not that Jackie's not smart, it's that I had to speak in a different way to explain it to him. And Anthony Hopkins is looking at me like, "Who are you talking to?" A lot of times the English ones like Ralph [Fiennes] would come in with a preparation. These guys do it two hundred times in the mirror, or whatever their process is. But I completely throw them off. I go, "Guys, we have got to go in the other direction." But they're such good actors, since they're from the theatre, that they can do that. Whereas Edward Norton, probably being used to the laziness of American filmmakers and the confidence in his own memory and skill, won't work as hard on it but will rely on instinctual stuff. So everyone has a different way of working, and they don't all like the way they work together. I have to be the kind of intermediary. What I do have, I think, is an ear for dialogue. I know it when I've got it. And I do whatever I have to do to get it. I've given some of the worst direction ever, but I've gotten the performance.

*It seems like you've made a conscious effort to jump around between different genres thus far.*
BR: The good thing about me is that I've made movies in three or four different genres now. *Family Man* doesn't look like *Rush Hour*. *Red Dragon* doesn't look like *Rush Hour*. *Red Dragon* doesn't look like *Money Talks*. It's like a good record producer makes the artists sound like themselves and doesn't force a sound on them. There are some directors where you see their movies and every movie looks the same, no matter what the genre. It doesn't mean they're not good directors. Michael Bay, whether you like his films or not, I admire that when you see the film, you know it's a Michael Bay film.

*So does part of you want your films to be as identifiable as a Michael Bay film is? Do you want a viewer to immediately know they're watching your work?*
BR: Every film director wishes for that, I think. People see my trailers and they say, "That's a Brett Ratner film, just because of the energy and the humor." I get that all the time: "I knew that was your film when I saw it. I didn't see the opening and then I saw the film and I was like, 'Brett must have directed this film.'" And that's the biggest compliment I can get. That's why Nic Cage agreed to do *Family Man*. He saw *Rush Hour* and he met me and he said, "You're *in* that movie!" But there's no particular shot that you could point to and say, "That's a Brett Ratner film."

*After the Sunset was your first film that didn't succeed from a commercial perspective.*
BR: That was the hardest movie I'd ever done. I was really lost in that film, because I didn't have a clue as to what the tone was. It had four different genres in it. I was like, "Fuck, this is crazy." It's kind of an amalgamation of all these different movies, which is why I was less sure of myself when I was giving the actors directions. It's all about finding the language of the film. I think aside from being a filmmaker, I'm a student of social behavior. I'm in the mix. Yeah, I live in a big house in Beverly Hills, but I'm not sitting there all day long. I'm going

out. I'm interacting with people. I'm not just having lunch meetings at the Ivy. *After the Sunset* wasn't a hit, but I'm not hiding out in a penthouse in Vegas, you know? (laughs)

*You seem to have made an effort thus far in your career to work with people who have more experience than you behind the camera.*
BR: Because I learn from them. When I'm fifty or sixty years old, then *I'm* going to get the young, hip video guy. Now I'm all the hip you need. I want the guy who's made thirty movies. I recognize talent. And I surround myself with the best people because that makes me look better. I know my position. I don't think I'm better than anybody. I know I'm talented. I know what I'm good at and I know what my weaknesses are. I know that I'm young and have a lot more to do. I don't feel like I've arrived. I have so much more to learn. I have so much more to do.

*Do you get final cut on your movies?*
BR: I don't ask for it and, believe it or not, I've never had one frame of my movies changed. My director's cut of *Rush Hour* is ninety minutes. Why do I need final cut? Final cut is for artistes quote unquote— directors whose movies don't make a lot of money. Maybe Scorsese should have final cut because a guy like Harvey Weinstein or a studio might change it to make it a little more accessible or a little more commercial and he has a vision of what he wants it to be. He wants it to be four hours long or whatever.

*Do you worry about losing touch? A lot of the of the great filmmakers of the seventies have been accused of losing whatever it was that made them great to begin with.*
BR: I think a lot of that has to do with final cut. A lot of that has to do with guys that don't have to answer to anybody. They don't have to test the movie. I like sitting in the middle of an audience and seeing how people vibe and how they react and how they respond. That's how I learn from an audience. I'm making movies for an audience, not just for myself.

*Do you think you have a smaller, less mainstream film in you?*
BR: My taste is accessible to what audiences want. Some people just have certain sensibilities, and I'm not going to apologize for mine. I was always envious of Paul Thomas Anderson because he was like, "Oh, me and Jonathan Demme are buddies and me and Kubrick hung out on the set with him with Tom and Nicole." I was jealous of that and I was like, "Shit, I want to be friends with these directors," and I thought I have to make my personal film about someone dying of brain cancer or whatever to get the respect. But then, after *Rush Hour*, when I got calls from Demme and Beatty and Bob Evans and all these guys I'm like, "You know what? Directors aren't snobs." They love a movie no matter what the genre is, if it works. It gave me so much confidence because I was just like, "OK, I don't have to go make *Boogie Nights*."

*Do you think about a legacy for your work?*
BR: I want to be remembered. I want my films to be remembered. Two hundred years from now I want people to say, "Oh, that's what it was like in that era." *Y tu mama tambien* is the only film that has captured what was going on today with the youth. If they pull out *American Pie* and look back, the future's going to think these people were fucking retarded. I want my movies to represent my generation or my era just like *Mean Streets* represented Scorsese's youth.

## THE DIRECTOR'S TAKE
## BRETT RATNER

*What is the first film you ever saw?*
Star Wars

*What is your favorite film of all time?*
Being There

*What's your favorite line in a film?*
"Don't ask me about my business."—Al Pacino, in *The Godfather*

*What movie made you realize that film was an art?*
The Bicycle Thief

*What movie do you consider your guilty pleasure?*
Scarface (1983)

*Who is your favorite movie character of all time?*
Tony Montana

*What's your favorite movie snack food?*
Icee

*Who is your favorite director of all time?*
Roman Polanski

*Who is the most impressive filmmaker working today?*
Clint Eastwood

*What quality do the best directors share?*
A personal style and vision

*Who is your favorite actor or actress of all time?*
John Cazale/Sterling Hayden

*Who is your favorite actor or actress of today?*
Al Pacino

*Who would you cast as yourself in a film about your life?*
Sean Penn

*If you could remake one movie, what would it be?*
The Killing of a Chinese Bookie

*What is your best quality as a director?*
My passion

*What is your greatest weakness as a director?*
My cell phone

*Finish this sentence: I'll never direct a movie about . . .*
what I did last night . . . unless I really need the money.

*Finish this sentence: The perfect movie is . . .*
one that makes me laugh and cry!

*What will they be saying about your work fifty years from now?*
"His movies have definitely gotten better."

*What piece of advice do you have for aspiring filmmakers?*
Never give up.

*What are you as passionate about as moviemaking?*
Movie-watching

# KEVIN SMITH

"Every fucking day I sit there going, 'Oh my God, am I any good at this whatsoever? Is today the day they're going to realize I'm fucking shit at my job?'"

## SELECTED CREDITS

*Clerks* (1994)–writer/director
*Mallrats* (1995)–writer/director
*Chasing Amy* (1997)–writer/director
*Dogma* (1999)–writer/director
*Jay and Silent Bob Strike Back* (2001)–writer/director
*Jersey Girl* (2004)–writer/director
*The Passion of the Clerks* (2006)–writer/director

It is difficult to come up with a filmmaker today who has engendered more loyalty from his fans than Kevin Smith. Perhaps it's because he is a writer and director without a hint of pretension, always quick to knock himself down before anyone else can get a chance. Or perhaps it's because he simply knows of what he writes. In 1994, after all, he created a living, breathing document that spoke to a generation in *Clerks*. Since then, with films like *Chasing Amy*, *Dogma*, and *Jersey Girl*, he's jumped in and out of his so-called view-askew universe of characters, tackling adult issues like sex, religion, and loss without ever apologizing for an obvious love for the profane and scatological. He's also well known for a frankness that is all too rare in Hollywood today. This conversation was no exception.

---

*Can you tell me a little bit about where you were raised in Highlands, New Jersey?*
KS: At one point in an interview in *Time* magazine I was quoted as saying that I was raised in a white-trash town. And boy did they hate that.

*So set the record straight here and now.*
KS: Apparently what I should say is I was raised in a very blue-collar town. Those of us downtown were regarded as white trash and clam diggers because fishing was the big industry. Apparently the uptown folks who raised the red flags about the quote didn't consider themselves white trash at all. I always liked Highlands. It was a really nice place to grow up.

*Your dad worked in the post office. Is that right?*
KS: He was the dude that cancelled your stamps. He was never a letter carrier, which I think he would have enjoyed more.

*Why do you say that?*
KS: He liked being out, actually. When he joined the post office, he was something of a young go-getter, and then the post office just kind

of crushed his spirit. He once told me that when he'd been there for about a month, he was pulled aside by a coworker who was like, "You really have got to slow down and pace yourself. You're making the rest of us look bad." He just hated it, because he wasn't allowed to excel at his job. So an early lesson he instilled in me was that whenever I eventually got a job, it should be something I really enjoyed doing.

*Do you think you take after him in other ways?*
KS: My sister always says that I take after my father. My father later in life became something of a recluse. He didn't want to go out and interact with the world, and that's kind of how I've always felt about the world.

*It's surprising to hear you say that. You seem like such a public person.*
KS: Well, right now I'm sitting in an office with the curtains drawn, so it has a dark cavelike atmosphere. It drives my wife up the fucking wall. Maybe it has something to do with the fact that so often I have to go out and do things in terms of work or Q&As and stuff like that. So when there's downtime, I'm like, "Let's sit at home and draw the curtains and watch a lot of TV." And that was my old man. My sister maintains I stole the Silent Bob character off Dad because he was a dude that never really spoke and then when he did speak, he usually said something that went right to the funny bone.

*What are the first moviegoing experiences that you remember?*
KS: I remember my parents taking me to drive-ins quite a bit, and the first movie I remember seeing was *The Gumball Rally*. It was essentially like *Cannonball Run* without celebrities. It was either that or *The Land That Time Forgot* or *Jaws*. The only real clear memory I have of *The Land That Time Forgot* is I went with my aunt Judy, who wasn't really an aunt but one of those people you call aunt. She had packed up a bunch of peanut-butter sandwiches in tinfoil, and while everyone was watching the movie, I went through every fucking sandwich and ate each one. So about halfway through the film she was like, "Hey, pass up one of those sandwiches." And I was like, "There are no

more." And the whole car freaked out. The whole car looked at me like, "Are you insane? How could you eat five or six sandwiches?" I didn't have much interest in the movie, but really was kind of taken with the notion of eating, which is something I've never been really able to separate myself from.

*You've said before that you think you grew up to do what you do because you grew up overweight?*
KS: Pretty much. I got into trying to be funny because I grew up fat, and you tend to overcompensate when you don't look like everyone else. I did grow up kind of hefty, and because of that I was very aware that I would have to come up with something other than a trim, tight body to attract the opposite sex or also to keep dudes from beating me up.

*And yet that's never been a subject you've really mined in your films.*
KS: Once I saw the movie *Heavy* I figured, "OK, that story's been done." It just seemed to me like that's rather obvious for me, for the fat guy to make the fat-guy movie. I don't know.

*It's telling that the actor you've used most often as your proxy onscreen is Ben Affleck.*
KS: Right, who's very far from heavy. I remember identifying a hell of a lot more with Affleck during *Chasing Amy* when he was a little paunchier and his teeth weren't capped. It's been almost a full decade now of the trim, shapely Affleck, which has been very good for his career but not very good for my self-esteem.

*So going back to your childhood, what was the earliest dream for you of a career?*
KS: I guess the earliest dream would have been writing for *SNL*. And then later on I would trade that dream in for the dream of owning a deli.

*Those two dreams don't usually go hand in hand.*
KS: Well, from high school through the age of twenty I really wanted to write for *SNL*. Before that I always wanted to be a writer, but I

didn't quite know how. I figured, like, maybe I'll wind up working at a newspaper, because the *Asbury Park Press* is something that I could conceive of working for. The idea of writing for TV or movies was just such a foreign notion. After high school I went to college for a semester at the New School for Social Research. There's a bunch of schools within that university, and the school I attended was Eugene Lang. I chose Lang because it billed itself as a writer's school and because it was in New York, which would put me close to Rockefeller Center, which was where *SNL* was made. A lot of times I would just blow off class and go sit in the lobby of 30 Rock and wait to be discovered, which was so stupid. I assumed that one day Lorne Michaels would walk by and be like, "Hey, you look funny. Can you write?" There would be times I would just sit there and kind of cry because I would be like, "Oh my God. I don't know how to accomplish what I want to accomplish." I finally dropped out of Lang after only doing one semester, and I went back to living in Highlands and worked in convenience stores. I had given up on the notion of being a writer and decided, "OK, I know how to make a sandwich." I've worked in convenience stores and delis all my life. The best I could hope for was one day to own a deli. When I dropped out, I figured—

*"That was my best shot and I missed it."*
KS: I missed it, and I should just resign myself to a normal life. It wouldn't be until a few years later, on my twenty-first birthday, when I went to see *Slacker* at the Angelika in New York that film presented itself as an option.

*You saw* Slacker *with your friend Vincent Pereira, right?*
KS: Yeah. He was the first person I'd ever known who talked about wanting to make movies. He worked at Quick Stop. He'd come in at nine at night and stock the milk room and then mop the floors. It took us a few months to actually start talking to each other, and when we did, we bonded over this love of *Twin Peaks*. Vinny was the one that was first like, "Did you ever think about directing?" And I was like, "Well, I didn't ever think about making a movie. I just like to

write." He was like, "The problem with just being a screenwriter is that somebody else controls the material." And that lodged in my mind.

*So what clicked when you saw* Slacker?

KS: *Slacker* had this kind of inspiring effect on me. I viewed that movie with a mixture of awe and arrogance. Awe because I couldn't believe what I was seeing. It opened a whole new world to me. It was the first independent film I'd seen. And arrogance because I was like, "Oh my God, if this counts, I could do this. I could make one of these." So when we're driving home from the theater that night I remember saying to Vincent, "I'm going to be a filmmaker. I think I would want to make a film." So I started looking into film schools, but they were all too expensive and too long. At this point in my life I'm twenty-one; I just want to do it! I don't want to sit around and talk about doing it. I just want to throw myself into the process and learn while doing. So that ruled out places like Tisch or USC or UCLA. So it was in the *Village Voice* that I found this ad for the Vancouver Film School, which had a 1-800 number. I figured, all right, it's eight months long; it's not a degree program, but that's cool because they're going to put equipment in my hands. I'm actually going to get to make a film and it's only going to cost me nine grand, which is way less than even one year of film school elsewhere. So I applied and was delighted to find out I got in, but when I got there I realized they let every applicant in. I went for about four months before I was like, "Fuck this," because it was a lot of theory and there wasn't a lot of hands-on stuff. I started talking to the front office and I was like, "If I drop out, do I get my tuition back?" And they told me, "If you drop out by this Tuesday, you get half of your tuition back." I knew it was a big deal dropping out, because at home everyone would be like, "Oh, fucking big shit said he was going to film school and then he fucking dropped out." And my parents would be like, "There's yet another thing that Kevin quit." But internally I was like, "This is a good idea because I'm going to take that money I'm going to save and I'm going to sink it into a feature." I'd met Scott Mosier, my producer, at Vancouver. So I said, "Look, man, whichever of us comes up with a script first, the other one will help that person go out and shoot their movie." And he was like, "Oh, absolutely. Sounds like a good idea."

*What did your parents say when you told them your plan to make a film?*
KS: My parents, to their credit, were never like, "What are you, fucking stupid?" But they were puzzled because it's not like we had somebody in our family who was in entertainment in any way, shape, or form. It was as if I'd said to them, "I'm going to go discover the nineteenth dimension." It was a foreign fucking notion to them. They were like, "OK. Good luck with that. We support you, but if it doesn't work out, go get a real job." My mother was like, "Your brother's a waiter; why don't you go be a waiter?" But to their credit, they never tried to dissuade me. And then, when we finally got around to making *Clerks*, we were doing it on credit cards and renting the camera package was going to be about a thousand dollars a week. So for the three-week shoot it was going to be three thousand dollars and they wouldn't take credit cards. So I went to my parents and I was like, "Look, I need three thousand dollars cash to rent from this place." My old man, my mother told me, never made more than, like, thirty grand a year. So for my parents to say, "OK, we can lend you the three thousand dollars," that was everything they fucking had. So it was really kind of a beautiful and big gesture that I never appreciated until later on in life when I found out we were as broke as we were.

*Did you have any fear during the making of* Clerks?
KS: Never any fear. That's the weird thing. The fear didn't kick in until the first screening at the Angelika. Up until that point it was all passion. At that first screening at the IFFM [International Feature Film Market], it felt like, "Oh my God, this is it." We worked this hard to get here and nothing was going to happen to this movie. That's when I started breaking down. I was like, "Why's everyone cursing? Everyone curses so much in this fucking movie. And it looks terrible! Why'd we go black-and-white?" I had a really hard-core panic attack for about ten minutes in that nearly empty theater.

*If the IFFM screening was the low point, was the high point when Harvey Weinstein said he wanted to buy* Clerks?
KS: Absolutely. That was definitely the high point. We went to Sundance with the assumption that it's dead. Nobody's going to buy this movie. But it didn't matter, because we'd been selected and I felt like, "Wow, the ball is rolling. It will be easier to make another movie next time." I could show them this movie, say we'd gotten into Sundance, and find financing for the next flick. So just getting into Sundance was the high point until Harvey bought the fucking movie.

*In retrospect, how much does* Clerks *feel like it was simply a case of the right film at the right time?*
KS: *Clerks* definitely was right film, right time. That's all that movie is to me at this point. I mean, the movie of course means the world to me, but I look at it and I don't go, "Man, you can fucking feel the talent burning." It was just like we said something about being a twenty-something slacker when everybody was curious about what it was like to be a twenty-something slacker. A year later, nobody would give a fuck. That movie is very much me in a nutshell at that point in my life and, ironically, it's me in a nutshell at this point in my life. I am still one of the laziest people, which is ironic because I tend to do a lot of things but ultimately, given my druthers, I would do nothing. I always look for the easiest way out. It's one of the reasons I don't want to make a big action movie. It's too much work. It's just much easier for me to write people talking and shoot that.

*With the success of* Clerks, *did it feel like you'd arrived? Did it feel like, "Now this is my life; I'm a filmmaker"?*
KS: The weird thing that happened is how quickly you slip into the new role that is your career. Film went from something that I wanted to do to it becoming my career overnight! And the transition happened so seamlessly that it was almost as if I'd been doing it forever. It was kind of creepy, like Nicholson in *The Shining* where Grady tells him, "You've always been here." It's one of those things where you hit the ground running. So we immediately set about making another

movie as quickly as possible. And that's what it's been like with every movie since. I still have that fear in me that the moment we stop—

*They'll forget about you?*
KS: Yeah. They'll forget, or it won't be as easy to make another movie. You're like, "I don't want to give them time to think, because with enough time they'll be like, 'What the fuck are we funding this idiot for?'" I remember reading a review in *The Washington Post* of *Chasing Amy* where this dickhead wrote, like, "I can't believe Miramax continues to fund this person. If you see the words 'film by Kevin Smith' written large on the screen, run, don't walk from the theater.'" At the time I was fucking devastated by it. It played on my insecurity. I was like, "What if he's right? What if Miramax reads this review and goes, 'Yeah, fuck this Kevin Smith guy!'"

*Do you think your work is ever overrated?*
KS: Some people will say, "Oh, he's overrated." And they're probably right to a large degree. To other people I'm incredibly underrated. And the truth is it's probably somewhere in between. I know I've gotten far more breaks than most people, and it's simply based on sheer goodwill and likability. I've never been a real prick, so they let shit slide. Look how much shit they let slide on our first movie. Our first movie looks terrible, and yet people let it slide because they liked the jokes and they kind of liked the idea of it. I've got a lot of people out there rooting for me not because they necessarily believe in me as an artist, but just because they like me. I'm not one of these people who's like, "I am a born filmmaker and my legacy is fucking resolute." Every fucking day I sit there going, "Oh my God. Am I any good at this whatsoever? Have I just been cruising by on nothing but goodwill? Is today the day they're going to realize I'm fucking shit at my job?" I've always kept my budgets kind of low, so that helps. I've never been like, "Give me $80 million because I have got to make my fucking dream film." The fact that I've always been able to return on the investment of what we've done helps a lot. Because at the end of the day, I assure you, no matter how much goodwill people have for you, if you don't

make any money, they don't fucking want to know you. Does it mean the world has embraced our shit? No. But enough people have embraced our shit that it's enabled me to continue going.

*Mallrats was the first time you had to work in collaboration with a studio.*
KS: Yeah. That was an interesting process. I really wasn't prepared for people telling me, "You've never made a movie, so we're going to tell you how to do it."

*Do you think you were too much of a pushover at that point, that you didn't hold your ground enough?*
KS: Absolutely. I wish to God I'd had a little more stones at that point, but I was so terrified that they'd kick us out of the fucking moviemaking club or some shit. I remember talking to Nina Jacobson, who was working at Universal at the time, about cutting out the scene of boys sitting around talking about scars they've gotten from eating pussy, which was a scene that was later put in *Chasing Amy*. And Nina was like, "You know, Kevin, it's not like anyone's trying to hammer out your originality. Don't you want your film to be seen by the widest possible audience? How is that a bad thing?" And I was like, "I guess it isn't." They win you over that way. It wasn't her going, "Surprise! You've come to the dark side!" It was just her making the studio's point of view evident. At the end of the day, they're just in it as a business. That's what they do for a living. They make movies. Of course studios want to reach the widest possible audience. They don't want to make movies like I do. I wanted to make movies for me first and my friends second and if anyone else liked it, great.

*How would you respond today to the kinds of things Nina said to you back then?*
KS: I'd be like, "I appreciate that, but then I guess we shouldn't be working together." On *Jersey Girl* I had to actually listen to studio notes and Harvey, but it wasn't that bad, because I knew it was coming from a guy who ain't fucking corporate. But at the same time we

had a problematic movie on our hands—a movie that featured two people that the world couldn't care a fuck less about at that point. So we had to make it more palatable to the fucking masses, otherwise the studio was afraid it was going to be seen as *Gigli 2*. So there were changes made on the movie. Having gone through that with *Jersey Girl*, it made it like I never want to go through this shit again. I don't want to work with fucking really famous people. It got me to a point where I was like, "I don't want to fucking work with a lot of money, because that means that the studio is going to make you do whatever you can to make it more palatable to the masses." It's why I eventually wound up walking away from *Green Hornet*. Because after *Jersey Girl*, the notion of working on this movie that would never be my movie but was made to sell action figures or to play multiple times to the same popcorn-eating audience over the summer where it was just going to get trashed by fucking critics for being yet another comic-book movie . . . none of that seemed appealing to me. So I was just like, "Run, don't walk, from that idea."

*You say the experience of* Jersey Girl *made you walk away from* Green Hornet. *Each of your films seems like a reaction to the one you've just completed.*

KS: Very much so. I'm kind of a reactionary filmmaker. *Chasing Amy* was definitely a reaction to *Mallrats*. *Jay and Silent Bob Strike Back* was a reaction to the process of releasing *Dogma*, which was so hellish with all the protests and hate mail and death threats. I just wanted to make a movie that went down smooth. Then with *Jersey Girl*, I'm thinking, "There's nobody that can protest *this*." Little did I know that the protesters wouldn't be people who were protesting the movie as much as the cast of the movie. And *Clerks 2* is definitely a reaction to having gone through the process of making a $35 million movie and watching it not reach $35 million theatrically. I felt like because of what I went through on it I wanted to go and do something where I didn't have to worry about a budget or making a bunch of money back or a cast.

*How much do you agonize over your film's box-office prospects? All of your films seem to top out at making $30 million domestically.*
KS: I always have this fear that *Fletch Won* is the movie that breaks through and does like $100 million in business. It would break my heart a little bit, because it ain't mine. I'm very elated and still amazed in this day and age that there's still $30 million worth of interest in one of my stupid ideas, but at the same time if I'm going to make a movie that really breaks through and crosses into the mainstream—

*You want it to be yours.*
KS: Yeah. I always thought the closest we would get would be *Jersey Girl*. So there's a part of me that's like, "Wow, if *Fletch* is the one that really breaks through, I'm going to have mixed feelings about it." It would be kind of like how did Gus Van Sant feel when *Good Will* broke through? Don't get me wrong, I love *Good Will Hunting*, but I wonder if there are days when he's like, "Why'd it have to be that one?"

*After* Mallrats *bombed did you feel like your career was in jeopardy?*
KS: The career didn't feel like it was in jeopardy after *Mallrats*. The career felt like it was just flat-out dead. The reviews were so bad and it just made no noise. There were no calls coming in after that. I remember the morning after the opening night we were just completely in the dumps. And the worst part about it was that Monday I was supposed to go to Boston College. I had agreed to go out there and speak. So me and Mosier drove to Boston and gave perhaps the most depressed, blue lecture of all time. We were just, "What's the point? Don't bother trying. You'll only fail."

*How did* Chasing Amy *start for you?*
KS: *Chasing Amy* kind of started while we were in post on *Mallrats* in the early days of my relationship with Joey [Lauren Adams]. It really started idea as an idea about a guy who falls in love with a lesbian. Mosier and I had met and started hanging out with the girls who

made *Go Fish* at Sundance. Gwen Turner and Scott in particular hung out and hit it off. And it was clear that Scott was kind of smitten with her, but things weren't going to go very far, so I suggested to Scott that he should write a movie about falling in love with a lesbian and how fucking fruitless it is. And after I kept bugging him about doing it for like a month or so and he didn't show any interest in it, I was like, "Fuck it. I'm doing it." Also at this time Joey and I were getting deeper into our relationship and I started to feel really insecure about the amount of experience Joey had in terms of not so much dating, but fucking. And we would get into fights about that because I didn't know how to deal with it. So yes, *Chasing Amy* is a movie about a guy who falls in love with a lesbian, but really the problem is that he's more hung up by the fact that she's had sex with [other] guys than the fact that she has sex with girls. So I started writing it as kind of therapy for the relationship.

*The case could be made that* Chasing Amy *was the most important film for your career.*
KS: The credibility that movie afforded me was insane. *Mallrats* did its very best to erase any credibility I'd garnered with *Clerks*. There are many who'd gone before me who were fucking ruined by the sophomore slump.

*With all your speaking engagements and activity on the Internet, you might be one of, if not the most, accessible filmmakers in history.*
KS: I've always felt like I am not the most successful filmmaker, but I'm definitely the most accessible filmmaker. Some people are like, "Aren't you worried about having stalkers and shit?" I'm like, "You can't have a stalker if you're as accessible as I am. Stalking is about people who aren't accessible. You can see me at a college Q&A. You can find me on the Internet. You can always find me." That's been a big part of my success. I spend a lot of time on the Web, and if film enthusiasts feel like they can talk to you, you create this kind of Internet family. I always feel like that's helped grow the fan base.

*There's also a loyalty your fans have to you that is very strong. They feel like you're one of them.*
KS: Totally. They feel, and rightfully so, that you're one of them who's just kind of made it to the other side of the fence.

*Does your interaction with fans inform the work?*
KS: It really gives me instant feedback, which is phenomenal. Before the Internet all you really had to go on were reviews and box office. Post-Internet it was like, "Wait a sec, I can finally figure out what people who buy tickets think about the movie," because you could jump in there and pretty much learn about what they thought right away.

*You were talking once about John Hughes saying that perhaps he can't tell any more stories of youth because he may have outgrown them. Do you think that may be the case for you? Does* Jersey Girl *represent the beginning of a new stage for you?*
KS: I don't know if it represents the beginning of the trend of, like, I can't tell stories about youth, but maybe it does. Because when I think about the *Clerks* 2 script, it's really not about being young. It's about what happens when you can't be young anymore. What happens to the angry young man when he turns thirty-two? The shit that used to work for you doesn't really work anymore, and you have to figure out a new way to be and interact with the world.

*Do you worry about falling into the habit of making films for the wrong reasons? Do you think audiences will notice if it happens?*
KS: I think the way you would recognize a big change is me making a lot of money doing stuff that I'm obviously not that comfortable with. There're people who will say the worst thing is to be a sellout. Well, did you like *Clerks?* Because I sold out in that movie. Somebody bought it and put it in the theater and that, technically, is selling out. But there's selling out and there's selling out. There's doing movies purely for the paycheck.

*I would think you've had many opportunities to do that. Any close calls?*
KS: I came very close to directing a movie that I didn't write and orig-inate. It was going to be with Ben. And it was this movie we were go-ing to do after *Jersey Girl* called *Ghosts of Girlfriends Past*. It was yet another variation on *A Christmas Carol*, and it was Ben playing a char-acter who's going to a friend's wedding and he fucking gets visited by three ex-girlfriends in the night who show him the error of his ways and blah, blah, blah. Could I have been matched up with that mate-rial pretty well? Sure. Was I doing it because I was like, "Man, this is a story that must be told and I really believe in this?" No. It was me doing it because Ben was like, "Let's do it together. It'll be fun." It didn't come to pass, thankfully, but that was the closest I came.

*Do you envision a scenario where you're accepting an Oscar one day?*
KS: Never. I don't think it'll ever happen. I just don't work in the same way that the Academy seems to like to work.

*I assume that doesn't keep you up at night?*
KS: Not in a million years. You know, what would bother me a lot more is if one day I woke up and the fan base wasn't there anymore. That to me is the fucking award, and I know that sounds fucking corny to say, but I find it far more rewarding to know that I can jump onto the board in the morning and find a bunch of people who fuck-ing love our stuff. Who cares if a bunch of people in film like what I do? Most of those cats see the shit you do for free at premieres and whatnot. It's much more rewarding to me that the person who's not in film, who can't fucking see this shit for free, takes part of their hard-earned fucking buck for that week and blows it on something you've created. That's far more rewarding for me.

## THE DIRECTOR'S TAKE
## KEVIN SMITH

*What is the first film you ever saw?*
It's either *The Gumball Rally* or *Jaws*.

*What is your favorite film of all time?*
*Jaws, JFK, A Man for All Seasons, Do the Right Thing, The Last Temptation of Christ*

*What's your favorite line in a film?*
"One dog goes one way, the other dog goes the other way, and this guy's sayin' 'Whadda ya want from me?'"—Joe Pesci in *Goodfellas*

*What movie made you realize that film was an art?*
Hal Hartley's *Trust*. It feels like a painting that talks.

*What movie do you consider your guilty pleasure?*
*Mystery Men*

*Who is your favorite movie character of all time?*
The one I most identify with is Holden McNeil from *Chasing Amy*.

*What's your favorite movie snack food?*
Chocolate-chip cookies.

*Who is your favorite director of all time?*
Quentin Tarantino

*Who is the most impressive filmmaker working today?*
Quentin Tarantino

*What quality do the best directors share?*
A sense of how the world should be

*Who is your favorite actor or actress of all time?*
Ben Affleck

*Who is your favorite actor or actress of today?*
Ben Affleck

*Who would you cast as yourself in a film about your life?*
Affleck. He would have to put on some weight, though.

*If you could remake one movie, what would it be?*
*A Man for All Seasons*, but I would never do it, because it was so perfect the first time.

*What is your best quality as a director?*
It's always handy to have a director who can give you new lines on the set.

*What is your greatest weakness as a director?*
I'm not as interested in visual storytelling as I should be.

*Finish this sentence: I'll never direct a movie with . . .*
a huge cock in my pants. That's the only "never" I can think of. I know
I'll never direct a movie while sporting a huge cock.

*Finish this sentence: The perfect movie is . . .*
one that I can watch back to back to back for a week straight.

*What will they be saying about your work fifty years from now?*
"Kevin who?"

*What piece of advice do you have for aspiring filmmakers?*
Never write or direct anything that you are not interested in yourself.
Never be afraid to lay yourself bare on the canvas.

*What are you as passionate about as moviemaking?*
Fucking my wife

# CHRIS & PAUL WEITZ

"We were thinking about directing only in the way that you think about dating one of the models in one of the *Sports Illustrated* swimsuit issues. It was a nice idea, but to get there seemed completely implausible."—Paul Weitz

## SELECTED CREDITS

*Antz* (1998)–Chris & Paul, cowriters
*American Pie* (1999)–Chris: producer, Paul: director
*Down to Earth* (2000)–Chris & Paul: codirectors
*About a Boy* (2002)–Chris & Paul: cowriters/codirectors
*In Good Company* (2004)–Chris: producer, Paul:
writer/director/producer
*American Dreamz* (2006)–Chris: producer, Paul:
writer/director/producer

Making movies was never the plan for Chris and Paul Weitz. That's something of a surprise, considering their lineage. Their grandmother, Lupita Tovar, was a famed Mexican actress, their mother, Susan Kohner, an Academy Award–nominated actress in films like *Imitation of Life*. Yet, to hear them tell it, these brothers virtually fell into the business. One was a struggling playwright, the other on a path to the State Department. Yet once they began collaborating, film emerged as the destination for both. Paul is the elder by three years. Otherwise, they're pretty much in sync, as evidenced by the cohesive vision on display in films like *American Pie* and *About a Boy*. While those two films wouldn't seem to have much in common, it is clear both are preoccupied with the challenges of being a "good man" today. It's no wonder, since their father was such an intriguing man himself.

---

*Your father, John Weitz, was a pretty fascinating man.*
CW: He was a pretty extraordinary guy with no ties to Hollywood whatsoever. He had this kind of amazing World War II experience. He was born in Germany in 1923. He moved to London in 1933 when Hitler came to power; emigrated to the U.S., I think in '39; joined the army and was recruited into the OSS and had extraordinary undercover experiences toward the end of the war. And then subsequently he became a fashion designer.

*He was a very successful one too. In fact, he was something of a celebrity.*
CW: I guess he and Bill Blass and Geoffrey Beene were the American designers in the 1950s who sort of set the style of men's style. They became licensable names.

*He had so many interests, from fashion to racecar driving. What do you think you inherited from him?*
CW: Actually, it's funny. I think the flaw that he passed down to me is that I get bored really easily.
PW: I got different flaws. (laughs) I take things overly personally. There's some terrific German word he used in his biography of

Hitler's banker, the essence of which is "He had a great degree of 'here I am.'" Meaning that it was deeply important to throw himself out there, whether or not he was going to get hit on the chin. I don't actually think it's a flaw, but sometimes it can manifest itself in less than savory ways.

*What did he make of your film careers?*
CW: He loved it. He had a German sense of humor, which is very sort of bawdy and scatological, so I think he genuinely enjoyed *American Pie*. He was really proud and supportive, and I'm sure he was relieved too.
PW: He was more relieved on my part because I'm older and it took me longer to make a living. He was just extremely relieved that we were able to fare for ourselves.

*What did each of you imagine you'd end up doing with your lives when you were young?*
CW: I didn't really have an idea. I guess I could have imagined being, like, an English professor but that would have been terrible.
PW: I remember you were going to be a diplomat, right?
CW: Yeah, I almost became a diplomat. I almost went into the State Department.

*What about you, Paul? Was there anything you dreamed of becoming when you were a kid?*
PW: Umm . . .
CW: Drug dealer? (both laugh)
PW: I would say drug dealer, yeah. I would say an actor, then a drug dealer, then maybe bum off my dad for the rest of my life until I realized that was not particularly attractive to women. (laughs) And then the only other thing I could imagine besides doing what I'm doing was to be a teacher.

*Did any films have a big impact on either of you growing up?*
CW: *Star Wars* changed everything for me. We were driving to see it and I was pissing in my pants with excitement and my brother

was being kind of mentally sadistic. I didn't really know what it was about, and he told me it was a documentary of a debate between two astronomers. It was really just a big intellectual argument. (laughs)

*Paul, does that story ring a bell?*
PW: (laughs) Yeah, sounds about right. I also remember convincing Chris that it would be fun to team up shoplifting in the local bookstores. We would go in there with our book bags and then fit as many books in as possible. This is when Chris is maybe six. And then we would come home and add up the face value of all the books we'd stolen and sort of compete with ourselves.
CW: They were secondhand books, though.
PW: It was a lifelong love of reading.

*Did you have a camera around, growing up? Did you make any movies?*
CW: Absolutely not. We didn't have that childhood of making short films. We weren't driven to express ourselves in film. It all seemed to happen pretty much accidentally. I think we ended up as directors largely to protect our scripts, just to get as much control over it as possible.
PW: I guess the earliest thing I did was I wrote a play my mom sent to this thing called the Young Playwrights Competition. It got into the semifinals or something, and I got a one-day performance at a theater and my dad got a limo and took me and a bunch of my friends to it. Then in the middle of the play he was horrified to realize that the play was a parody of him.

*You hadn't bothered to mention this to him beforehand?*
PW: I hadn't. And he had a bunch of friends there, and it was really awful because it was an unfair parody. I remember him coming home late to dinner that night and at the table he was steaming, saying, "This is obviously what he thinks of me" and my mom saying, "No, darling. It's just a play." (laughs) So it had a rocky beginning, the whole writing thing.

*Paul, you were writing plays for a while in New York before you teamed up with your brother.*
PW: Yeah. I managed to get an agent in New York and then I managed to not find any work for about four or five years (laughs).

*Through the agent's fault or your own or just circumstance?*
PW: Completely not through the agent's fault. I was trying to get into a training program for writing soap operas.
CW: (laughs) I don't remember that! That's crazy.
PW: It is. I didn't get in. My agent told me it was "a piss-pot full of money." That was her quote. And unfortunately I didn't get in.

*So the dream was to get a writing gig on* Days of Our Lives?
PW: Yes, exactly. If you were an unsuccessful playwright in New York, this was one of your hopes—to pay your rent. Our dad was desperate for me to get a real job, but he felt like it would be too bourgeois to actually kick me in the ass and say, "Get a job" or, "I'm not going to help you out anymore." The thing is that Chris was younger, so he had less time to be unemployed.
CW: That's true, actually.

*Chris, you went to school in England for much of your education. You got your bachelor's and master's from Cambridge?*
CW: Yeah. I stayed through college at Cambridge and the master's degree actually they throw in two years after you leave Cambridge, provided you haven't committed a felony. It's kind of like a bonus for good behavior. You can really rack up the degrees there.

*Did you have any idea what you were going to do?*
CW: No. I didn't. It's a point of pride there that you don't do anything that would be considered vocational, with the result that you're left very confused at the end, with this weird arrogance that is associated with being at Cambridge but with no marketable skills.

*Did you have anxiety about not knowing what to do?*
CW: Tremendous anxiety. I worked for a freelance journalist for a while but really never got it together enough to be steadily employed. If it hadn't been for my brother, God knows what would have happened.

*What was the first thing you guys collaborated on?*
CW: Well, the first thing we successfully collaborated on was this screenplay, *Legit*, about porn actors trying to make an art film.
PW: I was probably about twenty-five.
CW: Yeah, I was twenty-one.

*How did screenwriting emerge as something for you two to try?*
PW: Well, I had been dumped by a girl probably partly because I was just bumming off of my dad. I had a couple of jobs, one of which was writing algebra videos, and I decided that a way to make a living was to write screenplays. I wrote *Legit* with Chris, and I wrote a romantic comedy on my own. The romantic comedy was pretty bad, and *Legit* was pretty funny. We pitched an idea called *Karma Cops*. It was about a nonviolent Hindu cop from New Delhi who teams with a tough New York cop and MGM paid us guild minimum for it, which was complete manna from heaven. It was like the greatest thing that ever happened.

*You worked for a long time before you started to get actual credits on films.*
CW: It was seven years before we got our first screen credit. But in the meantime we had been rewriting other people's stuff and writing our own things, plugging away.
PW: We were plankton-eaters for a long time.

*Was all the rewrite work you were doing rewarding?*
PW: The getting paid part was truly thrilling. I think I knew, more than Chris, that it was a distinct possibility to write a heck of a lot and not get paid, so I was determined to be the hardest-working guy in showbiz.

*Your first credit came for cowriting* Antz. *How did that come about?*

PW: It was DreamWorks' first animated movie, and the only reason we got into that meeting was that it was grade-D writers who were being considered. A meeting was set up with Jeffrey Katzenberg and we came in and said, "We're really quick, and we know how to do this," and pitched him a bunch of ideas and he sort of laughingly said, "What are you doing for the next three years of your life?" We thought he was kidding, but it turns out it was actually true.

CW: Writing for animation is kind of this war of attrition. It's really hard work.

PW: Also, watching Katzenberg gave us some good lessons about directing in that he was on top of every detail but at the same time he was really good at giving credit to other people when they had done a good job. And you would see him calculating which arguments were worth standing your ground on. He would give on a small point in order to get something that was more important to him, which I think is a good lesson about directing.

*By this time were you thinking about directing a project of your own?*

PW: I think we were thinking about directing only in the way that you think about dating one of the models in one of the *Sports Illustrated* swimsuit issues. It was a nice idea, but to get there seemed completely implausible.

*And yet it wasn't long after that* American Pie *came your way.*

PW: We were assuming that we were going to have to do something indie first.

CW: We were surprised that they brought us in to meet as directors. And then, once we got the meeting, one thing I distinctly remember is lying to them about having directed theatre. I sort of figured that they were not going to check up on me if I said that I had directed theatre in New York.

*Did you come close to landing projects to direct before* American Pie?
PW: There was a *Wonderful World of Disney* movie that we missed out on.
CW: Thank God! It was *Angels in the Endzone.*

*What did you respond to in the script for* American Pie?
CW: It was really funny and actually quite heartfelt. It's not the kind of movie that we watched at all, but it had some heart to it and some great set pieces.
PW: I remember sitting in Chinatown in San Francisco, reading through the script for the second time, and I think that we actually kind of knew the direction that we wanted to take, which was to make it more palatable for girls. Also I felt like it was something that would not be hurt by being shot unpretentiously. I instinctually felt that we were probably not visual geniuses at that point, and a lot of first-time film directors make a mistake in trying to be stylistically bold.

*Was there any awkwardness shooting the nudity in the film?*
PW: It was awkward because Chris would show up nude. (laughs) I think that we didn't really believe until the last moment that Shannon Elizabeth had read the part of the script where she was naked. I think we suspected that at the last moment we would say, "Yeah, and then you take your robe off and you're naked," and she would balk at it, whereas she was completely ready to do it.

*Because you were making a relatively low-budget studio film, were you pretty much left on your own?*
CW: We were sort of under the radar. And then we had this insane test screening that was really, for us, unprecedented. It's the only time we've ever done that well in a test screening. We had the perfect audience, who thought it was just the greatest film ever made. That's because they were fourteen. It was like crack for these kids.

*Even though you codirected it, the Guild wouldn't let you share the credit. How was it decided Paul would get the director credit? Was there a coin flip?*
CW: No. It was seniority. (both laugh)
PW: Yeah, plus Chris knew that I was the less secure of the two of us.

*The film came to be lumped in with other films, like* There's Something About Mary, *as gross-out movies, accused of lowering the bar on humor. What did you make of that conversation?*
PW: It was interesting, because it came out right after the Columbine murders and there was this hue and cry about kids getting into R-rated movies when they were too young for it. And it was really interesting to see the degree in which society lumps in sex with violence and what a blind eye they turn to violence in film. Suddenly *American Pie* was part of a larger societal discussion, which actually was great. I don't think that being lumped in as a gross-out movie ever bothered me actually. I didn't give a damn. I think the film was more subversive because it was sweet.

*The film was hugely successful. Did you suddenly find yourselves being treated differently?*
CW: Afterwards we thought it was sort of routine to have a movie that grossed $100 million, which really disappointed us when our next movie didn't. It was this kind of bizarre, surreal experience when suddenly I remember we were invited to a lot of parties we had no business being in. But we were pretty much offered the same kind of stuff as *American Pie* after that, because people feel more comfortable with you as a bankable commodity with something you've done before.
PW: I remember one of the producers of *American Pie* coming in very excited and saying, "Hey, guys, I have a film to offer you; you're gonna love it. It's called *Chick Masters.*" Things did change overnight for me, because someone having a manic episode broke into my apartment and it terrified me so much that I ended up moving within two days of the film's release. They had a delusion that I was running a pornogra-

phy ring. (both laugh) I'm not kidding. I remember this person inside the apartment, ranting and raving, and having a delivery guy arrive at my house with a congratulatory basket for the film opening and trying to tell him not to go inside the house because there was somebody crazy in there.

*You followed up* American Pie *with a retelling of* Heaven Can Wait *in* Down to Earth. *It's not considered your best work.*
CW: I think in retrospect it's very difficult to remake a beloved film and distinguish yourself. It's much better to remake a bad movie. Chris Rock wanted to make a very sweet romantic comedy, and we probably wanted something more edgy from him. So I don't think any of us were working at the top of our abilities. That's why we sort of sleepwalked through that one, not that we weren't trying hard. We just approached it as business as usual and didn't shake ourselves up in terms of thinking of doing things differently, which is probably what we should have done.
PW: That movie would have been helped if we had brought a degree of visual inventiveness to it.
CW: We should have been more pretentious on the second one. When we did *About a Boy* afterwards, we felt we had every reason to kind of let it all hang out and do something totally different and mess around with the camera a lot more.

*So by the time you filmed* About a Boy *you realized it was now or never.*
CW: I think we felt that we got such a hard kick in the ass from *Down to Earth* that we had nothing to lose. I can remember there were specific shots on *About a Boy* where we had our initial plan and then we had a bail-out position of shooting them more conventionally and then being on set and saying, "Screw the bail-out position; let's just live or die with this."

*You wrote the film to Badly Drawn Boy. Do you always write to music?*
PW: For me it's really important in almost like a Pavlov's dog way. The most terrifying moment in writing is the moment of sitting down and

beginning. So if I put on a particular piece of music it almost tricks me into thinking, "It's time to write."

*Do you play music on the set for your actors?*
PW: No. I think only Cameron Crowe can get away with it.

*You were both nominated for an Oscar for the screenplay. What do you remember from that experience?*
PW: The whole thing is a cringing experience. It's one of those moments when you have no control. You go from making a film where you have the illusion of control to experiences which are more or less humiliating because they bring out the worst aspects of you. And it was almost immediately after the invasion of Iraq.
CW: That totally spoiled it for us. (both laugh)
PW: So not only was there the slight feeling that the Kodak Theater was going to be blown up [by terrorists], but there was also the slight feeling that everyone involved there was in some macabre dance of death.

*Has the system for how you've worked together, particularly in the writing process, changed over the years?*
CW: It varies. I'm not sure we've figured out the ideal way to work together. In terms of writing, we've gone from sitting in the same room for hours at a time to working more separately. I think Paul is probably more disciplined about things, and I tend to procrastinate more and do things quickly at the last moment.
PW: I think there's two ways to allay one's natural fears about writing: One is to just sort of hope that the gods will descend, and the other way is to try to be a banker about it and sit there regardless of whether you feel particularly inspired or not. And while the banker looks like he's doing more work, I've noticed that Chris actually gets down to it more easily than I sometimes. But I do think that, in terms of collaboration it's all to do with prep, and aside from that, just respecting what the other guy does. It's very fun for me, when we're working on something together, to look at the new pages that Chris has done, because it's all stuff that I generally find very good and very funny.

*And hopefully it inspires your creative end?*

PW: It's more like I'm thinking, "Oh, good, I don't have to do that." It's also just fun. Unfortunately we've both noticed that the things that crack us up about each other's writing are misspellings. There's nothing that will make us laugh like a good typo.

*What about in terms of story sensibilities? Are you pretty much on the same page?*

CW: I think we're wired pretty similarly for comedy. Part of the reason I didn't codirect with Paul on *In Good Company* was that it was a subject and themes that were very important to him at the time, and I was more attracted to doing a different kind of movie.

*Coming out of* About a Boy, *you wanted to do something on a much larger scale and for a while you were going to direct a big-budget film based on the fantasy series* His Dark Materials.

CW: Yeah, I think that probably Paul thinks about contributing to a body of work piece by piece, whereas I am always thinking that the next movie is going to be the last movie for me because I find it to be a kind of exhausting process. I wanted to bite off as much as I could chew. It was probably a bit more than I could chew.

*Do you regret leaving it now?*

CW: Sometimes I definitely do, because those books are incredibly important to me. I think the lesson is that a movie of that kind, which is sort of a CGI epic, is incredibly difficult to make, and you need a certain form of mania and insanity to make it. I gradually realized that I was going to have to convert myself into an obsessive-compulsive person to get it done. And I was also realizing that it was going to be a matter of two to three years, which is a different order of magnitude from anything we've done before. If I were in a different place in my life, then that might be something I could contemplate. It would essentially mean that I wouldn't have a life for two to three years, and I wasn't ready to do that.

*Paul, you seem to be in a different place than Chris, being a husband and now a father. It seems like that had to inform* In Good Company.

PW: There is the father-daughter relationship that's at the core. I like to learn things when I'm writing something, because you have to empathize with the characters and you have to try to listen to them and there were a couple of areas there that I wanted to learn about. I wanted to project myself into what it might be like to try to be a good person in the thick of being middle-aged. And then the other character, Topher Grace's character, is very work obsessed and able to hide an emotional life by achieving certain things, such as having a beautiful wife or having a certain career track or buying a Porsche, and I could identify with that guy as well. So, to some degree, that part of the movie was me trying to make sense of myself in what I'd been like when I was a bit younger. But what was also interesting to me was that it was a realistic story. I felt, for instance, there was a certain point where I was tempted to have Dennis Quaid's character sabotage the younger character because that would add more drama.

*According to filmmaking doctrine it seems almost like that's what the character is supposed to do.*

PW: Exactly. In order to dramatize, or to have a sort of fake act one or act two swing but I thought, "Well, the character wouldn't do that." And I ended up, sort of consciously, opting for realism more than basing it on another movie.

*Most of your films have dealt with, in one way or another, the difficulties of trying to be a "good man" in today's society. Is that a theme you've been surprised to see emerge again and again?*

PW: Well, to me that's funny because it's definitely the central theme of a few of the films, certainly *American Pie*. But I think now it's bothersome to me that it's so clearly a theme. It's muddying the waters, because if you are working on a theme, you don't necessarily want to think about it. You should be dealing with it primarily on a subconscious level.

*Is it important to both of you that all of your films be "about something"?*
*It seems like you always want your films to work on multiple levels.*
CW: I think so. I mean, I don't think we ever want to make a "message movie." I find those kinds of movies sort of boring.
PW: I think that things are either about something or about the avoidance of something. In other words, most Hollywood entertainment is about the avoidance of reality, but reality still lurks beneath it. So the answer is yes. For me, it's not about saying anything in particular, but just to acknowledge that there are layers of meaning beneath what we're seeing.
CW: Movies today are made backwards. Most movies made today are business propositions, really. If they're about anything, they're about getting people's asses into the seats and then selling the DVDs and stuff. We have a rougher road convincing people to make our movies, because they're not always obvious business propositions. It's the idea that there are good people in it and it's a good script and people will like it because it's good.

*There must be a temptation by this stage of your careers to go down the easier road and make a more overtly commercial film.*
CW: Well, the safety valve is that we get depressed when we contemplate that.
PW: Yeah, there are low moments when you think about how easy it would be to do this interesting film with some megastar, but then you project yourself ahead to when you're sitting in the editing room and you're only one of the schmucks who gets to determine what the tone of the piece is, as opposed to being the primary schmuck.

*What's your take on contemporary American filmmaking? How does it compare to, say, the supposed glory days of the 1970s?*
PW: It's less clearly an interesting state than the seventies, but personally I think you get a false sense about how good things were in earlier days because you don't see all the crap that was being made.

CW: There's just such a huge market that there's enough room for good films to be made, but also there are a lot of really scary tendencies that make me not want to go out and see a movie.

*What tendencies?*
CW: (laughs) I think that sadism is a weird tendency in films at the moment—enjoying seeing people get killed or mangled. I find that disturbing, and it makes me feel like I'm out of touch.
PW: There are a lot of violent films today by people who have not personally experienced violence.
CW: Yeah, that's part of what upsets me. It's violence without regard for the consequences, really. It's no longer cartoonish violence where people sort of bounce back. You actually have enjoyment of mutilation. I can definitely tell I am not in the same mood as the audience when I'm watching that. And that part of it scares me in terms of wanting to make movies and wanting people to appreciate them.

*Were you going to say something, Paul?*
PW: No, I'm just thinking how there's an air of delightful innocence to *American Pie*. (laughs)

## THE DIRECTORS' TAKE
## CHRIS & PAUL WEITZ

*What is the first film you ever saw?*
Chris: *Midway*
Paul: *Jaws*

*What is your favorite film of all time?*
Chris: *Lawrence of Arabia*
Paul: *The Four Hundred Blows*

*What's your favorite line in a film?*
Chris: "Nobody's perfect."—*Some Like It Hot*
Paul: "It goes up to eleven."—*This Is Spinal Tap*

*What movie made you realize that film was an art?*
Paul: That was always apparent.

*What movie do you consider your guilty pleasure?*
Chris: *Point Break*

*Who is your favorite movie character of all time?*
Chris: Max Fisher from *Rushmore*
Paul: I feel like I identify with the characters in almost any film I see. And for a few hours afterwards, I'm acting like the characters.

*What's your favorite movie snack food?*
Chris: Goobers
Paul: Popcorn

*Who is your favorite director of all time?*
Chris: Kurosawa
Paul: Truffaut

*Who is the most impressive filmmaker working today?*
Chris: Scorsese

*What quality do the best directors share?*
Paul: Humility toward the thing that they're making
Chris: Stubbornness

*Who is your favorite actor or actress of all time?*
Paul: Humphrey Bogart

*If you could remake one movie, what would it be?*
Paul: *Down to Earth*

*What is your best quality as a director?*
Paul: Politeness

*What is your greatest weakness as a director?*
Chris: Need for sleep

*Finish this sentence: I'll never direct a movie with . . .*
Paul: someone who sticks a gun in someone else's mouth.

*Finish this sentence: The perfect movie is . . .*
Chris: an hour and twenty minutes long.
Paul: cast entirely with monkeys.

*What will they be saying about your work fifty years from now?*
Paul: Nothing
Chris: "Yeah, I think I heard of that. . . ."

*What piece of advice do you have for aspiring filmmakers?*
Chris: Don't.
Paul: Remember that film is a mirror of life and not life itself.

*What are you as passionate about as moviemaking?*
Chris: Food
Paul: My family, and perceiving the stories that are in front of your nose every day